I0813936

TURNED AROUND

Related Works from the Same Author

Resurgent in the Midst of Crisis

Noble Beauty, Transcendent Holiness

Tradition and Sanity

John Henry Newman on Worship, Reverence, and Ritual

And Rightly So: Selected Letters & Articles of Neil McCaffrey

Reclaiming Our Roman Catholic Birthright

The Holy Bread of Eternal Life

Ministers of Christ

True Obedience in the Church

From Benedict's Peace to Francis's War

The Once and Future Roman Rite

Good Music, Sacred Music, and Silence

Illusions of Reform

Bound by Truth

Ultramontanism and Tradition

Unresolved Tensions

TURNED AROUND

Replying to Common Objections Against the Traditional Latin Mass

Peter A. Kwasniewski

TAN Books
Gastonia, North Carolina

Cover design by Michael Schrauzer

Cover image: Jindřich Tomec, *Solemn Mass in the Hofburg Chapel* (1917), Wikimedia Commons

Library of Congress Control Number: 2024941221

ISBN: 978-1-5051-3362-2
Kindle ISBN: 978-1-5051-3462-9
ePUB ISBN: 978-1-5051-3461-2

Published in the United States by
TAN Books
PO Box 269
Gastonia, NC 28053
www.TANBooks.com

Printed in India

Et dabo tibi thesauros absconditos, et arcana secretorum: ut scias quia ego Dominus, qui voco nomen tuum, Deus Israel.

And I will give thee hidden treasures, and the concealed riches of secret places: that thou mayest know that I am the Lord who call thee by thy name, the God of Israel.

Isaias 45:3

Contents

Publisher's Note ix
Preface xi

1 Why We Worship Facing East 1
"The priest has his back to me. I can't engage with him."

2 Why the Priest Is Separated from the People 29
"At Mass, the priest is doing everything and I'm just watching him."

3 Why the Traditional Mass Is Kingly and Courtly 56
"It's all fancy, like a royal court. It doesn't fit with a democratic society like ours."

4 Why We Follow Inherited Rituals and Strict Rubrics 79
"Everything's scripted and regimented—no room for spontaneity or adaptation."

5 Why We Repeat Ourselves in Traditional Worship 109
"There's so much repetition. Do we have to say things three times or more?"

6 Why We Use a One-Year Lectionary of Readings 133
"We read a lot more of the Bible in the Novus Ordo, so it's clearly better."

7 Why We Pray in Latin 167
"The Mass is in a foreign language. I can't follow it."

8 Why It Is Better Not to Understand Everything Immediately 191
"The new Mass is clear, easy, accessible. The old Mass is obscure and demanding."

9 Why We Kneel for Communion and Receive on the Tongue 213
"No posture is better or worse than another if your heart is in the right place."

10 The Mass Is the Faith and the Faith Is the Mass 234
"Why are you people always going on about 'the TLM this' and 'the TLM that'?"

Epilogue 241
What Next? 246
Acknowledgments 250
Bibliography 252
Index 263
About the Author 274

Publisher's Note

Since our founding in 1967, TAN Books has published works that preserve and promote the spiritual, theological, and liturgical traditions of Holy Mother Church. Our works on the Holy Sacrifice of the Mass—our greatest treasure—are at the heart of TAN Books's extensive catalog.

Everything flows from the Holy Sacrifice of the Mass, most especially the Holy Eucharist. In an age of secularism, relativism, ecclesiastical confusion, and growing disbelief in the Real Presence, Catholics must better grasp the roots of our present liturgical crisis. Dr. Peter Kwasniewski's *Turned Around: Replying to Common Objections Against the Traditional Latin Mass* sheds light on the beauty of the patrimonial Latin liturgy as practiced by the Church in an unbroken line from early centuries through Pope Pius V down to our own days. This work aims to articulate a position that is of maximum consistency with Catholic tradition, history, and teaching as well as one that is intellectually honest, even if it leads to conclusions that run against the grain of current thought. TAN Books, in its loyalty to the Church's teaching, has taken measures to ensure that what is opinion and what is dogma are clearly distinguished. The author herein published is, and intends to be, in all of his works, acts, and writings, a loyal son of the Church, and writes as such. The author holds, as do all Catholics, that the Novus Ordo is a valid Mass, in which the Body and Blood of Christ are confected.

It is our sincere prayer that those who read this book will find their understanding of the Roman Rite deepened, will fall ever more in love with Christ and His Church through a greater love for the Holy Sacrifice of the Mass, and will grow in holiness and love of God in their daily pursuit of what the Mass points to: union with God forever in heaven.

Preface

"Mystifying Tridentine priestcraft!" is the sort of insulting phrase that an English Protestant of the Baroque period might have hurled against the "Mass of the Roman Catholicks." It is highly doubtful that anyone at present would use this particular combination of words. Nevertheless, as I will show in this book, the *idea* behind it—and even something of the feeling of contempt—is still alive and well in the criticisms made by certain Catholics, whether prominent or pedestrian, when they talk about the classical Roman Rite of Mass, the so-called traditional Latin Mass or "Tridentine Mass," which they accuse, in various ways, of an unhealthy obscurity or mystification and of a "clericalism" that blocks popular participation.

Everyone who has attended a traditional Latin Mass (or "TLM" for short), which in an earlier book I called "the once and future Roman Rite," instantly recognizes that it is a very *distinctive* liturgy: it has many sharply defined traits that make it itself and nothing else, and—what is more controversial in our times—make it very different from the modern rite or Novus Ordo introduced by Pope Paul VI in 1969. So different, in fact, that one who falls in love with it feels "turned around" as regards all or most of what he formerly thought about the liturgy of the Church. He feels as turned around as the priest and the ministers when they face the altar instead of facing him. He may even feel turned inside-out and upside-down by all that he must learn, unlearn, and re-learn. Many Catholics have even called it a kind of "conversion," which, of course, literally means a turning around.

The distinctiveness of this ancient rite takes many forms: whether it be the offering of the Mass with the priest and the faithful facing in the same direction, namely, *ad orientem* or *versus apsidem* ("toward the east" or "toward the apse"), with much that is unseen and unheard; or the use of an ancient sacral language, Christian Latin, which few people today can read or speak fluently; or the great distance, both physical and psychological, that separates the clergy ministering in the sanctuary from the people in the pews and seems to give the former the lion's share of activity while consigning the latter to passivity; or the accentuated "regal" character of the old rite, especially in its more solemn forms and ceremonies, which are endowed with a pomp and pageantry reminiscent of the monarchs' courts of a bygone Christendom; or the insistence on communicants kneeling in a line at a rail, tilting their heads back to be fed directly into the mouth by the hand of an ordained minister; or the pervasive role of repetition, whereby the prayers of Mass remain much the same from day to day, and within Mass, some formulas are repeated many times; or the compact one-year lectionary, which is also characterized by repetition; or the military orderliness of the ceremonial choreography, dictated by super-refined, comprehensive rubrics that leave nothing up to chance, choice, charisma, or community; or, finally, the steady sense that, in spite of what one already knows and in spite of glimpsing more and more, there is so much one does not yet understand and may never understand in this life—a realm not only of mystery, but of humbling obscurity.

These are indeed formidable barriers for a lot of modern Catholics (and, it goes without saying, positively scandalous in the eyes of modern liturgists), but curiously, these things never prevented innumerable men, women, and children in centuries past from adoring God and nourishing their spiritual life in the context of the old rite, nor do they prevent a dedicated and growing minority from doing so today, even in the face of obstacles and challenges of many kinds. On the contrary, it is these very features of the old rite that lovers of the TLM find *attractive* and *rewarding*. There must be *something* to tradition, after all! What is it? Can we spell it out clearly and convincingly? Can we make a case for all that is distinctive, potently countercultural, vexingly premodern and even anti-modern in the classical Roman Rite of Mass?

Of course, there are plenty of other aspects of the TLM that some Catholics today object to or are puzzled by (and that other fellow Catholics find appealing and helpful); this book makes no attempt to canvas them all, which would require an encyclopedia.[1] Two examples of aspects on which I do not focus here would be the unbroken traditional practice that only males, properly vested, minister in the sanctuary of the church and the normative use of Gregorian chant and polyphony as the liturgical music.[2] All the same, I am convinced that the nine themes tackled in these pages cover a lot of this territory, and that a patient look at the profound reasons behind these distinctive aspects will bring the reader to a new appreciation—or will deepen his existing appreciation—of why this venerable liturgical rite operates the way it does. My method is to defend the most controversial premodern aspects of the TLM by raising common objections against them and then replying to the objections in some detail. While the wisdom of tradition is often surprising and paradoxical, even provocative, it is never random or pointless. I often feel that moderns have so tied themselves up in peculiar knots that it's harder for them to perceive what was once evident. The title *Turned Around* reminds us that for every argument, there is a counterargument, and that the combination of better understanding and repeated experience can drastically change one's perception of the value of a certain good. In my interactions with people over the past several decades, I've learned that critics of the TLM, so far from demonstrating its mortal flaws (as they have been trained to regard them), manage to exhibit an utterly superficial grasp of *how* it works and *why* it works—the sort of things the "little ones," children in age or in spirit, can easily relate to, as did generations of our forefathers.

As is often the case in traditionalist literature, this book focuses on the Holy Sacrifice of the Mass. This is *not*, mind you, because I consider it the only liturgical ceremony worth talking about or participating in; quite the contrary. Yet the Mass is indisputably the font and apex of our Christian life, and its healthy or unhealthy condition largely determines the health or sickness of the entire Mystical Body of Christ on earth (see 1 Cor. 11:30). It is where the faithful encounter Christ and the Church most regularly.

---

[1] Happily, there's an abundance of literature on the TLM by which one can pursue the understanding of any aspect of it: see the list of books across from this book's title page, as well as the recommendations at the end.

[2] Part of the reason for this choice is that I have already written books precisely on these two topics: *Ministers of Christ* and *Good Music, Sacred Music, and Silence.*

It has seen the worst profanation and abuse. Through the Mass, the work of our redemption is shown and carried out; no wonder the devil targets it with his most open and most subtle attacks. The objections raised and the arguments presented in the following pages do, however, have bearing on *all* of the sacramental rites of the Church, as well as her Divine Office, blessings, and special ceremonies.

Learning about a treasury as vast and intricate as ours takes time; indeed, it takes a lifetime. The more one learns, the more one appreciates; the more one appreciates, the more one internalizes the benefits. That is why, at the end, I have recommended a few next steps that a reader might consider taking to deepen his or her appreciation of the liturgical patrimony that is ours to love and to pass on.

Peter A. Kwasniewski
February 2, 2024
Purification of the Blessed Virgin Mary

1

Why We Worship Facing East

"The priest has his back to me. I can't engage with him."

Catholics who delve into serious discussions of liturgy, wishing perhaps to know what all the fuss is about, quickly discover that one of the hottest of hot-button questions is the orientation of the liturgy. Msgr. Klaus Gamber once claimed that turning the altar and priest around to face the people was the single most destructive change that occurred in the celebration of the Mass (and he was not favorable to most of the other changes either). What *is* the big deal, then, about the direction the priest is facing at Mass?[3]

I would like to begin with two testimonials. Both are taken, on purpose, from Catholics who would not call themselves "traditionalists." To my mind, this gives their perspectives more weight, inasmuch as they cannot be accused of wanting to "turn the clock back." Their views are based simply on how things appear to them. The first is from a layman, David Clayton, the impresario of Pontifex online university and the author of many books and articles on "the Way of Beauty," who says the following about his experience of worship facing eastwards:

> This is perhaps the most striking and immediate way of symbolizing that we look to and recognize a Higher Power. My own conversion was influenced by seeing an *ad orientem* Mass in which the priest was

[3] This topic has been taken up many times at the website *New Liturgical Movement* (hereafter "*NLM*"), but there are always more angles from which to pursue it, and we will never leave it alone. Those who wish to read more should search *NLM* with the keyword "ad orientem."

> seen as the head of a body of people, leading us towards a common destination. This impression just described was accentuated by the architecture and art [of the church—the Brompton Oratory in London], which served to focus my attention on and present to me visually images of what I otherwise would not have intuited.[4]

A diocesan priest, Fr. Dwight Longenecker, wrote some years ago about offering Mass *ad orientem*:

> I celebrate facing the same way as the people because I actually feel closer to them that way. I also feel closer to God. When I . . . face the Lord with the people I find that my own celebration of Mass is more intimate and mystical. I feel like I am able to focus more on the Lord and what is happening. If I need to weep I can do so without people seeing me. If I need to pause and pray I can do so without worrying what people are thinking.[5]

He then comments on one particular experience that he believes was made possible for him, in part, by the fact that he was not, so to speak, "on display," but focused on the prayer, with nothing before his eyes except the missal, the altar, and the holy oblations:

> As I celebrated Mass a strange awareness came over me. As I read the words from the missal it was as if the words themselves were alive and vivid. I cannot explain what I was seeing except to say that the words were thronged with the meaning of the words. The words on the page were distinct and that made every doctrine and truth distinct. It was as if each word and even each letter stood out with cosmic significance—not that the words themselves were so alive, but that the eternal meaning and truths that the words communicated were alive and throbbing with the meaning—meaning that was alive as far above me as the stars, and as close to me as my own breath. Then I thought of the mysterious meaning of "In the beginning was the Word and the Word was with God and the Word was God...and the Word became flesh and dwelt among us." It was as if this eternal mystery of the

---

[4] Clayton, "Connecting *Ad Orientem,* Sacred Art, an Ordered Environmentalism, Social Graces, and a Hierarchical Society."

[5] Longenecker, "From a Priest at the Altar."

> Incarnation was coming true again within the simple speaking of the words. Something happened. A transaction was made between this world and eternity.

Now, the way things appeared to Mr. Clayton and Fr. Longenecker is, I maintain, the way in which they naturally appear, or have the potential to appear, to anyone who arrives on the scene without prejudices.

Imagine a person with no knowledge of the Catholic Faith or perhaps even of Christianity deciding, out of curiosity, to step from a bright sunlit street into an attractive Catholic church or chapel. As his eyes adjust, he sees a number of faithful dotted here and there in the pews, kneeling and looking ahead. At the far end of the church, in a more open area with more decoration than the rest of the building, he sees a group of men, dressed in strange and elaborate garb, clustered round a large marble object with candles across it. They are all facing the same direction as the faithful in the church; they are intensely focused on what they are doing; their bodies block his view of their work,[6] but they look for all the world as if they might be huddling around a sacrificial victim to kill it. It is clear, at any rate, that their attention is *not* focused on the people. Our observer feels that something very solemn and serious is happening, and that everyone in the building is, in their different ways, utterly united in this action, whatever it may be. If, in addition, our hypothetical visitor hears chant or polyphony, and smells incense, and feels the hard wood against his legs, worn smooth by so many worshipers over the years, four of his outward senses will be, like the four evangelists, proclaiming a presence to him, even if he is not yet able to recognize it or call it by name.

Clayton speaks in a very similar way about that first Mass he attended at the Brompton Oratory:

---

6 How often have we heard, as an objection to *ad orientem:* "The people should be able to *see* what's going on"? Those who say that must never have read *The Little Prince,* which transmits the wisdom of mankind: *"On ne voit bien qu'avec le coeur. L'essentiel est invisible pour les yeux"* (Saint-Exupéry, *Le Petit Prince,* 76: "You can see well only with your heart. What is essential is invisible to the eye"). No one can *see* the miracle of transubstantiation. What we *can* see are the sacramental signs of the Lord's presence—and *those* are shown to everyone in the elevation of the host and, less directly, the elevation of the chalice.

> I couldn't understand the words. The three priests, one central and two flanking, each in ornately embroidered vestments, and the acolytes in white cotton had their backs to me and were facing towards the east (*ad orientem*), towards the giant altar. All the congregation faced east too, bowing, kneeling, standing and sitting together; and the priests seemed to be directing a common focus beyond themselves towards something mysterious. While I could not tell precisely what it was, they acted in unison, and so their body language spoke to me of their faith. They believed that what they were doing was of profound importance, I could tell. The mystery as to what that was in some way cleared, but in others intensified, when the priest held the white host aloft. I did not really know what I was seeing, but, nevertheless, my instincts told me powerfully that this was the focus of everything that had preceded it.... At that point I was only vaguely aware of what this [beauty of the integrated whole of this spectacle] was telling me, but I knew at a deep unspoken level, however dimly, that I was grasping a profound truth communicated to me by music, art, architecture, and body language.[7]

A visitor to such a liturgy has already begun to receive the first and most important lesson in the Christian religion: that *God* is the center of our attention, the goal of our strivings, the purpose of our lives. This visitor is seeing played out before him the meaning of Psalm 144:15: "The eyes of all hope in thee, O Lord: and thou givest them meat in due season." We have here a representation—and with it, the possibility of an experience—of man turning himself toward the source of his being and destiny: as the old prayer says, "I acknowledge Thee to be my Creator and sovereign Lord." Nothing—no amount of catechesis or homiletics or pastoral programs—can ever substitute for this experience or even vie with it. Without this immediate and wordless awareness of God as the *mysterium tremendum et fascinans*, the fearful and fascinating mystery for whose sake we stop paying attention for a moment to each other and to this world and stumble up to the edge of His domain, where His presence may infiltrate and permeate *our* domain . . . without this, I say, there is no religion at all, no worship, no sacred liturgy. Without it, a liturgy may

[7] Clayton, *The Way of Beauty*, 14.

technically still happen, but the terrible words of the prophet Isaiah, cited by Our Lord, would then seem to fit the case: "This people honoureth me with their lips: but their heart is far from me. And in vain do they worship me, teaching doctrines and commandments of men."[8] The new forms of Catholic worship that came in after the Second Vatican Council so readily lend themselves to endless verbalization and explanation that they leave no place for Newman's *cor ad cor loquitur*, "heart speaks to heart." "This people honoureth me with their lips: but their heart is far from me"; and why? Because the minds of all are captured by a swirling anthropocentric vortex animated by "the doctrines and commandments of *men*,"[9] that is, the false philosophical principles that guided the process by which we arrived at such novelties as *versus populum*, with the church reconfigured as a closed circle presided over by a sort of clerical chairman.

Historical Foundations

To avoid any risk of worshiping the Most Holy Trinity in vain, let us try to discover the deepest reasons for the ancient and, until recently, uninterrupted custom of praying eastwards—a custom that we find from the East to the West, in every traditional rite of Christian worship, be it Byzantine or Latin; Slavic or Greek; Roman, Gallican, Ambrosian, or Mozarabic; Chaldean, Coptic, Armenian, or Ethiopian.

For starters, the custom of all Christians either offering or participating in the Eucharistic liturgy facing east has the same apostolic roots and the same universality in Church history as the use of water baptism, the praying of the Psalms, the worship of the risen Christ on Sunday, the honoring of the Mother of God and the saints, and the veneration of their relics. As a matter of fact, eastward orientation *predates* the use of official priestly vestments, consecrated church buildings, and the very Niceno-Constantinopolitan Creed that we recite every Sunday.[10] Does

---

8 Matt. 15:8–9.

9 Matt. 15:9, emphasis added.

10 The archaeological and documentary evidence for this claim is overwhelming: early Christians built (and understood themselves to be building) real and proper altars, not merely "tables," and they prioritized facing eastwards to offer the sacrifice. The evidence has been painstakingly compiled and analyzed in Heid, *Altar and Church*. It is therefore of only marginal interest to note that some churches, owing to peculiar circumstances, were so situated that the altar had

that make it old enough and widespread enough to take seriously? If not, why do we take any of these other things seriously? They should be just as dispensable.

Think of it this way: Would you, if you are a practicing Catholic, want the Lord's Day to be abolished, replaced by another day of the week, or simply taken off the roster? That would be an unthinkable deviation from Christian practice. Would you want all the Psalms removed from the Mass and the Divine Office? Should we replace water baptism with a civil naming ceremony, or stop honoring our Blessed Mother because it might make us feel like immature children or offend anti-maternal feminists? Should priests celebrate Mass in jeans and T-shirts because that's the common clothing of our day, as robes and cloaks were the common clothing of ancient times? Impossible! It cannot be that something we have done for millennia should suddenly be dropped. But this is exactly what has been done with *ad orientem* worship.

For nearly 2,000 years, clergy and faithful together faced the same direction in expectation of Christ and in adoration of Him, the One who already comes in mystery in the Most Holy Eucharist, the One who is to come manifestly at the end of the world to judge the living and the dead and the world by fire. *Ad orientem* preserves the eschatological orientation of the liturgy. When Christians first gathered on Sundays to worship the Lord, they were anticipating the second coming of Christ—this seems to be the oldest characteristic of our corporate worship. The "primordial form" of Sunday was not so much a feast looking back to the resurrection of Christ on the first Easter, or to any particular mystery or moment of His earthly life, as it was a looking *forward* with longing to the Lord's return in glory, imploring Him to deliver us from the evils of sin, death, and hell.[11] Sunday

---

to be placed at the western end and the celebrant had to face the nave and thus the congregation; for he did so *in order* to face eastward. He was only incidentally standing "toward the people." Such anomalies show that, even where topography forced alternative designs, *ad orientem* remained a priority. Once the principle of a general unified orientation within a church (i.e., everyone facing the same way toward the apse) gained absolute precedence in church design, the literal or cosmic east was sometimes passed over in favor of the "liturgical east," i.e., *versus apsidem*. It is nevertheless far from ideal to sever the direction of the building from its cosmic framework, and every effort should be made to keep the architectural orientation in line with the cosmic orientation that is its foundation.

[11] Dix, *The Shape of the Liturgy*, 336–37, 359–60, 368.

Mass was about *the life of the world to come*, which the early Christians, suffering bitter and horrific trials, must have thought about a great deal as they hoped and prayed that they would remain faithful: "lead us not into temptation but deliver us from evil."[12] For this reason, the eastward focus of prayer was a poignant symbol: after the dark and cold night, the sun will rise gloriously on the eastern horizon, shedding light and warmth.

This mindset found both inspiration and confirmation in the Scripture passages that call Christ "the Orient" or say that He ascends to the east, or that He will come from the east. For example, Jesus says of Himself, in Matthew 24:27: "As lightning cometh out of the east, and appeareth even into the west: so shall the coming of the Son of man be."[13] The prophet Zechariah announces the Messiah in this way: "Behold a man, the Orient is his name."[14] The prophet Malachi calls Christ "the Sun of justice."[15] The canticle of Zechariah, sung every day in Lauds, describes the Messiah as "*Oriens ex alto*," the "dawn . . . from on high."[16] God is called "Light" in John 1:5, and later in verse nine, His Son is called "the true light, which enlighteneth every man that cometh into this world," as indeed the physical sun does.[17] Implicit in the description of King Solomon's dedication of the first temple is an *ad orientem* priestly gesture: "And Solomon stood before the altar of the Lord in the sight of the assembly of Israel, and spread forth his hands towards heaven."[18] This verse puts us in mind of the "Sursum corda" in the Preface dialogue, when the priest raises up his arms to God, gesturing that we should lift our hearts on high, to Him who lives and reigns forever, enthroned above the cherubim. The Divine Liturgy of St. John Chrysostom features a still more extroverted gesture, as the priest repeatedly bows and lifts his hands aloft during the Cherubikon or cherubic hymn.

Verses and practices like these were repeatedly commented on by the Church Fathers, such as St. Basil the Great (330–379), defender of the

---

[12] See Oppenheimer, "Towards the Second Coming."

[13] cf. Acts 1:10–11.

[14] Zach. 6:12.

[15] Mal. 4:2.

[16] Lk 1:78 RSVCE. Or, in the Douay-Rheims, with its customary literalism: "Through the bowels of the mercy of our God, in which the Orient from on high hath visited us."

[17] All these texts and more, with good commentary, may be found in the article by Hayden, *"Convertere, Israël, ad Dominum Deum Tuum!"*

[18] 1 Kgs 8:22.

divinity of the third Person of the Blessed Trinity, and St. John Damascene (c. 675–c. 749), defender of icons. One of the most famous passages on our subject comes, in fact, from Basil's treatise *On the Holy Spirit*, published in the year 375. The Cappadocian father writes:

> Of the beliefs and practices whether generally accepted or publicly enjoined which are preserved in the Church, some we possess derived from written teaching; others we have received delivered to us "in a mystery" by the tradition of the apostles; and both of these in relation to true religion have the same force. And these no one will gainsay—no one, at all events, who is even moderately versed in the institutions of the Church. For were we to attempt to reject such customs as have no written authority, on the ground that the importance they possess is small, we should unintentionally injure the Gospel in its very vitals.

Basil then offers a lengthy list of beliefs and practices not contained verbatim in Scripture but handed down by tradition:

> What writing has taught us to turn to the East at the prayer?[19] Which of the saints has left us in writing the words of the invocation at the displaying of the bread of the Eucharist and the cup of blessing? For we are not, as is well known, content with what the apostle or the Gospel has recorded, but both in preface and conclusion we add other words as being of great importance to the validity of the ministry, and these we derive from unwritten teaching. . . . We all look to the East at our prayers, but few of us know that we are seeking our own old country, Paradise, which God planted in Eden in the East.[20]

He then argues—bear in mind that this is a treatise in defense of the divinity of the third Person of the Trinity against those who deny it—that there is no more reason to worship eastwards than there is to worship the Spirit, since *both* are handed down by tradition. But since we all agree about worshiping eastwards, we should likewise all adore the Holy Spirit as God! How is it possible for us to ignore the force of such a witness from the early Church?

---

[19] "The prayer" in the sense of the greatest prayer: the Eucharistic offering.

[20] Basil, *On the Holy Spirit,* 27:66.

One is reminded of a similar argumentative move in St. Cyril of Alexandria's defense of the oneness of Christ, true God and true man, against Nestorius: we all know that the Holy Eucharist was given in order to divinize us; but if Christ is not truly the Son of God, receiving Him in Communion would never give us a share in the divinity; hence, He must be the Son of God. In arguing that way, Cyril, who died in 444, takes for granted a universal belief in the Real Presence of Christ in the Eucharist and deduces the divinity of Christ from it! Such examples are extremely embarrassing for Protestants, it must be admitted; but they are, sadly, no less embarrassing for modern Catholics, who seem only too willing to turn their backs on tradition—even when it can lay claim to apostolic origins.

Later, St. John Damascene ably summarized this particular tradition:

> It is not without reason or by chance that we worship toward the east. . . . Since God is spiritual light and Christ in sacred Scripture is called "Sun of Justice" (Mal 4:2) and "Orient" (Lk 1:78), the east should be dedicated to His worship. . . . Also, the divine David says: "Sing to God, ye kingdoms of the earth: sing ye to the Lord; who mounteth above the heaven of heavens, to the east" (Ps 67:33f.). And still again, Scripture says: "And the Lord has planted a paradise in Eden to the east; wherein He placed man whom He had formed," and whom He cast out, when he had transgressed, "and made him to live over against the paradise of pleasure" (Gn 2:8; 3,24 LXX), or in the west. Thus it is that, when we worship God, we long for our ancient fatherland and gaze toward it. . . . As a matter of fact, when the Lord was crucified, He looked toward the west, and so we worship gazing toward Him. And when he was taken up, He ascended to the east and thus the Apostles worshiped Him and thus He shall come in the same way as they had seen Him going into heaven (cf. Ac 1:11), as the Lord Himself said: "As lightning cometh out of the east and appeareth even into the west: so shall also the coming of the Son of man be" (Mt 24:27). And so, while we are awaiting Him, we worship toward the east. This is, moreover, the unwritten tradition of the Apostles, for they have handed many things down to us unwritten.[21]

[21] John Damascene, *De fide orthodoxa* 85 (IV 12), in *Writings,* 352–54.

The 180-degree turn in the stance of the priest—let's not forget that colloquially, someone who "does a 180" is someone who suddenly and completely changes his mind or course of action, implying a rejection of what came before—decisively severs us from that which is most ancient, most intrinsic, and most distinctive in our worship as Christians. Whenever people return to *ad orientem* worship, they return decisively to the fundamentals of Christian faith and its original practice. Ironically, in adopting the novelty of *versus populum*—a supposed "return to the earliest practice" in the judgment of (some) mid-twentieth century scholars, whose conclusions have been overturned by the work of subsequent scholars—*we ended up losing one of the most ancient elements of all.*[22]

The Theological Meaning

It is not hard to see why this custom should have been nearly convertible with Christian worship as such—above all in the Mass, the highest act of worship. The Mass is both Patricentric and Christocentric: these are different but complementary perspectives. Because Christ is both Head of the Church *and* our God, one in His divinity with the Father and the Holy Spirit, we can be at one and the same time on our way *with Him* to the Father in the power of the Spirit, and on our way *to Him* as our ultimate end. It is therefore correct to say that the priest, praying *ad orientem*, is facing Christ (the Orient), and to say that he is praying, as *alter Christus* or *in persona Christi*, toward the Father. In fact, the clear symbolic proclamation of the twofold mystery of Christ as both our God and our mediator with God is completely lost in the *versus populum* stance. To face Christ, and to face the Father with Christ, are mutually implicated, just as they are in Scripture: "You call me Master, and Lord; and you say well, for so I am"; "I and the Father are one"; "he that seeth me seeth the Father also"; "I go to the Father: for the Father is greater than I."[23]

---

[22] It is interesting to note that Fr. Joseph Jungmann, otherwise so influential in the liturgical reform, strongly defended the *ad orientem* posture. See his book (outdated in many ways) *The Early Liturgy to the Time of Gregory the Great,* 133–39. Similarly, although he expressed many criticisms of the Tridentine rite, Fr. Louis Bouyer staunchly defended the *ad orientem* stance in such works as *Rite and Man* and *Liturgy and Architecture.*

[23] John 13:13; 10:30; 14:9; 14:28.

Most simply, worship is about *God*, not about us. Or rather, it is about us only insofar as we are *from* God, *in* God, and *for* God, our Creator, Savior, Sanctifier, and Judge. Hence, even to the extent that, as St. Thomas Aquinas says, the liturgy is for our needs, since God who is infinitely good stands in need of nothing for Himself, it is still done for the love and praise and thanking *of God*, who is the source and fulfillment of our needs.[24] Our need, in short, is for *God*; our deepest need is to go beyond ourselves into Him. True worship takes us out of ourselves and establishes us in God, our ultimate end. In this sense, any aspect of liturgy that does not clearly terminate in God, Father, Son, and Holy Spirit, or any aspect that seems to terminate in *us*, is not liturgy, whatever else it may be (self-regard, social posturing, therapy, superstition).

Hence, the *ad orientem* stance simply expresses the act of worship as such, whereas the *versus populum* stance contradicts it outright. This is why the latter is not merely unfitting for worship but antithetical to the virtue of religion that adores God as first beginning and last end. The theologian Max Thurian, writing (somewhat surprisingly) in the official Vatican journal *Notitiae*, observed: "The whole celebration [of Mass] is often conducted as if it were a conversation and dialogue in which there is no longer room for adoration, contemplation, and silence. The fact that the celebrants and faithful constantly face each other closes the liturgy in on itself."[25] This observation anticipated Joseph Ratzinger's similar and more famous remark in *The Spirit of the Liturgy*: "The turning of the priest toward the people has turned the community into a self-enclosed circle. In its outward form, it no longer opens out on what lies ahead and above, but is closed in on itself."[26]

Along the same lines, the former papal master of ceremonies Guido Marini remarked at a conference in Rome:

---

[24] *Summa Theologiæ* II–II, Q. 81, art. 7: "We pay God honor and reverence, not for His sake (because He is of Himself full of glory to which no creature can add anything), but for our own sake, because by the very fact that we revere and honor God, our mind is subjected to Him; wherein its perfection consists, since a thing is perfected by being subjected to its superior, for instance the body is perfected by being quickened by the soul, and the air by being enlightened by the sun."

[25] Thurian, "La Liturgie, contemplation du mystère," 2.

[26] Ratzinger, *Spirit of the Liturgy,* II.3, in *Theology of the Liturgy,* 49.

> In our time, the expression "celebrating facing the people" has entered our common vocabulary. . . . Such an expression would be categorically unacceptable the moment it comes to express a theological proposition. Theologically speaking, the holy Mass, as a matter of fact, is always addressed to God through Christ our Lord, and it would be a grievous error to imagine that the principal orientation of the sacrificial action is the community. Such an orientation, therefore, of turning towards the Lord must animate the interior participation of each individual during the liturgy. It is likewise equally important that this orientation be quite visible in the liturgical sign as well.[27]

Marini helps us to see not only that the object of liturgy should always be God, or the God-man Jesus Christ, never mere man, but also that this objective *orient*ation (we cannot avoid the east even in our ordinary way of speaking!) should be *visible*, evident to the senses, easily grasped by the intellect, and easily translated into the movement of the will that we call love, which is ordered to the good—to a good outside of ourselves, in the case of our ultimate end.

The contrast between the postures can be articulated in terms of their subject/object signification. In the *ad orientem* arrangement, the subject/object appears as MAN/GOD. The priest both looks and acts like an image of Christ, the mediator between God and man, Himself always oriented to the Father.[28] Paradoxically, the ceremonial centrality of the priest in the old rite serves to emphasize that God is the one and only object of worship, since the priest is so obviously assimilated to his office as *alter Christus*, as the head of a people on pilgrimage to the Kingdom of Heaven.

In the *versus populum* arrangement, the subject/object appears as PEOPLE/PRIEST. The priest, even with the best of intentions and behavior, looks and acts like an empowered facilitator of a communal event; the *vis-à-vis* positioning confers on him a sort of autocratic prominence as the one to whom the congregation is subordinated and beholden. This may be the psychological reason why some priests overcompensate with informality, jokes, banter, smiles, waves, applause, or what have you—the priest's very "over-againstness"

---

27 Marini, "Clergy Conference in Rome: Address of Msgr. Guido Marini, Papal Master of Ceremonies."

28 See Kwasniewski, "The Sacrifice of Praise and the Ecstatic Orientation of Man."

in *versus populum* seems to demand a downplaying of the over-against by means of emphasizing that he's really "one of us" after all! How sad that the one true and obvious way of representing that the priest is "one of us"—namely, by having him face in the same direction as everyone else and offer the sacrifice on their behalf, the very same sacrifice they are offering in their hearts—has been discarded as an opaque and expired symbol, to be replaced by a format that turns the Mass into something done *toward* the people and, in a sense, imposed upon them. In reality, the Mass is something Jesus Christ, according to His human nature, does toward the Most Holy Trinity, as the great prayer "Suscipe, sancta Trinitas" in the traditional Offertory perfectly expresses—and we are permitted to join in. Ironically, for a rite that is supposed to be less clericocentric and more congregational, the priest in the new rite becomes far more central and attention-getting because his personality, his "vernacular style" or "way of being a priest," intrudes. *Versus populum* does nothing but underline this unfortunate amplification of human presidency, undermining assimilation to Christ's *kenosis* or self-empyting and diluting His unique mediation.

When I was teaching in Wyoming, I often engaged my college students in conversation about liturgical matters and enjoyed listening to their spontaneous ideas. Most of them had never picked up a book about liturgy, but they intuitively understood a lot, simply from reflecting on their experiences. One student, a senior, decided to send me an email one day:

> The more I think about it, the more significant the *ad orientem* debate seems to me. Praying eastwards just *makes sense.* All of a sudden, the priest's personality *doesn't matter.* It seems like such a small thing, but I am convinced that if priests didn't face "the audience," they would act *and perceive themselves* very differently. Why? Because they are human. And humans love feeling powerful, like rock stars. The priest has become a performer, and that has enormous implications. Not only has his importance eclipsed that of the Eucharist in the eyes of the everyday Catholic, but I think this is a fundamental reason the priesthood started attracting the wrong kind of man. Before, the priest was an instrument, a mediator; someone who sacrificed his life for Christ in the Eucharist and for His bride the Church. Now the role of priest is the opposite of humble. He's a guru, a prophet, a philosopher and psychologist, a rock star, the host

> of a show. Before, he was a man with a job; now he's *someone.* Praying *ad orientem* entails an immediate shift in consciousness—and it would have the fringe benefit of turning off seminarians who are attracted for the wrong reasons. I know it's not the only reason the role of priest has been completely changed, but I think it might be one of the most basic.[29]

The phrase "seminarians who are attracted for the wrong reasons" is a delicate reference to the problem of clerical homosexuality.[30] For, beyond the temptation to pride, there is also an inherent effeminacy to *versus populum.* Based on Manfred Hauke's discussion of the sexes,[31] one can associate the symbol for the male (♂), an arrow shooting out from a circle, with *ad orientem,* and the symbol for the female (♀), a statically mounted circle, with *versus populum.* The eastward-oriented priest looks outward and leads the people as their head, directing them to the divine beyond creation; the woman shelters, cradles, turns to the child, in an anthropological symbol of immanence, of rootedness in the created order. Due to the sacramental principle at work, the symbolic stance of the celebrant *effects a disposition,* a mentality, like that which it symbolizes. What is proper to a woman and a most beautiful perfection of hers becomes, in a priest or in men generally, effeminacy. The "mothering" of the congregation—particularly when it is done with a lecturey schoolmarm spirit—is deeply corrosive of spiritual virility. That is why Cardinal Heenan, as part of the group of bishops who were given a "sneak peak" of the Novus Ordo at the Synod of Bishops in 1967, predicted that the new rite would empty the churches of men; and it is no surprise that statistics show a much higher percentage of men in old-rite congregations today (sometimes more than 50%) than in new-rite ones.[32]

Kathleen Pluth brilliantly captures the problem and the solution. Having said that she hates being a cause of distraction to others by cantoring in the front of a church and that she much prefers the anonymity of the choir loft (singers should be heard and not seen), she then speaks about the celebrant of the Mass:

---

[29] Private correspondence.

[30] See Francis Magister, "What Attracts Homosexuals to the Priesthood?"

[31] See Hauke, *Women in the Priesthood?*

[32] For an extended reflection on these issues, see Shaw, *The Liturgy, the Family, and the Crisis of Modernity,* 215–72.

The role of the priest is exponentially more complex. He cannot hide. His role is inherently, and in some regards primarily, visible, leading the congregation through the veil, into the Holy of Holies. We follow him, as he expresses in the highest possible way his conformity to Jesus, our advocate before the Father. For centuries the symbolism of our "following" the priest was clear. However, in the postconciliar period, and without a direct referrent in the Council's documents themselves, the character of the priest's relationship to the people has been visibly distorted by the *versus populum* posture.

When people face each other, they aim to please. They make eye contact; they smile encouragingly. There is a word for such gestures: flattery. People flatter their priests and their priests flatter them, at an average ratio of, say, 500 to 1. None of this is encouraged in the Council documents. The *versus populum* posture is specifically worldly. It sets up the priest, not as a model to follow, but as a talk show host to be flattered insofar as he delights us. There are no good reasons for this.

The lines of sight to God should be made clear in the Liturgy (see Pseudo-Dionysius' *Ecclesiastical Hierarchy* for a beautiful exposition of how this should work), but instead our path towards God is obscured by the distracting cycle of eye-contact and feedback. The Sunday liturgy is for everyone their primary and for many their only contact with the Church. As such, its symbols should express the truth, including the truth about ecclesial relationships, which should not be a matter of flattery but of service. The Psalmist sings, "Let your priests be clothed with holiness/The faithful shall ring out their joy." The *ad orientem* posture lets priests be priests and [lets] the people be themselves too, all facing God together.[33]

Of Divine and Diabolic Symbols

Accordingly, it was much to the devil's advantage to turn the priest around to the people, creating a charmed circle of neighborly affirmation that brought the experience of the Mass down to the level of a horizontal exchange, a back-and-forth in everyday speech. There is nothing transcendent about that; on the contrary, God is domesticated, tamed, manipulable—not a recipient of

33 Pluth, "The First Step in Ecclesiastical Reform: Turn the Altars Around."

sacrifice but a subject of conversation. The liturgy comes to be *about* God instead of *for* Him. Indeed, as Ratzinger said, at times one wonders if there is any room left for God at all.[34] Reflecting on the symbolism of east and west at work in the Byzantine rite of baptism, David Clayton remarks:

> At one point we all turned as directed by our pastor to the west, in order to renounce Satan loudly and to make the gesture of spitting on him. We then turned around and to the east, *ad orientem*. This was as much, it seemed to me, to turn our backs on Satan as to look for the Risen Christ. It was a powerful moment. . . . Perhaps the same neglect [of piety in venerating holy images] opened the west door of the Church and left it ajar and unattended, drawing the "smoke of Satan" into the vacuum created by the absence of fragrant incense, followed (who knows?) by the entrance of Satan himself. If he did enter, he would likely not be greeted by a shower of spittle, but greeted in a spirit of diversity by a priest facing him directly, worshiping and making a sacrifice. What sort of message does that communicate, I wonder? Those who do realize the seriousness of what is going on and object to it are too often showered with spite, if not spittle, for their troubles.[35]

In the Western context, moreover, where the use of a sacral language had been the nearly universal and exceptionless practice for most of the Church's history, the sudden introduction of the vernacular—and until very recently, a bland and boorish vernacular at that—contributed to this serpentine leveling as well. *Ad orientem*, use of Latin and plainchant, and kneeling for Communion are simple but potent ways to remind ourselves that we are *not* "on a level playing field" with God, that He is truly Almighty and Pantocrator, and we are His creatures and His subjects. These traditional practices effectively repudiate the aberration of democratic horizontalism that has afflicted not only our entire social life as citizens but also, for more than half a century, the Church's social life, that is, her liturgy.[36]

---

[34] Ratzinger, *Milestones,* 148–49: "I am convinced that the crisis in the Church that we are experiencing today is to a large extent due to the disintegration of the liturgy, which at times has even come to be conceived of *etsi Deus non daretur,* in that it is a matter of indifference whether or not God exists and whether or not he speaks to us and hears us."

[35] Clayton, "The Smoke of Satan Enters From the West…at Our Invitation."

[36] See chapters 3, 7, and 9.

The dismantling of these things—the removal of Communion rails, the introduction of Communion in the hand while standing in line (again, I speak in reference to the Western experience as it developed over the second millennium), the disappearance of the acolyte with the paten, and so forth[37]—is consistent with the overall warping of the act of worship into an act of precipitous self-esteem, one that is disturbingly reminiscent of the scenario played out in the Garden of Eden, where Adam and Eve looked downward and inward, away from God, away from the world that had been gifted to them, and into their own vanity and pride; seeking a self-affirmation that resulted in their catastrophic alienation from God, from each other, and from their very selves. For these reasons, I concur with Martin Mosebach's assessment:

> The Missal of Paul VI did not . . . prescribe the turning-around of the altars—that is the most palpably felt transgression against the tradition of prayer in the whole world. The priest should turn himself, along with the congregation, to the Crucified and to the Christ who will return from the east; he should direct his prayers, in common with the congregation, to the altar and to Christ. . . . This change in the direction of prayer has caused greater harm in Europe and America than all of the relativizing, demythologizing, and humanizing theologies put together. It became patently clear to even the simple faithful that the prayers were directed, not to God, but rather to the congregation, which was to be put in the correct mood so as to celebrate *itself* as the "people of God."[38]

Contrary to a steady stream of progressive propaganda starting in about 1960, the Mass is not first and foremost a "communal gathering"—for there are many sorts of communal gatherings that are not Masses, and as the Church has consistently taught, a Mass celebrated by only a priest and a server, or in a case of necessity by a priest alone, with no congregation in sight, is still every bit as true and proper a Mass as one offered in St. Peter's Basilica with tens of thousands of faithful in attendance: each is the supreme sacrifice of Christ offered by and for the Church, His Mystical

---

37 I will come back to these topics in chapter 9.

38 Mosebach, *Subversive Catholicism,* 80.

Body. For the essence of the Mass is *not* the circle of people who may or may not gather around the table, but the all-pleasing immolation of the spotless Lamb who takes away the sins of the world: the sacrifice of Jesus Christ on Calvary, made present anew in the immolation of the Victim under the species of bread and wine, offered as a sweet-smelling oblation to the Father. Consequently, the Mass is a *theocentric* prayer: it is ordered *to God.* It is done, in the words of the *Gloria*, "*propter magnam gloriam tuam*" ("for the sake of Thy great glory"); in the words of the doxology at the end of the Canon, "All glory and honor are Thine, Almighty Father. . ." Yes, the Mass was given to us by Our Lord at the Last Supper for *our* benefit (since God does not benefit from our good actions!), but it benefits us precisely by ordering us to God first, giving Him the primacy that is His by nature and by conquest. We are benefited by being subordinated to God, yielding ourselves to Him as a rational sacrifice;[39] we profit from being decentered on ourselves and recentered on Him, our first beginning and last end. We stand to gain the most when we lose ourselves the most in Him.[40] *Convertimini ad me, et salvi eritis, omnes fines terrae, quia ego Deus, et non est alius.* "Turn to me and be saved, all the ends of the earth! For I am God, and there is no other."[41]

It is exactly for these reasons that celebration of the Mass *versus populum* or "facing the people" is not merely an unfortunate aberration based on poor scholarship and democratic habits of thought endemic to modern Westerners; it is a contradiction of the essence of the Mass and a distortion of the right relationship of man to God. Because of its inversion of the worshiping community's proper directionality (including the priest's) to the uncreated Font and Origin, it functions as a sort of "immunization" against the rational self-sacrifice that turns our souls and our bodies toward the Father, in union with His beloved Son, whose meat is to do the Father's will, not His own as a man.[42] This directional inversion substitutes a Protestant notion of worship for a Catholic one. Erik Tonning summarizes the critique made by the poet David Jones:

39 See Rom. 12:1.

40 This is the theme of my book *The Ecstasy of Love in the Thought of St. Thomas Aquinas.*

41 Is 45:22 RSVCE.

42 See John 4:34 and John 6:38; see also chapter 4.

> The reform played down the role of the priest as *sacerdos*, and the specifically cultic, sacral elements of propitiatory sacrifice, in order to cater to an ultimately Protestant-Humanist understanding of the liturgy as commemorative meal focused around preaching and imparting useful moral lessons.[43]

As Fr. John Hunwicke—himself a former Anglican cleric—explains:

> The sort of liturgical culture which Catholics have experienced since the 1960s is in fact a culture which was common in English Protestant Non-Conformity for many generations before the 1960s; and in a Protestant ethos it represents the theologically right and appropriate liturgical expectation. If the faith-feeling, *fiducia*, is the salvific reality to which the Christian must cling, then worship can have no other purpose than to produce and sustain it. It is not for nothing that Protestant ideologues have seen the Sacraments—on the rare occasions when they celebrate them—as merely "enacted Words." The problem for us is that for half a century most Catholics have been indoctrinated into that same essentially Protestant presupposition. When, now, they are exposed to something as ancient and authentic as *versus Orientem*, they can feel excluded by the celebrant—"Why isn't he attending to *me*?": the reaction of the toddler whose mother seems now to be devoting to the new baby all the love and attention upon which previously that toddler had an exclusive claim. "Leave your horrid private God alone and turn round and be my friend again." These poor layfolk are bound to feel repulsed; the outrage done to their gut-instincts may even make them revolted.[44]

In the pointed words of Fr. John Zuhlsdorf: "If your life is centered on Christ, you would more than likely be offended to see a priest turn his back to *Him*. If, on the other hand, you are centered on yourself, you would be offended to see a priest turn his back to *you*."[45]

---

43 See Shaw, *Latin Mass and the Intellectuals,* 315.

44 Hunwicke, "Facing the Mystery."

45 Zuhlsdorf, "More on liberal liturgists' attacks."

Emphasis or Distortion?

"But wait a minute," interrupts an objector. "Let's say, for the sake of argument, that eastward orientation is better—that it is more traditional and more theologically meaningful. But isn't it also true that Mass is a meal, like the Last Supper where it originated, in which we receive the Lord as food for the journey, and that emphasizing this side of the reality isn't false and can even be a good idea sometimes?" The objection, in other words, is that if there are a pair of truths, one of which has greater weight than the other, nevertheless the one does not cancel out the other: both deserve to be brought to the attention of the faithful. Might it not have been useful, after so many centuries of a mysterious, transcendent form of worship, to "flip things around" in order to make manifest the *other* side of the Mass?

The objection is well-intentioned, though deficient in historical basis.[46] My answer: to privilege a partial, secondary truth over the more fundamental truth is to inculcate untruth. We can see this if we look at the history of Christian heresy. When the Arians privileged the truth that the Son is in some sense less than the Father[47] but neglected the more fundamental truth that He is God—God from God, Light from Light, true God from true God—they inculcated an untruth; for the Son is not less than the Father simply speaking. When the Pelagians privileged the truth that man is not saved without his own effort but neglected the more fundamental truth that even our efforts are God's gift and that without His aid we can do nothing, they inculcated an untruth; for we are not saved by works, simply speaking. When the Protestants privileged the truth that Jesus Christ is our Savior but neglected the truth that He saves us in and through a visible body, the Church, of which we must become members in order to benefit from His saving action, they inculcated an untruth; for there is no salvation outside of the body of the Savior. A subjective conviction that "I am saved"

---

46 I will not give much attention here to the claim that the Last Supper was a *"versus populum"* affair and thereby justifies having the priest face the people. Ancient Mediterranean and Jewish banqueting customs make it virtually impossible to see the Last Supper as having been conducted either *versus populum* or *ad orientem,* at least in the literal sense of the terms. It was a *sui generis* Passover meal transformed into the kernel of a sacramental sacrifice; it was never taken as a simple model for Christian liturgy until the time of the Protestant reformers. For more on this point, see Kwasniewski, *Illusions of Reform,* 123–33.

47 See John 14:28.

has nothing to do with what we see happening in the New Testament, let alone the history of the early Church. When modern-day liberals privilege the truth that man has innate dignity but neglect the truth that his dignity is not absolute or independent of his social nature, with its ensuing obligations toward society and its susceptibility to just punishment up to and including death, they inculcate an untruth; for neither death nor the sovereignty of civil authority is contrary to human dignity, simply speaking.

In all of these examples (and they could easily be multiplied), we see how the emphasis of a partial truth, taken out of the context of the network of truths that gives it meaning, results in the establishment of a false system of belief, an "–ism" that separates itself from Catholicism.

The same is true of *versus populum.* When liturgical reformers privileged the idea of a communal gathering for table fellowship, but neglected the more fundamental truth (recognized as *de fide* dogma by Trent) that the Mass is the unbloody re-presentation of the bloody Sacrifice of the Cross, they inculcated an untruth; for the Mass is not first and foremost a group doing something together, but Jesus Christ offering Himself in sacrifice and granting us the opportunity to unite ourselves to this perfect, all-sufficient offering, the very cause of our salvation. It is the man who, over his lifetime, has become one with Jesus on the Cross who will be saved, not the man who gets together with friends to reminisce about the itinerant preacher of kindness from Nazareth. The emphasis of a partial truth (the Mass is a social or communal event involving edible refreshment), when taken out of the context of the larger dogma that gives this event its meaning and power (the Mass is the sacrifice of Christ, Head and members), falsifies the partial truth and in fact makes it to be harmful, in the same way as Arianism, Pelagianism, Protestantism, and Liberalism are harmful, although each is built upon a truth.

Celebration of the Eucharistic liturgy facing the people necessarily decontextualizes and falsifies the social nature of the Mass and unavoidably (even when the celebrant has a different subjective intention) suppresses its theocentric essence. For this reason, it inculcates a false understanding of the Mass, effectively *decatechizing* the faithful as to its true nature. It does not simply tilt the emphasis to one side or the other; it cancels out the orientation that is demanded by the holy sacrifice, which is to be offered to God alone, by a priest authorized to do so on behalf of the people. God alone, moreover, deserves and demands our adoration, and if it is not *clear* that we are united together in adoration of the One who alone is worthy of *latreia* (divine worship), then the unique right of God to such worship in spirit and in truth has been compromised or canceled out.

If we recall that for St. Thomas Aquinas, "religion" names the moral virtue by which we offer to God what is owed to Him by means of external signs and rites,[48] it would be accurate to say that worship *ad orientem* and celebration *versus populum* are the expression of different "religions," at least in the sense that something different is being displayed and given by the human actors. The problem, then, is not merely that the practice of celebrating Mass "toward the people" has no foundation whatsoever in the history of Catholic or Orthodox worship. No, it is much worse than an unfortunate sociological aberration, like the current fashion of body piercing. The use of *versus populum* erodes and corrupts the faith of the people as to the very essence of the Mass and the adoration owed to God for His great glory, since it takes away the most intuitive visual sign of God's primacy over man, and with its loss comes a severe weakening of the perception of man's duty to subordinate himself to God—in opposition to the ancient sophists and enlightened moderns who believe that "man is the measure of all things."

Clearing Up a Misunderstanding

I once received a forthright letter from a priest who argued strenuously against the position I have been explaining and defending. He wrote:

> May I ask a simple question? Where is God? Up there, out there? Or with us, among us?
>
> I imagine everyone would say he is both, he is everywhere, but clearly no arrangement of physical space in our churches or other buildings can adequately convey both his immanence and his transcendence. Seeing, however, that after centuries of *ad orientem* worship, emphasising the apartness, remoteness and unapproachable glory

[48] See *Summa Theologiæ* II–II, Q. 81.

of God, the Christian churches seem to be in continual decline, many would contend that it is high time to redress this distorted balance and emphasise the presentness of God *with* us. This is what reformed liturgy seeks to do. It is, of course, a senseless caricature to see it as priest and people greeting or confronting each other in an anthropocentric way; rather it is priest and people gathering *together* around the altar which is the focus of our worship, knowing that God in Christ is present in our midst. If we can rediscover God among us we might be able to realise more appropriately his glorious apartness as well. It is not a matter of contradictory theologies, but of complementary ones.

So far as I can see, we do not relate to God solely as an object of worship out there or up there, but also as a reality, a real presence in us and with us. Our symbolism cannot adequately convey all of this, so we make our choice of what we want to emphasise. Traditional worship has emphasised the glorious otherness of God; many now think we need to redress the balance towards his presence with us.

The very earliest forms of eucharistic liturgy were, I believe, domestic. The book of Acts records the first followers of Christ breaking bread *in their homes.* It is surely highly unlikely that they would have set up anything like the medieval church with nave and sanctuary, and far more likely that they would have gathered at or around a simple table. If anything, the earliest eucharist was probably more like our reformed liturgy today than the grandiose *ad orientem* High Mass.

To his credit, this priest quite capably presents some of the main arguments used by critics of *ad orientem* and/or advocates of *versus populum.* Here is how I responded.

Dear Reverend Father,

I think this is the wrong way to go about the question. God is indeed everywhere. That doesn't help at all with determining how liturgy should be done. Starting from the simple fact of His omnipresence, we might end up with the attitude of religion-free hippies: "I worship God on the beach or in the mountains." And while it is never wrong to lift one's personal praises to God in the great outdoors, this is not the path any orthodox Christianity ever took for its weekly or daily memorial of the saving death of Jesus.

The question should rather be put this way: "What *symbols* do we use in Christian worship to express our relationship to God and His to us?" And to answer that question, we have to look to the three principles of cosmos, history, and mystery, as Ratzinger argues in *The Spirit of the Liturgy.*

The universe (*cosmos*), which is God's "First Book," gives us the rising sun from the east. That is why God's Second Book (i.e., Sacred Scripture) talks so much about the Orient. The sun, the moon, and the stars were given to men "for signs and seasons" (Gen 1:14). If they are signs, what are they signs of? We ignore nature at our peril—now, more than ever, when artifacts and technology insulate or even alienate us from reality. That the sun rises in the east signifies that Christ is the true light who enlightens every man (Jn 1:9).

Church *history*, for its part, gives us a consistent witness of oriented churches where the nave gives way to the sanctuary, which gives way to the altar. How likely is it that the custom of facing east to worship, which came into public view in basilicas across the entire civilized world as soon as Christianity was legalized in the early fourth century, was something made up on the spot? The ancient Christians were far too jealous of their customs. It is far more likely that their preferred manner of praying was rooted in the habits of prayer handed down from the Apostles themselves, as St. Basil the Great testified. To remain symbolically effective, eastward prayer does not need to be set within elaborate architecture or ritual, although clearly all later architecture and ceremonial is like the pearl that forms around this initial grain of sand.

Mystery, the third criterion, tells us that we should not worship in such a way that we risk deifying ourselves or our community. Our worship has to be outward and upward in order to reinforce in us through sensible signs that we cannot save ourselves but must seek salvation beyond ourselves. True though it is that the soul is the temple of the Blessed Trinity, it can be dangerous to shape public worship in terms of God's immanence within us, since fallen human beings tend to be self-absorbed and self-exalting.

Traditional forms of worship greatly accentuate both God's transcendence and His immanence: His transcendence, in the various ways already mentioned; His immanence by the fact that our worship

> is physical, sensuous, and concerns food and drink and other ordinary things, through which the infinite and eternal God meets us in a definite place and time. I have never found that a Latin Low Mass or High Mass interferes with my awareness that God is within; on the contrary, the traditional rite's wide-open spaces for prayer, intensive preparation for Holy Communion, and facilitation of quiet thanksgiving for the gift of Our Lord have greatly strengthened my interior life as well as my sense of wonder at the astonishing humility of a God who comes to dwell with us.
>
> While a decline in numbers of Christian worshipers began in some places already in the middle of the twentieth century, it is a fact that the Catholic Church was booming throughout most of the world, with vocations, conversions, baptisms, and other statistics riding high. What happened? The increasing humanism of the twentieth century came to a head in the antinomianism of the 1960s, when progressivism, liberalism, and hedonism introduced profound unrest, malaise, and dissatisfaction with inherited forms of life and piety. But this was not the fault of the forms; it was the fault of those who rejected them in favor of sex, drugs, and rock 'n' roll—or, more innocently but no less fatally, felt banners, casual presidership, and folksy kindergarten churchsongs. The emphasis on God's "presentness"—"We are the People of God!"—coincided with the greatest exodus of Christians from public worship ever seen in the history of the world. If some reform was needed, what we got was certainly not it.

(I should mention that no reply was received from the priest.)

Temporary Expedients and Permanent Solutions

Years ago, the "Benedictine altar arrangement," named after Pope Benedict XVI, was all the rage in liturgically conservative circles. You have probably seen it: "the big six" (that is, six candles) and a crucifix are placed along the front edge of an altar, between the congregation and the celebrant, with the corpus on the crucifix facing the celebrant as a resting point for his gaze. Ratzinger's rationale was simple enough: the Mass is a transforming mystery through which we can come to grips with death and pass beyond it. The crucifix is central in worship, even as Calvary is central in salvation history. If, for whatever reason, we cannot or should not return to the *ad orientem* arrangement, we must at least face the cross together. In this way, the life-giving death of God is put before us. The candles, moreover, line the altar in a way that marks it off as a special place and helps us focus our attention on what transpires there, almost like lights that guide an airplane to a safe landing.

There was a time when I saw this set-up as a valid temporary solution to the dramatic pastoral crisis of the anthropocentric inversion of the Mass. Granting that it breaks up the closed circle and offers visual respite from the tête-à-tête, I can no longer see it as adequate to the magnitude of the *versus populum* error. The placement of six candles and a crucifix on the west side of the altar, though it may seem useful as an "instant fix," creates two major problems of its own. First, it leaves the false orientation intact, as the priest is *still* standing with his back to the east or to the apse that represents the east (and, in a church with a centrally located tabernacle, turns his back to the Lord!), and he is *still* facing the west which, as indicated in the Byzantine rite of baptism, symbolizes the kingdom of darkness. The idea of a "virtual east" represented by the crucifix, while clever, is too cerebral; it is contradicted by the "body language" of the sanctuary, the altar, and the priest. Second, this altar arrangement sets up an arbitrary barrier between the celebrant and the people, in a way that never happens in *ad orientem* worship, where everyone faces the same direction and feels the unity of this common orientation. In this way, it subtly accentuates the "priest *over against* people" mood that is already such an irritating characteristic of the Novus Ordo, which was composed by clericalists masquerading as populists.[49]

I am not at all opposed to the existence of real, permanent barriers in a church whenever they make sense liturgically and ceremonially: the ancient curtains around the baldachin, the chancel screen or rood screen, the iconostasis, the Communion rail. Such barriers articulate liturgical space and

[49] I hasten to add that, as I have demonstrated in a widely read article ("The Normativity of *Ad Orientem* Worship"), the missal of the modern rite does *not* require *versus populum* celebration; indeed, it presupposes the *ad orientem* stance, which is a strictly separate question from whether the altar is against the wall or freestanding. See, too, Schrader, "'Altared' States." Regrettably, Paul VI set the tone for the implementation of the liturgical reform when he offered Mass *versus populum* in Rome on March 7, 1965: see Augustinus, "50th Anniversary of Paul VI's First Italian Mass."

provide for a meaningful progression of ministers and actions, while catechizing the faithful about hierarchy, sacredness, and eschatology. But introducing a line of furnishings on the western end of an altar in order to make up (somehow) for the lack of a proper common orientation is arbitrary. It looks temporary and temporizing, as it is, and more often than not, marks an awkward caesura in the sanctuary, like a divider between office cubicles. Interesting, from this point of view, is the poet Paul Claudel's protest against the denuding of experimental *versus populum* altars in France, as well as the problem of trying to load them up again:

> Naturally, as the convenience of the faithful [for "seeing the Mass"] was held up as the guiding principle, it was necessary to rid the aforementioned table of the "accessories" cluttering it up: not only the candlesticks and the vases of flowers, but the tabernacle! The very crucifix! The priest says his Mass in a vacuum! When he invites the people to lift up their hearts and their eyes . . . to what [are they to look up]? There is nothing left in front of us to focus our minds on the Divine. If the candlesticks and crucifix were kept, [however,] the people would be even more excluded than in the old liturgy, because then not only the ceremony but the priest himself would be completely hidden from view.[50]

In *versus populum* is symbolized and promoted the anthropocentrism of modernity; its forgetfulness of God; its refusal to order all created reality to the uncreated source; its humanistic this-worldliness, which does not decisively subordinate the here and now to the Lord, the Orient, who has come and who will come again to judge the living and the dead. With this change alone, the liturgical ethos or consciousness of Christianity was shattered. We stopped facing God together and began looking at each other. If the old Mass were suddenly to be celebrated *versus populum*, in the manner in which the Novus Ordo generally is, it would be totally undermined by this one change; if the reformed Mass were to be celebrated *ad orientem*, this liturgical prodigal son would, by that *metanoia*, have already begun its journey back to the father's house.

---

[50] Claudel, "La Messe à l'envers" (written in 1955—which goes to show what busy beavers the liturgists already were before the Council!).

The eastward stance, with all that it symbolizes and implies, is not a mere accident, an incidental feature we can take or leave, like this or that style of chasuble. It is a constitutive element of the rite of the Holy Sacrifice. We should stop pretending that this is an instance of *de gustibus non disputandum*, where either "option" has something to be said for it. A Mass that refuses to orient itself in continuity with the universal tradition and theology of Christian worship is irregular and subversive—harmful to the priest and people whom it malforms in an anthropocentric mentality, harmful to the Mystical Body in which it perpetuates rupture and discontinuity, and less pleasing to God whom it deprives of due adoration. So much depends on the priest and the people facing east together that it is no exaggeration to say that orthodox Christianity will thrive where public prayer is thus offered and will suffer attrition wherever it has been abandoned. "Turn to him from whom you have deeply revolted, O people of Israel."[51]

May Christ, our true Light, the Orient and the Sun of Justice, who dawned on the world in His Incarnation and will return from the east as our Judge, grant each and all of us the grace to do our part in restoring this ancient tradition, *ut in omnibus glorificetur Deus*—that God may be glorified in all things.

[51] Is 31:6 RSVCE.

2

Why the Priest Is Separated from the People

"At Mass, the priest is doing everything and I'm just watching him."

Critics of the traditional Latin Mass and defenders of the modern rite of Pope Paul VI (usually the same people) often raise the objection that in the TLM, the priest is "far away" from the people, set apart as the only one offering the liturgy; that he "does everything" and they "do nothing"; that he ignores them, and they are lost.

These are the sorts of claims that drove the original liturgical reforms of the 1960s, although it should be noted that it was never the faithful who asked for the reforms, but rather the "experts" who claimed to know best what people needed. Perhaps the most perfect example of this attitude came from the pen of Dom Gregory Murray, OSB, writing in a letter to *The Tablet* on March 14, 1964: "The plea that the laity as a body do not want liturgical change, whether in rite or in language, is, I submit, quite beside the point. . . . It is not a question of what people want; it is a question of what is good for them."[52]

Experience has taught me, and study has shown me, that the professional liturgists' objections to the old rite are rather superficial and that, if we think about things more carefully, we will find, on the contrary,

[52] Cited in Davies, *Pope Paul's New Mass,* 91.

that the traditional approach makes much more sense of the paradoxes of divine worship. The hieratic distance between priest and people serves to accentuate the divine presence that invites *all* of us deeper into the liturgy and impresses on us the seriousness of our common work of worship; the priest's more involved role serves as a model and an invitation for the faithful's prayer, as they learn from watching and following, like apprentices from a master; and the apparent "ignoring" of us people in the pews by the clergy busy in the sanctuary liberates us from a merely horizontal and human "self-enclosed circle," in which the higher acts of prayer are suffocated in low-level communication and comprehension. Instead of being "on duty" and on display, we are free to be anonymous, hidden, and able to approach God in a variety of ways afforded us by the liturgy.

Propagandists of Revolution

Let's take as our point of departure half-a-dozen real-life examples of the basic critique made of the TLM. My first exhibit is from the blog *Where Peter Is*. In a title that would have served well for the *Babylon Bee*, the blog published an article called "Pope Francis: Guardian of Tradition." Its author, Terence Sweeney, launches broadsides against the "clericocentrism" of the Tridentine rite and insists on the dire need there was for a new Mass that would *at last* allow the people to have their proper role. He writes:

> The Tridentine liturgy centered on a cleric in a parish. All liturgical ministries are conducted by the one celebrant along with other clerics or altar servers dressed in clerical garb. The laity had little role—hearing little and saying less. . . . A liturgy in which the laity has no active role cannot express the ecclesial reality that the members of the laity do have active roles in virtue of Baptism and Confirmation. The liturgy of the Second Vatican Council is better because it is suited to this era of the Church. More importantly, it activates the full Body of Christ. In fully involving the laity (in the roles proper to them), Vatican II activated the whole Church. . . . To separate the active apostolate from the active liturgical practice is to foster an ecclesial incoherence. The Roman Rite [*sic*; he means the Novus Ordo or the modern rite of Paul

> VI], in contrast, fosters the full coherence of the Church by summoning all to active engagement in the liturgy in ways impossible in the Tridentine Rite.[53]

This way of arguing on the part of those who have little experience and even less understanding of traditional worship is so common as to be predictable. Only one who is profoundly ignorant of liturgical history and theology could forge a terminological contrast between "the Tridentine Rite" and "the Roman Rite" when, in reality, the former was the *only* Roman Rite the Church had—not just for four hundred years but for at least sixteen hundred years if we take into account its full historical sweep from the time before St. Gregory the Great to its culmination with St. Pius V to the eve of Vatican II, whereas, lamentably, the Novus Ordo bears little resemblance to *any* liturgy familiar to Catholics prior to the 1960s.

Here is a liturgist from Seattle, Fr. Jeffrey Moore, developing the same kind of critique as Sweeney's:

> One of the great scandals of the Roman Rite over the centuries has been its progressive disconnect from the people. Slowly over time, partly from a desire to preserve Latin as the language of worship, partly due to increased complexity and dramatic elements introduced by Frankish liturgists, and partly due to historical factors I will not rehearse here, the Mass became a purely clerical affair. The priests and other ministers would be gathered around the altar saying the Mass, and the people would be observing, almost like they were attending a play. By the end of the nineteenth century, the core of the Mass was said silently by the priest to himself or to the servers, with the empty silence filled by the choir singing complex Baroque compositions, or the people singing hymns or praying their private devotions. The Mass was schizophrenic, with the head separated from the body. . . .
>
> Why do you think the last 57 years have been liturgically so chaotic? Because the Church is suddenly trying to focus on something that she has not deeply considered for more than a millennium. The Church is trying to answer the question of how to include the people in the liturgical action of the Mass. . . .

[53] Sweeney, "Pope Francis: Guardian of Tradition."

My friends, the Second Vatican Council was an incredible gift to the Church, and the rediscovery of the dignity and role of the laity in both the liturgies and the mission of the Church is something we can never, ever, allow ourselves to lose sight of or back away from. . . . We live in a unique and blessed time, where the Church has turned her immense theological energies specifically toward the rediscovery of lay participation in the Mass. We have realized once again that the Mass belongs to us all, and it is in uniting our hearts and minds to the actions of the Mass that we will unite ourselves to Jesus and our salvation.[54]

Echoing Fr. Moore is the Jesuit Fr. Bruce T. Morrill:

Francis's directive [*Traditionis Custodes*] is about more than simply the ritual of the Roman Mass, for exclusive performance of the older rites by some Roman Catholics cannot but sustain, to varying degrees, ecclesial and social ideology inconsistent with Vatican II's entire reforming agenda for the church . . . The conversion from silent women, men, and children "attending" Mass to the assembled baptized people of God celebrating word and sacrament in their socio-cultural context is the seismic shift in Roman Catholicism at stake in Pope Francis's reversal of his two predecessors' incremental accommodations to arch-conservative, even reactionary clergy and laity.[55]

Allow me to provide just a few more examples. Here is Italian liturgist Andrea Grillo, rumored to be among the ghostwriters of *Traditionis Custodes*:

The liturgical reform has profoundly altered the understanding of the celebrating Church, the subjects involved in it, and the tradition to which they acknowledge they belong. The space of an "*actuosa participatio*" [active participation], which the preconciliar rite had profoundly forgotten, reappears at the center of experience and demands

[54] Moore, "Liturgical Participation." Fr. Moore and the others I am quoting here say nothing different from the talking points of the Liturgical Movement vanguard around the time of the Council. For example, Canon J.B. O'Connell, an "early adopter" of reform, opined as follows: "It is almost incredible to think that for a thousand years the vital link between the worshipping people in the benches and the ministers at the altar had been cut" (quoted by Fr. Bryan Houghton in 1967; see Shaw, *Latin Mass and the Intellectuals,* 53). We may gloss O'Connell: it is incredible, that is, unbelievable, because it is false, as Houghton shows.

[55] Morrill, "Tradition and the Roman Rite."

> new subjects, new actions, new spaces, and new times. To remain (or return) to Pius V is to have failed to understand this profound change and/or to want to explicitly contradict it.[56]

Preacher of the papal household Fr. Raniero Cantalamessa shows that he remembers exceptionally well the classes he took in the 1950s and '60s, for even today he repeats verbatim the standard line of the Liturgical Movement's *avant-garde* on the eve of and in the wake of Vatican II:

> At the beginning of the Church and for the first three centuries, the liturgy was truly a "liturgy," that is, the action of the people (*laos*—people—is among the etymological components of the word *leitourgia*). From St. Justin, from the *Traditio Apostolica* of St. Hippolytus, and other sources of the time, we obtain a vision of the Mass that is certainly closer to the reformed one of today than to that of the centuries behind us.

A brief digression: modern scholarship entirely rejects the notion that "liturgy" means "work of the people."[57] *Leitourgia* means "the work of One on behalf of many." This definition is properly theocentric and Christocentric; it justifies, even as it relativizes, the "sacerdotalism" of all traditional rites.

Cantalamessa presents with particular force the objection to which the rest of this chapter will be a response:

> What happened? The answer is an awkward word which, however, we cannot avoid: clericalization! In no other sphere was it more conspicuous than in the liturgy. Christian worship, and especially the Eucharistic sacrifice, underwent a rapid transformation, both in East and West, from being an action of the people into being an action of the clergy. For centuries, the central part of the Mass, known as the Canon or Anaphora, was pronounced by the priest in a low voice, in Latin, behind a curtain or a wall (a temple within a temple!), out of the sight and hearing of the people. The celebrant only raised his voice at the final words of the Canon: "*Per omnia saecula saeculorum*," and the people replied, "Amen!" to what they hadn't heard, let alone understood. The only contact with the Eucharist, announced by the sound of the bells, was the moment of the elevation of the Host.

56 Grillo, "Rito tridentino e nullità matrimoniale."
57 See Kwasniewski, "Refuting the Commonplace."

> There is an evident return [here] to what was going on in the worship of the First Covenant. The High Priest entered the *Sancta sanctorum*, with incense and the blood of the victims, and the people stood outside trembling, overwhelmed by the sense of God's tremendous holiness and majesty. The sense of the sacred is at its highest here, but, after Christ [has come], is it the right and genuine one? . . . The holy has changed the way of manifesting itself: no longer as a mystery of majesty and power, but as an infinite capacity of hiding and suffering.[58]

The last sentence betrays an oddly Marcionite point of view, in which there is a decisive break between the Old and New Testaments: the revelation of God in the Old Covenant, including how He is to be worshiped, has no abiding lesson for us under the New Covenant. On this account, salvation history is characterized primarily by rupture, not by continuity. How such a view can be seen as compatible with the birth of Eucharistic worship out of the confluence of synagogue, temple, and Passover is quite beyond me; it certainly bears no resemblance to the approach of the Church Fathers.

Last but certainly not least, we have Cardinal Arthur Roche, the prefect of the Dicastery for Divine Worship, who made a startling comment that, predictably, attracted a lot of attention:

> You know the theology of the Church has changed [with Vatican II]. Whereas before, the priest represented, at a distance, all the people. They were channeled, as it were, through this person who alone was celebrating the Mass. It is [now] not only the priest who celebrates the liturgy but also those who are baptized with him. And that is an enormous statement to make.[59]

But *did* the Church's theology change? Are Cardinal Roche, Cardinal Cantalamessa, Andrea Grillo, Fr. Bruce T. Morrill, Fr. Jeffrey Moore, Terence Sweeney, and others who say similar things actually in possession of a correct understanding of the "before" that they criticize, or of the "after" that they praise? As I will show, these critiques are premised on several

---

[58] Cantalamessa, "Mysterium Fidei! On the Liturgy—Fourth Lenten Sermon 2023."

[59] See, for the quotation and further commentary, Shaw, "Cardinal Roche on the Vatican II Rupture"; Baresel, "Archbishop Roche: 'The Traditional Mass Must Go.'"

misunderstandings that can only be called enormous, the recurrence of which under Pope Francis gives us a welcome occasion to delve deeper into the relationship between clerical ministry and the laity's offering of the Mass. In so doing, we shall arrive at a greater appreciation for the wisdom of tradition.

Distinguish in Order to Unite

One of Jacques Maritain's most famous books bore the title *The Degrees of Knowledge.* Its subtitle is, however, more intriguing: *Distinguish in Order to Unite.* That subtitle reminds me of a statement from Henri de Lubac: "The more you separate, the less do you really distinguish"—as if to say: by distinguishing two things well, you show how they are, in fact, united to one another in a relationship. We see this most luminously in the mystery of the hypostatic union: in Jesus Christ, the divine nature of the Word and the human nature consisting of a rational soul informing an organic body are perfectly united—"distinct but not separated, joined but not confused," in the classic formula of Council of Chalcedon.

How wonderfully the traditional Latin Mass *distinguishes* between the identity of the priest offering the Mass and the identity of the laity who assist in this offering—between his role and theirs! By clearly and consistently delineating what is a priestly act and what is a congregational act, the classical liturgy more deeply *binds together* the celebrant and the people in a common act of worship that is nevertheless hierarchically differentiated. By emphasizing to the maximum the priestliness of the priest, it brings him into the closest spiritual union with the people on whose behalf he serves and for whom he mediates. This, in turn, forms the laity in such a way that they can be mediators for the secular world, whose conversion and transformation is their special vocation.[60]

Christ is the mediator on behalf of mankind; the priest is a mediator on behalf of the faithful; the faithful are mediators on behalf of the unconverted world. The hierarchical action of the liturgy does not end with the clergy but extends, in this way, to the people and through them to every nook and cranny of creation. But it does so *in a hierarchical manner*, that is, in strict

[60] See Kwasniewski, *Ministers of Christ,* 65–102.

accordance with distinctions established by God, not in a disorderly and/or democratic way. This must be so, not only because God delights in order, diversity (rightly understood!), dependency, obedience, service, and sacrificial love, but also because He is, in some mysterious sense, hierarchical in Himself: He is order within absolute unity. The Father is the origin without origin; the Son is originated from the Father and, as one with Him, originates the Spirit; the Spirit is only originated. They are one, yet the Persons proceed in such a way that the "monarchy of the Father" is eternally established.

How We Learn to Offer the Mass

Paradoxically, it is by seeing what is proper to the priest that the faithful come to understand what is proper to them as a priestly people: *we* are doing, analogously, what *he* is doing. We come to know the marvelous truth of our participation in the sacrifice of Christ only by seeing this mystery enacted *outside* of ourselves, *beyond* our reach, and at a level that, in fact, does *not* belong to us—even as the salvific and sanctifying action of Christ the High Priest surpasses the capacity of any human being.

This is the way we learn almost anything: by watching it done or hearing it explained by someone who knows how to do it well, and then entering into it from below (as it were). The difference, of course, is that with something like literacy, we can eventually become the equal or even the superior of our reading instructor, because a natural skill grows with time and age; whereas with priesthood, there is a qualitative difference between the sacramental character of baptism and the sacramental character of the ordained.[61] The layman is equipped to offer himself, his actions and sufferings, his loved ones, and the world of his work to God through the sacrifice of Jesus Christ; the priest is equipped to offer the very sacrifice of Jesus Christ, on behalf of the same divine Person.[62]

---

[61] As, indeed, Vatican II taught in *Lumen Gentium,* no. 10, in continuity with Pius XII's *Mediator Dei,* nos. 40–43, 69, 84, 92, et passim.

[62] It bears emphasis that the laity's offering of the sacrifice of the Mass, albeit in a different mode from that of the priest, was well and widely recognized in theological and devotional writing for many centuries prior to Vatican II, showing just how wrong Cardinal Roche et al. are in their sweeping claims. For evidence, see the magisterial (in every sense of the word) treatment by Pius XII in *Mediator Dei,* nos. 82–104; cf. "Is the Laity's Offering of Mass a Postconciliar Rediscovery?," in Kwasniewski, *Illusions of Reform,* 83–92.

We see this qualitative difference emphasized again and again in the prayers themselves of the old Roman Missal: the separate Confiteors of the celebrant and the servers; phrases in the Offertory like "which I, Thine unworthy servant, offer unto Thee, my living and true God, for my countless sins, offenses, and negligences; likewise for all here present" and "that it may avail both me and them . . ."; and plenty of similar lines, to which I shall return in a moment.

That the Mass is a true and proper sacrifice is far more evident in the *Vetus Ordo* than in the *Novus Ordo*. In its prayers and gestures, the traditional Mass readily presents itself as the fulfillment of the Old Covenant in the institution of the New Covenant. I, the worshiper, can see that the priest is going up to the altar on my behalf to offer sacrifice to God for my sins, in continuity with the old priesthood ministering in the Temple with symbolic animal sacrifices and incense—now truly accomplished once for all in the self-offering of the divine Victim. At the *Hanc igitur*, prior to the consecration, the priest puts both hands over the bread and wine as the Old Testament priest would put his hands over the head of the sacrificial victim—a clear connection between the Old and the New. Sadly, in the Novus Ordo Mass, the language of "calling down the Spirit" has been artificially grafted on to this gesture, completely changing the meaning into a *faux* Byzantine epiclesis, which the Roman Rite never had and never needed.[63]

No "Separation Anxiety"

At a sung or High Mass, the salutary separation between priest and people becomes much clearer because of the phenomenon—native to all traditional rites, Eastern and Western—called "parallel liturgy." Multiple things are happening simultaneously. In the Tridentine Mass as in the Byzantine Divine Liturgy, the faithful or the choir may be singing a chant while the priest is saying or doing something else. The liturgy is a complex action with many participants who have different works to perform, yet these diverse participants and works coalesce around and culminate in a unity. Very different is the rationalistic construct of "sequential liturgy" favored by the architects of the Novus Ordo, where usually only one thing is allowed to be happening at

63 DiPippo, "Reforming the Canon of the Mass."

a time, and everyone must wait until a particular task is done before moving on. This, again, seems to downplay the idea of multiple distinct roles that can overlap like the lines of polyphony in a motet by Palestrina.

The traditional rite makes manifest the nature of the ordained ministerial priesthood and the salutary separation between this and the universal priesthood of all baptized believers. The Novus Ordo with its *versus populum* stance, permeable sanctuary, lay lectors and extraordinary ministers, and so forth, blurs the line between the two, blunting the many lessons and insights that the distinction imparts. The beautiful ways in which the old Mass distinguishes between the priest and the faithful, with so many signs, at so many levels, serves rather to unite the members of the Mystical Body in a common act of worship, where the eye, the hand, the head, and the feet are content to be what they are and to do what belongs to them.[64] One might say: there is no body-part dysphoria.

In the traditional Latin Mass, I find great comfort in the fact that the priest is offering the Mass on my behalf to Almighty God. He was and is ordained to do so; that is his place, and it helps me to find my own. When a parent must deal with a fussy baby and can't follow along, he or she can rest in the peace of the rite, knowing that the father of the ecclesiastical family is taking care of it, on the laity's behalf, and with the awesome power of Christ the Eternal High Priest carrying and empowering the worshipers. One can simply revel in God's presence. One doesn't feel as if one needs to "actively participate" *in the Novus Ordo sense* to feel like one has "been to Mass"; the action is so mighty and mysterious that simply *being there*, with faith and love, is already a tremendous grace, a privilege, a participation deeper than external words or actions. One has been drawn into a Mass that seems, in a way, to emerge from eternity and to merge back into it. I *hear* the Mass and I *assist* at it, but I am not carrying it myself, nor is it directed to me; it carries me to the Lord, to whatever extent His grace permits. The rite carries me; I do not carry the rite. The priest, too, though uniquely empowered to offer the holy oblation, is also carried by the rite, no less than the rest of us. Ultimately, we are all drawn by the Cross into the glory of God the Father "of whom all paternity in heaven and earth is named."[65]

---

64 Cf. 1 Cor. 12:15–26.

65 Eph. 3:15.

What Anglican Converts Noticed

St. John Henry Newman vividly describes what traditional Catholic worship is like, in a passage of his novel *Loss and Gain*:

> Reding thought he never had been present at worship before, so absorbed was the attention, so intense was the devotion of the congregation. What particularly struck him was, that whereas in the Church of England the clergyman or the organ was everything and the people nothing except so far as the clerk is their representative, here it was just reversed. The priest hardly spoke, or at least audibly; but the whole congregation was as though one vast instrument or Panharmonicon, moving all together, and, what was most remarkable, as if self-moved. They did not seem to require anyone to prompt or direct them, though in the Litany the choir took the alternate parts. The words were Latin, but everyone seemed to understand them thoroughly, and to be offering up his prayers to the Blessed Trinity, and the Incarnate Saviour, and the great Mother of God, and the glorified Saints, with hearts full in proportion to the energy of the sounds they uttered. There was a little boy near him, and a poor woman, singing at the pitch of their voices. There was no mistaking it; Reding said to himself, "This *is* a popular religion." . . . "How wonderful," said Charles to himself, "that people call this worship formal and external; it seems to possess all classes, young and old, polished and vulgar, men and women indiscriminately; it is the working of one Spirit in all, making many one."[66]

Another great English convert from Anglicanism in yet another great English novel—Msgr. Robert Hugh Benson in *By What Authority?*, set during the reign of Queen Elizabeth I—features a Calvinist named Isabel, who has gradually warmed to the Catholic Faith. Benson imagines her thoughts when witnessing her first Mass. The Mass is said silently in the home of a recusant family by a priest who, not long before, had been tortured on the rack. The passage deserves to be quoted at length, so well does it present the contrast (also remarked on by Newman) between Protestant and Catholic worship:

---

[66] Newman, *Loss and Gain,* pt. III, ch. 10, 426–27.

Isabel had a missal, lent to her by Mistress Margaret; but she hardly looked at it; so intent was she on that crimson figure and his strange movements and his low broken voice. It was unlike anything that she had ever imagined worship to be. Public worship to her had meant hitherto one of two things—either sitting under a minister and having the word applied to her soul in the sacrament of the pulpit; or else the saying of prayers by the minister aloud and distinctly and with expression, so that the intellect could follow the words, and assent with a hearty Amen. The minister was a minister to man of the Word of God, an interpreter of His gospel to man.

But here was a worship unlike all this in almost every detail. The priest was addressing God, not man; therefore he did so in a low voice, and in a tongue as Campion had said on the scaffold "that they both understood." It was comparatively unimportant whether man followed it word for word, for (and here the second radical difference lay) the point of the worship for the people lay, not in an intellectual apprehension of the words, but in a voluntary assent to and participation in the supreme act to which the words were indeed necessary but subordinate. It was the thing that was done, not the words that were said, that was mighty with God. Here, as these Catholics round Isabel at any rate understood it, and as she too began to perceive it, though dimly and obscurely, was the sublime mystery of the Cross presented to God. As He looked down well pleased into the silence and darkness of Calvary, and saw there the act accomplished by which the world was redeemed, so here (this handful of disciples believed), He looked down into the silence and twilight of this little lobby, and saw that same mystery accomplished at the hands of one who in virtue of his participation in the priesthood of the Son of God was empowered to pronounce these heart-shaking words by which the Body that hung on Calvary, and the Blood that dripped from it there, were again spread before His eyes, under the forms of bread and wine.

Much of this faith of course was still dark to Isabel; but yet she understood enough; and when the murmur of the priest died to a throbbing silence, and the worshippers sank in yet more profound adoration, and then with terrible effort and a quick gasp or two of pain, those wrenched bandaged hands rose trembling in the air with Something that glimmered white between them; the Puritan girl too drooped her head, and lifted up her heart, and entreated the Most High and most Merciful to look down on the Mystery of Redemption accomplished on earth; and for the sake of the Well-Beloved to send down His Grace on the Catholic Church; to strengthen and save the living; to give rest and peace to the dead; and especially to remember her dear brother Anthony, and Hubert whom she loved; and Mistress Margaret and Lady Maxwell, and this faithful household: and the poor battered man before her, who, not only as a priest was made like to the Eternal Priest, but as a victim too had hung upon a prostrate cross, fastened by hands and feet; thus bearing on his body for all to see the marks of the Lord Jesus. . . .

Isabel went to her room as one in a dream. She was soon in bed again, but could not sleep; the vision of that strange worship she had assisted at; the pictorial details of it, the glow of the two candles on the shoulders of the crimson chasuble as the priest bent to kiss the altar or to adore; the bowed head of the server at his side; the picture overhead with the Mother and her downcast eyes, and the radiant Child stepping from her knees to bless the world—all this burned on the darkness. With the least effort of imagination too she could recall the steady murmur of the unfamiliar words; hear the rustle of the silken vestment; the stirrings and breathings of the worshippers in the little room. . . .

Mistress Margaret was only one of thousands to whom this little set of actions half seen and words half heard, wrought and said by a man in a curious dress, were more precious than all meditation and prayer put together. . . . Was it, indeed,—this half-hour action,—the most august mystery of time, the Lamb eternally slain, presenting Himself and His Death before the Throne in a tremendous and bloodless Sacrifice—so august that the very angels can only worship it afar off and cannot perform it?[67]

The Priest Praying for Himself

Let us take a closer look at why so great a benefit accrues to the people precisely from the priest himself in the traditional Mass carrying the burden of his unique role as *alter Christus* or "another Christ," acting *in persona Christi capitis* or in the person (that is, on behalf of and by the authority

[67] Benson, *By What Authority?*, 339–41, 342, and 343.

of) Christ the Head of the Church, with numerous ministerial tasks never shared out to the laity—responsibilities specific to himself and to his fellow clergy in the sanctuary. A proper "priestly domain" is traced out, so to speak, by the number of prayers and gestures that only the priest performs, as the model of the Christ who alone is our Redeemer and Savior.

In the mad race to make liturgy more communal, more active, and (consequently) more egalitarian, the postconciliar liturgical reform reduced this "priestly domain" more and more, like the Indian territories in early America that kept getting smaller and smaller as settlers moved in and took over the ancestral lands. The role of the priest was re-conceived in a functionalist or utilitarian manner; his new work was to engage the people as their dialogue partner, to animate them, to occupy them with pious thoughts (in a best-case scenario); and even when he addressed God in prayers, he must do so out-loud and *versus populum*, which creates cognitive dissonance as to who is really being addressed and why. These factors tend to evacuate his ministry of its own interior spiritual density and earnest focus on God, its mediation of divine gifts, and turn it into an extroverted presidency of a social gathering.

Now, there are a lot of problems with this sudden and radical change in the basic conception of what liturgy is and what the priest's role within it should be. Here, I want to focus on the spiritual side of things. What might have been "self-evident truths" once upon a time are no longer evident to many clergy, to their superiors, and to their flocks. One such truth is staggeringly obvious: *the priest, too, has a soul to sanctify and save*. One might as well say that water is wet, or fire is hot. Yet the implications of this truth seem not only to be ignored, but to be suppressed, especially in the period after the Second Vatican Council, when pastoral activism has threatened to turn the priest into a glorified social worker, a man so oriented to others that he ceases to be oriented to God. As we saw in the last chapter, the *versus populum* stance at Mass, so far from being just a groundless bit of false antiquarianism, becomes emblematic of a way of life: instead of offering a sacrifice to God on behalf of the people *and of himself as a member of the Church,* the celebrant appears rather to be offering a service *to* the people, with himself in the role of teacher (at best) or showman (at worst).

Consider, in sharp contrast, how often the Order of Mass in the traditional Roman Rite makes the priest pray for himself in a deliberate and earnest way—not for someone else; not for the people; not for a vague set of intentions; but specifically *for himself.*

After the sign of the cross, the first words: "I will go in to the altar of God." The whole of Psalm 42 is recited, alternately with the ministers, as a personal preparation. Here are the priest's own verses:

> Judge me, O God, and distinguish my cause from the nation that is not holy; deliver me from the unjust and deceitful man. . . . Send forth Thy light and Thy truth: they have conducted me and brought me unto Thy holy hill, and into Thy tabernacles. . . . To Thee, O God, my God, I will give praise upon the harp: why art thou sad, O my soul, and why dost thou disquiet me? . . . Glory be to the Father, and to the Son, and to the Holy Ghost. . . . I will go in to the altar of God.[68]

Then comes the priest's *own* Confiteor—not a shared and therefore comfortably untargeted confession, but a personal one to which the rest of the Church bears witness, and after which the lowly servers or subordinate clerics beg the Lord to forgive him specifically:

> *I* confess to almighty God, to blessed Mary ever virgin, to blessed Michael the archangel, to blessed John the Baptist, to the holy apostles Peter and Paul, to all the saints, and to you, brethren, that *I* have sinned exceedingly in thought, word and deed: [the priest strikes his breast three times saying:] through *my* fault, through *my* fault, through *my* most grievous fault. Therefore *I* beseech the blessed Mary ever virgin, blessed Michael the archangel, blessed John the Baptist, the holy apostles Peter and Paul, all the saints, and you, brethren, to pray to the Lord our God for *me.*

As the priest mounts the altar steps, he prays in the plural, but surely with himself most of all in mind: "Take away from us our iniquities, we beseech Thee, O Lord; that, being made pure in heart we may be worthy to enter into the Holy of Holies. Through Christ our Lord. Amen." Then

---

68 Translations are taken from either *The New Roman Missal* (1945) by Father Lasance or the *St. Andrew Daily Missal* (1945).

bowing to kiss the altar, he prays in the singular: "We beseech Thee, O Lord, by the merits of those of Thy saints whose relics are here, and of all the saints, that Thou wouldst vouchsafe to pardon me all my sins. Amen."

Before the Gospel, the priest recites these prayers at the center of the altar:

> Cleanse my heart and my lips, O almighty God, Who didst cleanse with a burning coal the lips of the prophet Isaias; and vouchsafe in Thy loving kindness so to purify me that I may be enabled worthily to announce Thy holy gospel. Through Christ our Lord. Amen. Vouchsafe, O Lord, to bless me. The Lord be in my heart and on my lips, that I may worthily and becomingly announce His gospel. Amen.

Perhaps the most striking example of a priest's prayer for himself is to be found in the traditional Offertory of the Mass, which emerged in the early Middle Ages and is to be found, with similar texts, in all Western liturgical rites.[69]

> Receive, O Holy Father, almighty and eternal God, this spotless host, which I, Thine unworthy servant, offer unto Thee, my living and true God, for my countless sins, offenses, and negligences; likewise for all here present, and for all faithful Christians, both living and departed, that it may avail both me and them to salvation, unto life everlasting. Amen.

The *Lavabo* is found in its full form:

> I will wash my hands among the innocent, and will compass Thine altar, O Lord. That I may hear the voice of praise, and tell of all Thy wondrous works. I have loved, O Lord, the beauty of Thy house, and the place where Thy glory dwelleth. Take not away my soul, O God, with the wicked; nor my life with men of blood. In whose hands are iniquities: their right hand is filled with gifts. But as for me, I have walked in my innocence; redeem me, and have mercy on me. My foot hath stood in the right way; in the churches I will bless Thee, O Lord. Glory be to the Father . . .

69 See DiPippo, "The Theology of the Offertory."

Of course, many other prayers in the Order of Mass would *include* the celebrant, but I am keeping my gaze on those that tie in more personally with the priest's own role, his sinfulness and sanctification. The next obvious candidate, then, would be the "*Nobis quoque peccatoribus*" of the Roman Canon, when he strikes his breast and gently lifts his voice in humble confession:

> To us sinners, also, Thy servants, who put our trust in the multitude of Thy mercies, vouchsafe to grant some part and fellowship with Thy holy apostles and martyrs; with John, Stephen, Matthias, Barnabas, Ignatius, Alexander, Marcellinus, Peter, Felicitas, Perpetua, Agatha, Lucy, Agnes, Cecilia, Anastasia, and with all Thy saints. Into their company do Thou, we beseech Thee, admit us, not weighing our merits, but freely pardoning our offenses: through Christ our Lord.

The embolism after the Lord's Prayer:

> Deliver us, we beseech Thee, O Lord, from all evils, past, present, and to come: and by the intercession of the blessed and glorious Mary, ever a virgin, Mother of God, and of Thy holy apostles Peter and Paul, of Andrew, and of all the saints, graciously grant peace in our days, that through the help of Thy bountiful mercy we may always be free from sin and secure from all disturbance.

The three prayers of preparation, *all* of which must be said:

> O Lord Jesus Christ Who didst say to Thine apostles: Peace I leave you, My peace I give you: look not upon my sins, but upon the faith of Thy Church, and vouchsafe to grant her peace and unity according to Thy will: Who livest and reignest God, world without end. Amen.
>
> O Lord Jesus Christ, Son of the living God, Who, according to the will of the Father, through the co-operation of the Holy Ghost, hast by Thy death given life to the world: deliver me by this Thy most Sacred Body and Blood from all my iniquities, and from every evil; make me always cleave to Thy commandments, and never suffer me

> to be separated from Thee, Who with the same God the Father and the Holy Ghost, livest and reignest God, world without end. Amen.
>
> Let not the partaking of Thy Body, O Lord Jesus Christ, which I, all unworthy, presume to receive, turn to my judgement and condemnation; but through Thy loving kindness may it be to me a safeguard and remedy for soul and body; Who, with God the Father, in the unity of the Holy Ghost, livest and reignest, God, world without end. Amen.

At the moment of Communion, still facing east, head bowed to the Lord—and crucially, in the midst of *a Communion rite of his own* that completes the offering of the sacrifice,[70] before he turns to hold aloft the Lamb of God for the congregation—the priest prays privately:

> I will take the bread of heaven, and will call upon the name of the Lord. Lord, I am not worthy that Thou shouldst enter under my roof; but only say the word, and my soul shall be healed [thrice]. May the Body of Our Lord Jesus Christ keep my soul unto life everlasting. Amen.
>
> What shall I render unto the Lord for all the things that He hath rendered unto me? I will take the chalice of salvation and will call upon the name of the Lord. With high praises will I call upon the Lord, and I shall be saved from all mine enemies. May the Blood of Our Lord Jesus Christ keep my soul unto life everlasting. Amen.

Having distributed the Body of Christ, he recites two prayers after Communion:

> Into a pure heart, O Lord, may we receive the heavenly food which has passed our lips; bestowed upon us in time, may it be the healing of our souls for eternity.
>
> May Thy Body, O Lord, which I have received, and Thy Blood which I have drunk cleave to mine inmost parts: and do Thou grant that no stain of sin remain in me, whom pure and holy mysteries have refreshed: Who livest and reignest world without end. Amen.

---

70 See chapter 5, pp. 124–25.

Of greatest importance in grasping the theology and spirituality of the Roman Mass is the last prayer said by the priest prior to his giving the final blessing:

> May the lowly homage of my service be pleasing to Thee, O most holy Trinity: and do Thou grant that the sacrifice which I, all unworthy, have offered up in the sight of Thy majesty, may be acceptable to Thee, and, because of Thy loving kindness, may avail to make atonement to Thee for myself and for all those for whom I have offered it up. Through Christ our Lord. Amen.

The Mass does not suddenly end but merges into the Last Gospel, a gentle moment of meditation, gratitude, and farewell, when the Beloved Disciple proclaims the Word made flesh, full of grace and truth, whom we have just offered and received.

The Scandal of the Removal of These Prayers

Now, we can all agree that the prayers I have just quoted are extremely rich in their theological and devotional content and in the intensity of their focus on the reality of God with whom, above all, the priest is dealing at Mass. God is more real than a million members of the congregation, more real than a million priests, more real than the liturgy: He is an infinite living fire that consumes with love those who love Him, burns away the iniquities of those who repent, and punishes the wicked with flames of justice. With this God of eternal splendor and righteousness, the Mass brings the priest face to face, breath to breath, heart to heart. The prayers given to the priest to say must somehow be suitable to the truth of this encounter at the burning bush, at the top of Mount Moriah, at the edge of the celestial Jerusalem. They must plunge him into it and make him recognize the gravity and grace of what he is doing. Not even a thousand prayers could ever be sufficient compared to the one Word uttered from all eternity in heaven; but at least the liturgical rite must show a truthful apprehension of what is taking place, in and through the priest, at his hands, by his voice. The rite will make him pray earnestly for himself and on behalf of the people, for purification, worthiness, and divine help; it will be theocentric, fixed—even fixated—on God; it will take the time and the silence and the gestures needed to approach the mysteries thoughtfully and to handle them reverently. That is what we see in abundance in any traditional liturgical rite, including the Latin Mass with its obvious orientation to Our Lord and Savior Jesus Christ and through Him to the God and Father of all, who is above all, and through all, and in all.[71]

Is it not, then, a monumental scandal, a frightening departure from wisdom, that nearly all of the priestly prayers I have quoted above were simply struck from Pope Paul VI's Order of Mass, which is denuded and exiguous by comparison, and which, practically speaking, is almost totally extroverted and procedural in nature?[72] Not only that, it took away most of the kisses given to the altar, many genuflections, many signs of the cross, a multitude of gestures that tied the priest to the altar, the sacrifice, and the person of Jesus Christ whose high-priestly character he bears. The modern rite barely addresses the subjective disposition of the one offering and the need for careful preparation; it hardly touches on his unworthiness and need for purification and mercy. It includes remarkably few signs by which an observer unfamiliar with the Catholic Faith could detect that something wondrous, astonishing, and awesome is taking place, before which angels veil their faces and men beat their breasts.[73]

---

[71] See Eph. 4:6.

[72] Abolished: the prayers at the foot of the altar; the separate Confiteor; the prayers said while mounting the steps and kissing the altar; the burning coal prayer; the Offertory prayers (all of them, replaced with texts from rabbinical Judaism); the embolism in its full form; the prayers immediately before the priest's reception of Communion; the second prayer during the ablutions; the *Placeat tibi;* and the last Gospel. All are gone from the Novus Ordo. The priest is asked to make a choice between two prayers of preparation before Communion (in the old rite he says both). The Roman Canon is, on average, rarely used.

[73] Thus, the number of osculations (kissings) of the altar has been pared down from eight to two; the number of signs of the cross the priest makes over himself has been reduced from as many as eight to only one; the triple sign of the cross, from two to one; the sign of the cross over the bread and wine, or with the host and chalice, from several dozen to only one; the blessing over persons was reduced to the end of Mass, leaving out blessings made over the readers of the Epistle and the Gospel and the recipients of Communion; the dozens of beatings of the breast, reduced to one or none; the multiple bows of the head and genuflections, cut to a mere fraction of what they were. All these signs were meaningful and reinforced associations of the sacred; their elimination should be seen as a major cause of the desacralization of the Mass.

What were the liturgical reformers thinking? For them, the prayers of the priest for himself must have looked like exaggerated medieval piety and devotionalism, too introspective and clericocentric; the liturgy is "for the people," after all. But this is manifestly a false view both of what liturgy is and of what these specific prayers are meant to accomplish. Because the liturgy is above all *God's work* on behalf of the people, with the priest at their head by divine appointment, it follows that the priest must be especially solicitous *for himself*, that he may offer the oblation in holiness, in atonement for his own sins and for the sins of the people, and for the strengthening of the inward man, the new Adam, in everyone. To remove or downplay this dimension is to strip the liturgy of that quest for righteousness that makes it serve the foremost need of *every* Christian, regardless of his place or role in the Mystical Body of Christ.

Looking over the Order of Mass,[74] we cannot help noticing that the Novus Ordo has largely purged this element of the priest praying for himself. While we can readily admit that moral and doctrinal problems existed among clergy before the Council, we have nevertheless seen an exponential rise, a tidal wave, of clerical dereliction and corruption *since* the Council, and particularly since the introduction of the modern rite of Pope Paul VI. If we actually believe in the power of prayer, can we not attribute much of our current crisis to the fact that priests (with the exception of the 1% or so that are celebrating the traditional liturgy) are not habitually *praying for themselves* and making confession and reparation for their sins in the context of the Church's highest and most powerful prayer—that very sacrifice of the High Priest to whom their ordination configured them, and for the offering of which they have been separated and empowered? Such sacerdotal prayers are meant to guide and inspire the priest to offer the liturgy "in spirit and in truth," imbuing him with the gravity and grandeur of what he is daring to do. When God says to St. Catherine of Siena: "I am *He who is*, you are *she who is not*," He is stating a basic truth of the spiritual life—one that must not be forgotten in one's private rooms or in the Church's public worship.

---

74 For a convenient side-by-side comparison, see "New and Traditional side-by-side," *The Latin Mass Society of England & Wales*, https://lms.org.uk/missals.

The Priest's Unique Role—for the Benefit of All

Narrating his conversion from the New Age to traditional Catholicism, Roger Buck quotes a priest who sent him the following description:

> Unlike the Mass of Vatican II [*sic*] in which a dialogue between celebrant and congregation carries most of the ritual, the prayers and rituals of the Tridentine form demand that the celebrant be continually attentive to the rites he is enacting. His voice varies from being audible to a quiet whisper; his eyes regularly turn to the crucifix; the movements of his hands are conscious and deliberate. Even when he turns to the congregation the greetings are brief, his glance downward, his gestures precise. The Priest is servant of the ritual, and the rubrics foster a mindfulness and self-awareness which not only focus his own attention, but *also that of the faithful*, as they kneel once more at the foot of the cross of Calvary. Each time before he turns to the congregation the Priest kisses the altar. Priest, altar and sacrifice are at the core of Catholic worship. When he is at the altar offering the sacrifice a Priest's ministry finds its most sublime expression. His kiss of the altar is not only a sign of honor and respect for the source of his identity, but also an expression of his own affective attachment to his vocation.[75]

It is no form of clericalism but simply Catholic truth to say that the priest is given to the people as a model and a guide. All Christians in their baptism—and priests in a new way by their ordination—are ontologically configured to the priestly office of Christ.[76] The priest above all should be setting the example of pursuing the holiness of a priestly people, so that we, in turn, might catch fire from that example. The liturgy ought to be the image of the Christian life, not a mere "filling station" where the tank is filled, or a meeting place where we exchange greetings and announcements.

Thus, the priest's offering of the sacrifice devoutly and earnestly *for himself* models to the entire congregation how they, too, must offer the sacrifice of themselves with Christ upon the altar. What *he* does and says in the liturgy is exemplary for *all* of us. Lay Catholics who follow along in their

---

[75] Buck, *Cor Jesu Sacratissimum,* 303–4, emphasis added. Chapter 4 will focus on the fittingness of such "precise gestures" and detailed rubrics. Regarding the number of times the altar is kissed, see Kwasniewski, "'For I Will Not Give You a Kiss as Did Judas.'"

[76] See 1 Pet. 2:5; see also Rom. 12:1.

daily missals learn how to apply these priestly prayers analogously to themselves, too; they learn how to enter into the supreme offering of Christ to His Father, uniting themselves to it.

In short, *as prays the priest, so pray the people.* If the liturgy is reduced to a priest's engagement with the people, the people's liturgy will be reduced to their engagement with the priest. If the liturgy is oriented to God, with the priest offering intense pleas for his own forgiveness and purification and earnest appeals for sanctification and salvation, the people, too, will ask for the same—often with the same words and even with the same or similar bodily attitudes; they will be habituated to seeing liturgy as the locus of God's work of salvation among us.

I am reminded here of a saying recounted by Dom Jean-Baptiste Chautard: "If the priest is a saint, the people will be fervent; if the priest is fervent, the people will be pious; if the priest is pious, the people will at least be decent. But if the priest is only decent, the people will be godless."[77] Actually, I first heard this saying in another form that is perhaps more striking, although melodramatic: "If the priest is an angel, the people will be saints; if the priest is a saint, the people will be good; if the priest is good, the people will be mediocre; and if the priest is mediocre, the people will be beasts."[78] Is this a clericalist sentiment? No more than it would be militarist to recognize that the quality and success of an army depends to a huge extent on its generals, colonels, captains, and lieutenants. Chautard is simply expressing a fact about our communal life as Christians that we would be hard-pressed to deny or refute. There will *never* be an orthodox Christianity in which the priest does not have the primary role in liturgy, as the mediator and the model of our approach to God. This cannot but have ripple effects in every aspect of the Christian life. Are we really surprised that holiness flourished in the parish run by St. John Vianney, or near the confessional of Padre Pio? Examples could be multiplied endlessly. As prays the priest, so pray the people; and a priest who lives from and for the altar, the sacrifice, the bread of life, will raise up a people who live from and for the altar, the sacrifice, the bread of life.

---

77 Chautard, *The Soul of the Apostolate,* 39.

78 This quote is attributed to St. Pius X.

The Right Clothing for a Kingly-Priestly Sacrifice

Over and over again, experience has impressed upon me the importance not only of what the priest *says*, but of what he *does*, and *how* he does it—the ceremonial aspect, the "clothing" of the words. The way the priest is dressed, the way he behaves, his gestures and his movements; beyond that, the way the acolytes fulfill their tasks, the handling of sacred objects in the sanctuary and at the altar: all of these are like the clothing of mysteries too dazzling to behold in their naked purity, and beyond our earthborn powers of perception. We can compare it to the clothing of Mary, the Mother of God. Would Our Lady wear immodest or ugly clothing unworthy of her dignity? Of course she would not, and neither should our public worship of God. All of our rites should be fully and magnificently clothed in the vesture of royalty.[79]

This is how, for example, we should see the use of the noble Latin language—specially set apart after untold centuries of use in the sacred liturgy, consecrated, as it were, to divine service. When we hear the sonorous, lofty, unchanging sound of Latin, we know instantly that we are at worship; the Church's public homage has commenced. It is offered not for the instant and simple grasp of the people, as a didactic lesson would be, but for God first and foremost, as a sweet offering of incense, the fragrance of ancient orthodoxy and timeless praise, uniting us with the saints of our history and the saints in heaven. The worship thus rises above the bounds of this present moment in society and culture. Latin, together with Gregorian chant and periods of silence, serves as a "sonic iconostasis," a symbolic barrier that, on the one hand, tells us we are on sacred ground and should not succumb to the temptation of a chummy familiarity with God, and, on the other hand, reminds us forcibly that we are now being invited into the embrace of His divinity, summoned to a foretaste of beauty and happiness that exceeds our earthly concepts and projects.[80] The very *differentness* of traditional worship is its chief strength, helping us to overcome the "domestication" and the "secularization" of God that is a perennial human temptation, whether in the form of a rank idolatry by which one would try to control the divine,

---

79 See the next chapter, as well as Kwasniewski, "Clothed in the Vesture of Royalty."

80 See Kwasniewski, *Reclaiming Our Roman Catholic Birthright*, 28–33.

or in the more subtle forms we see in the modern West, like the pursuit of a humanistic interreligious global fraternity that elbows out the Gospel of Jesus Christ.

Two truths are impressed on us when we hear the priest speaking or singing Latin: first, we learn that the realm of the divine, though it penetrates into our world and surrounds it, is also a realm of its own, above and beyond our world. A thousand years ago, when more people spoke and understood Latin, its linguistic beauty and nobility would still have been admired, but it would not have seemed so foreign; and to that extent, I maintain we are more fortunate than they were, because Latin is now so stamped and impregnated with sacred significance that it functions nearly as a sacramental, like holy water that blesses those who use it and those upon whom it falls. At the same time, as rational animals, we should be moved by a desire to grasp the meaning of the Latin—not only its generic symbolic value, but the intelligible content the liturgy is offering us. That is where education comes in: we *should* pay attention, at least sometimes, to the prayers of the liturgy, starting with the translations in a daily missal; and, as time and opportunity allow, we should learn some ecclesiastical Latin. The special character of the language is not in the least diminished when we start to grasp its meaning; on the contrary, we come to appreciate its incomparable vividness, its poetic beauty, and the subtlety with which it conveys the truths of our Faith. It truly is a perfect instrument for its purpose in worship, and as we grow in our awareness of it, we see and marvel at that perfection all the more, and we penetrate more deeply into the truths expressed in the language. Mystery and catechesis, liturgy and education, go together as natural companions. Even though the traditional Latin Mass does a lot more "silent catechizing" than the Novus Ordo does, much of the liturgy will remain a closed book unless we take some time to deepen our understanding of its prayers, readings, and ceremonies. Fortunately, it has never been easier to do this than it is today, when we have access to books and articles that can serve as guides on this road of discovery.[81]

---

[81] My book *Reclaiming Our Roman Catholic Birthright* is designed as a helpful resource of this kind, and it contains an annotated bibliography, including books for younger readers and recommended websites. I return to the topic of Latin in chapter 7 below.

Another example of how the traditional Mass is clothed in the vesture of the royalty of Christ is the customs surrounding the Most Blessed Sacrament, which is, after all, Our Lord Himself. The Host and the chalice are treated with the utmost reverence at every moment. An elaborate offertory and the unsurpassable Roman Canon make it clear that the bread and wine are intended to become, and do become, the sacrificial Victim, the Lamb of God, in the sacramental separation of His Body and Blood. The priest once again relates to the people in a specifically priestly way by being the only one who handles the Body of Christ and gives Him to the faithful.[82] When the faithful kneel to receive Communion on the tongue, the divine nature of the food we are receiving is emphatically proclaimed: we did not earn this food, we could not obtain it for ourselves through our own efforts, and we cannot even feed it to ourselves. Only Christ our Lord can feed us with Himself, and thus His minister, empowered by the Sacrament of Holy Orders to stand in His place and to do His work, feeds the faithful who, like little children, allow themselves to be nourished by another's hand. The heavenly gift comes from above, down to our mouths; we obey God who tells us in Scripture: "Open your mouth wide, and I will fill it."[83] All the ceremonies surrounding the Body and Blood—be it the many genuflections, the priest holding together his thumb and forefinger, the thorough ablutions of the fingers and vessels—everything conspires to show us, to reinforce our faith, that we are in the presence of God Himself, whom we must *never* treat in a casual, sloppy, ordinary way, for that would be no better than contempt. Surrounded by angels, we do not think it too much to imitate, however poorly, their perfect service, which tirelessly attends to every detail.[84]

To conclude, the sorts of things I have described in this chapter—the hieratic distance between clergy and people in the old Mass; the dense content of the priest's own prayers, which are often heard by no one else; the use of Latin, chant, and silence as a sonic iconostasis; the manner of handling and distributing Holy Communion—can all be taken as illustrations

---

[82] A deacon, ordained to the ministry of service, is also permitted to distribute Holy Communion in the *usus antiquior*.

[83] Ps 81:10 RSVCE; Ps 80:11 in the Vulgate. See Kwasniewsk, *The Holy Bread of Eternal Life*, 89–103.

[84] Chapter 9 will focus on the pronounced and pervasive Eucharistic reverence of the TLM.

of a general principle: catechesis is more or less worthless if the signs of the liturgy contradict it.[85] To put it positively, the first and most elementary catechesis is *how we act in the liturgy.* How we act, in turn, shapes and is shaped by what we *say* we are doing in the liturgy—and I mean, not what we say *about* the liturgy outside of it, but what is said *within* it and *by* it. Of Jesus Christ, we read in the first verse of the Acts of the Apostles: "Jesus began *to do* and *to teach.*"[86] The doing precedes the teaching. In its *acta et dicta,* the traditional form of the Mass more fully exemplifies and more intentionally inculcates the virtues at the heart of the Christian life than does its 1969 replacement.

If we want to take Christianity seriously—if we really believe in the existence of truth, virtue, prayer, holiness, and eternal life—we will return, as swiftly as we can, to a liturgical rite that takes these things seriously and, in its texts and rubrics, *imposes* them on the celebrant, as a sweet yoke and light burden uniting Him with Christ. The traditional Latin Mass is the ideal form of liturgical prayer not only for the laity but also, in a very special way, for the priest, who, thanks to it, is able to present to the faithful an image of God-centered prayer, culminating in the mystical sacrifice that unites men to God, earth to heaven, time to eternity.[87] May more and more priests discover this truth and embrace it wholeheartedly, for *their* benefit, as well as for the benefit of the faithful, living and dead. A holy and zealous priest, plunged into the mysteries of Christ, united with the Savior's own prayer before the throne of grace, will always benefit the people of God far more than the people-centered or outward-oriented priest that the post-conciliar era sought and still seeks to produce.

---

[85] See Kwasniewski, "Formation and Malformation."

[86] Acts 1:1, emphasis added.

[87] See Kwasniewski, "Not Abandoning the Flock."

3

Why the Traditional Mass Is Kingly and Courtly

"It's all fancy, like a royal court. It doesn't fit with a democratic society like ours."

It's already clear from the last two chapters that the traditional Mass goes against the grain of our times. The priest "ignores" the people to give all his attention to the Lord. The ministers are separated off in an elevated space of their own, divided from the people by a barrier; to them belongs most of the conduct of the ceremony. The language is strange and lofty, unknown to many who are assisting at the liturgy. It seems, evidently, that these things are "features, not bugs," since they are internally consistent and mutually reinforcing. This liturgy must be working from a deliberate idea, intending to evoke that idea in all who assist at it. It is the purpose of this chapter to say what that idea, or rather, reality, is.

Heavenly Blueprint

Let us begin at the end of the Bible. According to Joseph Ratzinger, the Book of Revelation, or the Apocalypse of St. John, shows forth a kind of "archetypal liturgy" to which all our earthly liturgies must bear resemblance:

> With its vision of the cosmic liturgy, in the midst of which stands the Lamb who was sacrificed, the Apocalypse has presented the essential contents of the eucharistic sacrament in an impressive form that sets a

> standard for every local liturgy. From the point of view of the Apocalypse, the essential matter of all eucharistic liturgy is its participation in the heavenly liturgy; it is from thence that it necessarily derives its unity, its catholicity, and its universality.[88]

Pope John Paul II made a similar observation about the Canticle in chapter 5 of Revelation, saying it "belongs to the solemn opening vision" that "presents a kind of heavenly Liturgy to which we, still pilgrims on earth, are also associated during our ecclesial celebrations." He continues:

> The hymn from the Book of Revelation we are meditating on today ends with a final acclamation shouted by "myriads of myriads" of angels (cf. Rev. 5:11). It concerns "the Lamb that was slain," who is given the same glory destined for God the Father, because "he is worthy to receive power and riches, wisdom and strength" (5:12). It is the moment of pure contemplation, joyful praise, and the song of love to Christ in His paschal mystery. This luminous image of heavenly glory is anticipated in the Church's Liturgy. Indeed, as the *Catechism of the Catholic Church* reminds us, the Liturgy is the "action" of the whole Christ (*Christus totus*). Those who celebrate it here already live, in some way, beyond the signs, in the heavenly Liturgy, where the celebration is totally communion and feast. It is in this eternal Liturgy that the Spirit and the Church make us participate when we celebrate, in the sacraments, the Mystery of Salvation.[89]

In his book, *The Lamb's Supper*, Scott Hahn writes: "I suspect that God revealed heavenly worship in earthly terms so that humans—who, for the first time, were invited to participate in heavenly worship—would know how to do it."[90] The Book of Revelation, Hahn suggests, offered help to the nascent Church in discerning which elements of Old Covenant worship should be retained in the New Covenant, inasmuch as the new both *concludes* and *includes* the old.[91] The Church can, and should, have buildings,

---

88 Ratzinger, *Pilgrim Fellowship of Faith,* 110–11.

89 John Paul II, General Audience, November 3, 2004, drawing on *CCC* 1136 to 1139. The quotations are directly translated from the Italian by the author.

90 Hahn, *The Lamb's Supper,* 122.

91 In Matt. 5:17–18 ("Do not think that I am come to destroy the law, or the prophets. I am not come to destroy, but to fulfil. For amen I say unto you, till heaven and earth pass, one jot, or one tittle shall not pass of the law, till all be fulfilled"), the Greek verb for "fulfill" means both

ministers, candlesticks, chalices, incense, and vestments, because her worship, being ordered to and derived from Jesus Christ, is the perfection of all that the old worship, with these typological symbols, pointed to as yet to be fulfilled. They do not cease to be the symbols we need in order to perceive and enter into communion with Christ; they acquire a *new* purpose as symbols that point to a reality now accomplished, a salvation won on the Cross, a glory shared with the faithful who may now enter heaven. Indeed, since our earthly worship is still imperfect as compared with that of the heavenly kingdom, it is appropriate that we retain symbols that cannot be mistaken for the ultimate reality and yet not only bring it to mind but bring us into living contact with it. It is not that Old is related to New merely as symbol to reality; rather, if I may use a bit of shorthand, there is a double proportion, Old : New :: New : Heaven.[92]

Who is the central figure of the Book of Revelation? The slain and risen Lamb, the Paschal or Passover Lamb that is given to us in the Holy Eucharist, instituted by Jesus at the last meal He celebrated with the disciples before His atoning death. What is the central activity depicted in the book? Worship—either true worship (directed to God and the Lamb) or idolatrous worship (directed to Babylon, the beast, the whore, etc.). And what is the central metaphor? Marriage. Either we are united as "one flesh" with the Lamb, washed clean in His blood and feasting at His table, or we are fornicating with the devil. The two cities are contrasted as a whore (the old, unfaithful Jerusalem) and a virgin bride (the new Jerusalem, the Church). The very term for revelation—*apokalypsis*—means "unveiling." At the time Revelation was written, this term was used to describe, among other things, the unveiling of the virgin bride as part of the wedding festivities. In short, the Book of Revelation is about true worship of the true God, a mystical marriage with Him; and this is brought about through the Church's worship, especially in the sacraments of baptism and the Eucharist. Apart from this sacramental life, there is error, folly, despair, horror, and destruction—the history of fallen mankind, which wages war against the Lamb.

---

to bring something to completion *and* to bring it to an end. The perfection of the Law both embodies all that is good in it and surpasses it with unexpected fullness.

92 Spelled out: the mere symbol (or anticipatory sign) is to the reality-symbol (or efficacious sacrament) as the reality-symbol is to the ultimate reality (the face-to-face vision of God).

It is interesting to note that this book has received a title of honor that was subsequently extended to, or rather, recognized in, the entire body of Scripture, namely, "revelation"; and it is not by chance that *this* book, called "Revelation," is about true worship of the true God—for, indeed, *all* of Scripture is about true worship of the true God. Christianity is a religion principally and fundamentally concerned with adoring, loving, and serving the one true God, in which man's salvation consists (spilling over into the love of neighbor). Put differently, there is no such thing as an "ethical reduction" or a "philosophical distillation" of Christianity; it is inherently bound up with sacrifice and sacrament, by which we profess our faith in God and yield ourselves to Him in love.

Why does Sacred Scripture *end* with the Book of Revelation? The reason is as simple as it is profound: Revelation is not merely or even primarily the closure of a written book but the beginning of, or aperture to, something *else* that is intrinsically greater than Scripture—the living worship of the living Body of Christ, on earth and in heaven. This is the subtle but potent response, far ahead of time, to the Protestant invention of *sola scriptura:* Revelation ends the Bible because it depicts and invites us to the Eucharistic banquet of the Lamb, which is where the *things* that are spoken of in Scripture are *really present*. The written signs lead us to the reality signified; the bread of the word leads to the bread of life, the book to the altar. As Hahn writes:

> For most of the early Christians it was a given: the Book of Revelation was incomprehensible apart from the liturgy. . . . It was only when I began attending Mass that the many parts of this puzzling book suddenly began to fall into place. Before long, I could see the sense in Revelation's altar (8:3), its robed clergymen (4:4), candles (1:12), incense (5:8), manna (2:17), chalices (ch. 16), Sunday worship (1:10), the prominence it gives to the Blessed Virgin Mary (12:1–6), the "Holy, Holy, Holy" (4:8), the Gloria (15:3–4), the Sign of the Cross (14:1), the Alleluia (19:1, 3, 6), the readings from Scripture (chs. 2–3), and the "Lamb of God" (many, many times). These are not interruptions in the narrative or incidental details; they are the very stuff of the Apocalypse.[93]

93 Hahn, *The Lamb's Supper*, 66–67.

In the final pages of Revelation, we behold the new Jerusalem descending from heaven. Whither does it descend? It descends to Mount Zion, that is, the place where Jesus had eaten His last Passover and instituted the Eucharist, where the Holy Spirit descended at Pentecost, where the Christians were spared Roman destruction in the year 70. "In other words, the new Jerusalem came to earth, then as now, in the place where Christians celebrated the supper of the Lamb."[94] Liturgy is the anticipated Parousia, the "already here" entering our "not yet there," as beautifully expressed in the Collect of the Twelfth Sunday after Pentecost, which teaches that our Eucharistic banquet in church descends from and summons us to the heavenly feast:

> Almighty and merciful God, from whose liturgy comes the fact that Thou art worthily and laudably served by Thy faithful ones: grant, we beseech, that we may run without stumbling to Thy promises. Through Our Lord Jesus Christ, Thy Son, who liveth and reigneth with Thee in the unity of the Holy Ghost, God, world without end. Amen.[95]

On this prayer, Michael Foley comments:

> The Collect is essentially stating that God has a service, and from it flows our serving Him "worthily and laudably." Or to use another word for a public, religious service (this time from Greek), God has a "liturgy" (*leitourgia*), and it is by virtue of His liturgy, the divine liturgy, that humans are able to worship Him properly. . . . Even though human hands have obviously played a part in its historical development, sacred liturgy, which participates in and anticipates the cosmic liturgy described in the Epistle to the Hebrews and the Book of Revelation, is ultimately not the "work of human hands," but the product of the Holy Spirit and the ongoing action of Jesus Christ the High Priest. Divorcing the human from the divine in sacred liturgy is a fool's errand, as foolish as trying to separate the humanly composed from the divinely inspired in the Sacred Scriptures. . . . It is not the case that liturgy is a primarily human phenomenon, the concept of which we then apply to what is happening in Heaven, albeit weakly and metaphorically. On the contrary, the realest of real liturgies is

---

94 Hahn, 102.

95 A "slavishly literal" translation by Michael Foley.

> what is happening in Heaven at the altar of the Lamb who was slain and is now at His Wedding Feast; what we do on earth in our churches is the derivative act. But since it is derivative, our earthly liturgies are truly partaking of the Heavenly Liturgy right now.[96]

If Joseph Ratzinger, John Paul II, Scott Hahn, and Michael Foley are all correct in what they are saying about the connection between the earthly liturgy and the heavenly, we have a powerful and truly unanswerable argument in favor of the restoration of the sacred, the recovery of signs and symbols in every aspect of the liturgy from architecture, furnishings, and decorations to the ceremonial and the sacred music. It is an argument in favor of the preservation or reestablishment of continuity with traditional Catholic worship, and the overwhelming need to enrich and "celestialize" the often sterile and impoverished vocabulary of modern liturgical life. The music we hear, for instance, should be awe-inspiring, or, at very least, effective in elevating the mind to divine things, so that we may catch a faint echo of angelic music; the church building should be an evocation of the heavenly city, the sanctuary a magnificent image of the Holy of Holies. The ceremonies, in their solemn and ordered splendor, should draw the mind upwards into the majesty and mystery of God. If we do not strive to have and to do these things to the extent that it lies within our power, we are not just running away from a tradition stretching back 3,000 years (if we take into account the Jewish antecedents)—bad enough as that would be, and smelling suspiciously of the ancient heresy of Marcionism that pitted the Christian God against the Jewish God; we are showing that we have neither understood nor embraced the message of Divine Revelation *as a whole*. We are, in a sense, rejecting the root of our religion, which proclaims and actualizes the coming of the kingdom of God in our midst, "that we may receive the King of All, invisibly escorted by ranks of angels"[97] and accompany Him into glory.

What we can and must learn from the Book of Revelation is the essential vocation of the Church: the glorification of God and the sanctification of souls in time of tribulation. To do this, we first of all need to consider the

---

96 Foley, *Lost in Translation,* 165–66.

97 From *The Divine Liturgy of Our Father Among the Saints John Chrysostom,* 53, n259.

fundamental symbolic paradigm of worship according to Sacred Scripture and the entire Christian tradition—namely, that God is our great King, ruling over all with the scepter of righteousness; that Jesus Christ is the King of kings and Lord of lords, the Judge of the living and the dead; that heaven is His throne and earth His footstool;[98] and that, in His holy court, a vast multitude of saints and angels minister unto Him, with His holy Mother, Our Lady, as their Queen.[99]

Defending the Courtliness of the Liturgy

Yet an objection will arise: Isn't all this royal, monarchical, courtly imagery—together with the old liturgy that relies so heavily upon it—merely a time-bound cultural construct, ready to be replaced with a more democratic or populist convention in our times? Shouldn't each age have a liturgy that speaks to it from within its predominant political models? Progressivist Fr. Thomas O'Loughlin cannot contain his surprise at Catholics who prefer the older form of worship: "There are gestures—bowing and even genuflections—that are derived from the hierarchical world of the Byzantine imperial court, but now used by people who claim that they embrace human equality and democracy."[100]

Fr. Anthony Ruff, a Benedictine monk of St. John's Abbey in Collegeville, Minnesota,[101] hypothesizes that the bishops at Vatican II issued a blank check for radical reform that would finally bring the liturgy into modernity. He writes:

> The Council fathers didn't get into all the specifics of the reform of the liturgy. They left most of that to a future commission under the pope. The fathers approved a major paradigm shift—from liturgy as Carolingian clerical drama to liturgy as act of all the people—and

[98] See Is. 66:1; Acts 7:49; Matt. 5:35.

[99] As Pius XII writes of Our Lady in his encyclical *Ad Caeli Reginam* (October 11, 1954): "She bore a Son who, at the very moment of his conception, because of the hypostatic union of the human nature with the Word, was even as man King and Lord of all. So, rightly and justly, St. John Damascene could write: 'When she became Mother of the Creator, she truly became Queen of every creature.'" Thus, the traditional liturgy also features a large number of obligatory Marian feasts, characterized by elevated praises of the Virgin Mother.

[100] O'Loughlin, "Liturgy is not a visit to a museum."

[101] A monk and a monastery more akin in mentality to modern Jesuits than to classical Benedictines: see Kwasniewski, *Noble Beauty,* 115–33.

> then left open what the implications of that shift would be. No doubt some or many of the fathers didn't yet have in mind all the possible implications of the paradigm shift. Nor did they need to. . . . [102]

One wonders how many of the Fathers of the Council would have said that the traditional liturgy as they knew it was "Carolingian clerical drama" and that they wanted to shift liturgy to an "act of all the people" in such a way that they expected no limitations on how the liturgy would be modified in order to achieve this nebulous vision. In another article, Fr. Ruff states: "For liturgy, the paradigm shift is from Carolingian clericalized sacred drama to an act of the entire community. Just let the full weight of that shift sink in, including all the possible implications for liturgical practice."[103]

The Carolingians—that is, the Franks of the early Middle Ages, whose greatest ruler was Charlemagne, and in whose empire the papal liturgy mingled with Gallican elements to form the substance of the Roman rite in its high medieval maturity—are a rather easy target for liturgists with modern reform on the brain, who seem to feel little compunction for glossing over the immense complexity of the historical record as they indulge in comic-book generalities. As a matter of fact, the little we know about the liturgy of the *pre*-Carolingian period makes it relatively easy for liturgists to attribute to the Carolingians almost anything they personally dislike, giving them a perfect excuse for claiming it is not "primitive" and must therefore be expunged.

So let us then take up the implicit challenge in Fr. Ruff's words. Foes of tradition assert that the classical Latin liturgy is characterized by courtliness or court etiquette, and that, as time went on, it got mixed up with (and corrupted by) expressions of Baroque secular politics. In other words, the progressives hold that the traditional Mass—think especially of the Pontifical Mass—is an elaborate show of deference toward a prince or king, indebted

[102] Ruff, "Cardinal Sarah on Mass Not Facing the People."

[103] Ruff, "The Worst Reasons for *Ad Orientem.*" If "clericalism" is supposed to be the problem, the Novus Ordo does not overcome it, since "participation" in the new liturgy is often linked to laity performing historically clerical roles such as reading Scripture and distributing Communion—as if the most meaningful way for laity to be involved is for them to become minor or temporary clergy, a phenomenon John Paul II referred to as "the clericalization of the lay faithful" (*Christifideles Laici,* no. 23). See Kwasniewski, *Ministers of Christ,* 38, 67, 73, 157, et passim. The clerical nature of these roles is underlined by the fact that it is still illicit, even in the Novus Ordo, for a layman to read the Gospel or for the celebrant to *not* distribute Communion.

more to secular high culture than to sacred precedent, and detracts from the humility, simplicity, and immediacy of the presence of Christ in the community, the brotherhood gathered around the table.

However plausible this may sound to some, there are nagging counter-indications that deserve the attention of honest inquirers. In his work *The Treasure of the Church*, Canon Bagshawe argues to the intimate connection between royalism (or royalty) and temple liturgy, and how, as a result, the image of "the court of the great king" was taken up by Christian liturgy and everywhere accepted as a normative framework—something it obviously already is in both the Old and New Testaments. In Bagshawe's words:

> The very fabric of the church suggests the presence of God, and the adornment of the altar carries out the same idea. In principle it is very like the splendour and ceremonial of the king's court. It is impossible for men to have royalty amongst them, and yet not have some external sign by which the king is pointed out and honoured. The ceremonial has, of course, differed widely at different times, but from the earliest king that ever ruled amongst men down to our own time, there has always been a royal display of some kind. It is impossible, in the same way, for men to believe that our Lord is amongst them and not to lavish on Him their most precious treasures, just as it was impossible for St. Mary Magdalen not to pour out her precious ointment on His feet (Jn 12:3).
>
> The church is His palace, and the altar is His throne. We take that glorious court of Heaven described to us in Holy Scripture, and try feebly to imitate it on earth. The candles, and the incense, and the flowers—the vestments and the ceremonial of priests—what are they, but an earthly image of that "great multitude which no man could number . . . clothed with white robes, and palms in their hands," and of "all the angels who stood about the throne, and the ancients and the four living creatures, and they fell down before the throne upon their faces and adored God"? (Rev 7:9–11)[104]

We cannot dismiss this language or imagery, pervasive in Scripture and the Patristic period, as a mere epiphenomenon of ancient near-Eastern courts and kings or a superficial mood-setting backdrop easily left behind by

[104] Bagshawe, *Treasure of the Church,* 165–66.

"emancipated" modern minds. For, the same conceptual world extended throughout the Byzantine empire for over a thousand years after Constantine the Great; it embraced medieval courts, Renaissance courts, Baroque courts, and the professedly Catholic governments that existed well into the twentieth century. Monarchy or princedom, the oldest and arguably the most natural form of political organization, has been a far more consistent part of the human experience and of the formation of Christian culture than the democratic/egalitarian ideology of "self-evident truths" of which we have persuaded ourselves in modernity. It has continued to exercise a strange fascination in politics and literature, and wins huge popular support where it still exists.[105] Fr. Louis Bouyer observes that royal myths are among the primordial structuring elements of human consciousness implanted and fructified by the Word of God. As Bouyer scholar Keith Lemna summarizes:

> Our intellect requires attunement to the [religious] symbol in order to receive divine revelation, and the phalanx of religious symbols present in royal myths provided the matrix utilized by the divine Word, in transfiguring manner, to make himself known to us. . . . The glory of the cosmos reflects the transcendent glory of God the One, True King. God the King is, moreover, the one and only source, in and through His Word, of the one law that rules the cosmos as well as the hearts of humankind. . . . The myths of the first civilizations centered on the person of the king as mediatory figure linking heaven with earth. The biblical Word took up this theme but transformed it, asserting that God alone is true King, the King of all nations and people on earth as well as of the cosmic powers themselves. God is King of the cosmos.[106]

Regardless of whether we think democracy can be made to work or not,[107] democracy has no place in the realm of supernatural mysteries: Christianity is purely and entirely monarchical. Against the backdrop of the Old Testament revelation of God as the (one and only) great King over

[105] See Shaw, *A Defence of Monarchy.*

[106] Lemna, *The Apocalypse of Wisdom,* 25, 95, and 114.

[107] Its track record so far is vastly inferior to that of monarchy and aristocracy, if we look to the standard of beatified or canonized rulers and the preservation of the Faith in societies. See Kwasniewski, "Between Christ the King and 'We Have No King But Caesar.'"

all the earth, and of the people of Israel as a kingly, priestly nation ruled by prophets, judges, and ultimately the Davidic dynasty, we profess that Christ is our King, the Ruler of heaven and earth, of all times, past, present, and to come, of this world and of the next; that His angels and saints are His royal court; that while He deigns to call us His friends and brethren, we know that we never cease to be His servants, who long for His courts and tabernacles. As recently as 1926—not even a century ago—the Church believed the faithful needed to hear this message in the Postcommunion prayer of the then newly-instituted feast of the kingship of Christ: "Having received the food of immortality, we beseech Thee, O Lord, that we who glory in our service under the standards of Christ the King, may be able to reign with Him forever on His heavenly throne: Who with Thee liveth and reigneth . . ."[108] The thick "politicism" of the imagery points to the real, sovereign polity of the Roman Catholic Church as a perfect society (*societas perfecta*) altogether perfected in the heavenly Jerusalem, the city of the great King. Our ecclesial sacrifice, the Most Holy Eucharist, is a kingly and high-priestly oblation, a true *leitourgia*, which means the work of one on behalf of many—the work that explains the pervasive Christocentrism and sacerdotalism of traditional liturgical rites.

Consequently, the modern fixation on democracy, as if it were the best or the only good form of government, not only does *not* abolish our need for the language of kingship and courtliness, but makes it *far more needed* than ever before, in order to impress on our minds the way things really stand in the definitive reality of the kingdom of God. All of our democratic and egalitarian experiments will fall away at the end of time when the glorious reign of Christ the King is revealed to all the nations, and those who have submitted to His gentle yoke will be raised to eternal life in glorified flesh while those who have rejected Him will wail and gnash their teeth, condemned to everlasting torment. The liturgy should reflect the truth of God—His absolute monarchy, His paternal

[108] Foley, *Lost in Translation,* 243; "standards" as referring to the Cross and the various instruments of the Passion. Inevitably, a prayer like this—and most of the liturgy for the feast of the Kingship of Christ—did not survive the scalpels of the liturgical reformers, whose official theology disapproved of the basic concepts of the pope (Pius XI) who instituted it. Paul VI did not merely *move* the feast of Christ the King, he *replaced* it with another feast, on a different date and with different texts, all tending away from the truths discussed in this chapter (see Foley, 240–44).

rule, His hierarchical court in the unspeakable splendor of the heavenly Jerusalem—and not the passing truths of our modern provisional political organizations.

In short, to conduct the liturgy so that it appears to be *less* courtly, *less* regal, *less* hieratic, *less* splendid, is to make it appear to be something other than what it most deeply *is*—to make it, so far as we can, less true to itself, less heavenly, less real. A Mass deroyalized and decelestialized deceives the Christian faithful, who are led further away from an encounter with the God whom no hands have fashioned and no minds have fathomed. If the way the liturgy is conducted allows people to think that the Mass is about *them*—that *they* are the primary protagonists of a this-worldly gathering in which the priests are somewhat like hired public servants who administer, in the name of the community, the business that actually belongs to it—then such a liturgy is inculcating a pernicious lie.[109] The liturgy is not "of the people, by the people, and for the people." It is the saving act of Christ, done by Him first and always, and by the ordained ministers who act in His name and by His authority; it is done for the glorification of God *and only for that reason* does it sanctify the people. One can say the liturgy is "for us" in the same way that one can say we ought to love ourselves, namely, by loving God first and foremost, with the sacrificial offering of ourselves in mind and body,[110] which is how we truly love ourselves.

Therefore, one of the greatest blessings of the traditional Latin liturgy is its pure, open, unembarrassed representation of the court of the great King of heaven and earth in all of its prayers, rubrics, and ceremonies, in the magnificent art forms that emerged from its "courtliness" and reinforce the "drama" of the holy mysteries of our redemption. We find in it an uncompromised and unapologetic expression of the divine monarchy as it radiates through the panoply of sacred symbols and the ecclesiastical hierarchy endowed with fatherly potency. We are wrapped in an atmosphere of spiritual aristocracy, namely, the world of the saints, who reign with

[109] Ratzinger saw all this very clearly. In his address "The Ecclesiology of the Constitution on the Church *Lumen Gentium*," he noted that the phrase "the People of God" quickly gave rise to a fundamental and dangerous misconception of the nature of the Church, in a Marxist or democratic vein. He saw, too, the liturgical implications of this wrongly politicized ecclesiology; see especially his essay "The Image of the World and of Human Beings."
[110] See Rom. 12:1–2.

Christ. After all, this venerable liturgy was not produced by a committee of experts, as laws and bills are manufactured in contemporary parliaments or congresses; it emerged slowly over time from innumerable currents of doctrine and devotion introduced by pious monks or bishops and assimilated by God-fearing laity. In the words of Fr. Claude Barthe:

> Without going into great historical considerations, it is important to remember that this [ancient Latin] Mass was formed at the same time as the West was becoming and constituting itself as Christian. As far as the structure of the liturgy is concerned, the great period of its creation lies between the Constantinian and Carolingian eras, when the orations of the Canon, a veritable rule of Eucharistic faith, and the other great priestly orations, developed at the same time as the forging of this specific Latin language, which some have described as canonical. As for the "flesh" of this Mass (if we can use this term for the multiple prayers of gloss at the Entrance, Offertory, and Communion), its full flowering was achieved with the Gregorian reform [eleventh century]. The Roman Mass was fully constituted when the ideal of Christianity reached maturity. It is the Mass of Christendom.
>
> But above all, it should be noted that, theologically, this Mass, sacrificial in essence, is at the same time royal. It is Christ making His royal entrance at the first moments of the ceremony, revealing Himself in epiphany at the Offertory, "drawing all to Himself" from the height of the glorious Cross at the moment of the Canon, inviting His friends to His royal banquet at the moment of Communion. The adoration of the Lord, who manifests Himself to His faithful in this way, has been expressed since the age of cathedrals by the Elevation, a kind of ostension of the King's Body.
>
> Of course, to lay a cornerstone for the reconstruction of Christendom, it's not enough merely to celebrate Mass; other battles are necessary too. But the anti-modern character of our liturgy, quite the opposite of a liturgy that imitates worldly fashions and language, powerfully helps us to put the priestly and royal mark of Christ on the whole of our personal, family, and public lives.[111]

---

[111] Fr. Claude Barthe, "A Sacrificial and Royal Liturgy." For similar reflections, see Smith, "Jesus Christ Is Our True King and Priest."

The traditional liturgy, in short, challenges *everything* modern man has come to take for granted, everything he has persuaded himself to believe "self-evident." It throws down the gauntlet to our modern assumptions, routines, and expectations. It is an enormous challenge to our collective social hubris and post-revolutionary pride. This is why the traditional liturgy is hated and feared by those who embrace modernity as a primary value that gives value to all else; this is why it is passionately loved by those who recognize in it a higher, deeper, and better vision of ultimate reality.

The Byzantine Witness

When we are considering the courtliness of liturgy with its irreducible monarchical and aristocratic elements, we should not forget, moreover, to "breathe with both lungs" of the Church. The Byzantine Divine Liturgy is positively bursting with courtly imagery and gestures, as befits its long sojourn in Constantinople. The Byzantines have retained many of these features because they did not succumb to the pragmatism, utilitarianism, and democratic thinking that have poisoned the springs of Western social life and made of us men with hollow chests. Byzantine liturgy has all the same kinds of "courtly" rituals that the old Roman Rite has, such as the kissing of the celebrant's hands, the bowing toward persons, icons, and other objects, the processional candles, and the incense, rituals that had their origin in the veneration surrounding the emperor.[112] Nor should we be surprised: both the Byzantine court and the Carolingian court saw themselves as continuations of the Roman Empire, now consecrated in its new role as supreme governor of the Christian world, for the glory of God and the empire of Christ. It was completely natural to the clergy and faithful to adopt for their divine worship customs that accompanied the earthly ruler; indeed, in so doing, they restored the proper immovable and incorruptible object of veneration, bestowing on the ruler the privilege of being an earthly icon of the divine King. What began on earth

[112] As Martin Mosebach notes: "The liturgy had taken over from the court ceremonial of the pagan emperors the symbolic language for the presence of the supreme sovereign: candles, which preceded the emperor, and the thurible. Whenever candles and incense appear in the liturgy, they indicate a new culmination of the divine presence" (Foreword to Kwasniewski, *Noble Beauty,* xxii).

was raised to heaven and seated there at the right hand of the Father; thence it descended to the human throne as a mantle of authorization and a reminder of responsibility.

All four of the Cherubic hymns refer to Christ as *King*. The one for daily use sings: "We, who mystically represent the Cherubim, and chant the thrice-holy hymn to the Life-giving Trinity, now set aside all cares of life *that we may receive the King of all*, Who comes invisibly escorted by Angelic Hosts." At the Liturgy of the Presanctified is chanted: "Now the powers of heaven do serve invisibly with us. *Lo, the King of Glory enters.* O, the mystical sacrifice is upborne, fulfilled. Let us draw near in faith and love, and become communicants of life eternal." On Holy Thursday: "Of Thy mystical Supper, Lord, let me partake, O Son of God, for of Thy mysteries I will not speak to Thy enemies nor kiss Thee like Judas, but like the thief on the cross I will confess Thee: *In Thy Kingdom, Lord, remember me.*" On Holy Saturday: "Let all mortal flesh keep silent, and stand with fear and trembling, ponder nothing of earth; for *the King of kings and Lord of lords cometh forth to be sacrificed* and given as food to the believers; and there go before Him the choirs of Angels, with every dominion and power, the many-eyed Cherubim and the six-winged Seraphim, covering their faces, and crying out the hymn . . ."[113]

Thus, the Byzantine rite's four chants for the Great Entrance refer to the coming of the King, including His post-resurrection life as king of the heavenly city and of the entire cosmos. To circle back to our initial point, this is really nothing other than a consistent embrace of the imagery of kingship with which the Book of Revelation, the Apocalypse of St. John, is rife:

> And the seventh angel sounded the trumpet: and there were great voices in heaven, saying: The kingdom of this world is become our Lord's and his Christ's, and he shall reign for ever and ever. Amen. And the four and twenty ancients, who sit on their seats in the sight of God, fell on their faces and adored God . . . (Apoc. 11:15–16)

> Now is come salvation, and strength, and the kingdom of our God, and the power of his Christ: because the accuser of our brethren is cast forth, who accused them before our God day and night. (Apoc. 12:10)

---

[113] The Byzantines currently use the last of these only on Holy Saturday, but it was the daily-use Cherubic hymn for the Liturgy of St. James, which is currently undergoing something of a revival among the liturgically *outré*. The traditional Old Church Slavonic version is most impressive.

> And singing the canticle of Moses, the servant of God, and the canticle of the Lamb, saying: Great and wonderful are thy works, O Lord God Almighty; just and true are thy ways, O King of ages. Who shall not fear thee, O Lord, and magnify thy name? For thou only art holy: for all nations shall come, and shall adore in thy sight, because thy judgments are manifest. (Apoc. 15:3–4)

> These shall fight with the Lamb, and the Lamb shall overcome them, because he is Lord of lords, and King of kings, and they that are with him are called, and elect, and faithful. (Apoc. 17:14)

It was once common to say, and one still hears it said once in a while, that the Mass is a mystical representation of the life of Christ—that it makes His life present to us in all of its mysteries, as if recombining the spectrum into pure white light so that all the colors are virtually there in a single moment. Since this is true, we must say that *all* phases of the life of Our Lord are present and active, including the 2,000 years of His Mystical Body over which He reigns as the glorified King and Son of God (in the Davidic, and more than Davidic, sense). In fact, while the Mass is the sacramental renewal of the once-for-all sacrifice of Calvary, we know at the same time that it is the offering of the risen Lord in His royal dignity, power, and beauty. Thus, however much we rightly emphasize the Passion, the Mass should be for us a tangible (i.e., sacramental) encounter with our glorious King. The traditional Roman Rite, especially in its sung and solemn forms, has exactly this character, in company with all the Eastern rites.

It is currently, for some odd reason, fashionable to admire the colorful extravagance of the Byzantine liturgy while contemptuously dismissing anything in the Latin tradition suggestive of the same. People admire gigantic gold vessels and rich vestments in the East while settling for unsightly cups and drab drapes in the West; they catch their breaths at an impressive iconostasis, while shaking their heads at altar rails and other signs of separation between the nave and the sanctuary; they extol the marvelous poetry of the kontakion or troparion sung to a haunting traditional melody, while leaving their own incomparable Gregorian repertoire out in the cold. The ubiquitous presence of this peculiar double standard in the halls of academia and power suggests that we are dealing with a psychological disorder, a kind of self-loathing that compels some people to strip themselves of the treasures of "the other" and to force themselves into a plainness that is almost a punishment or an echo chamber of their own emptiness. We are permitted to lavish praise on beauty *elsewhere*, like a tourist passing through the halls of Versailles, as long as we deprive ourselves of it here and now, and suffer our democratic fate, which we deserve good and hard. A perfect expression of this disordered thinking may be found in the words of Cardinal Giovanni Battista Montini, the future Pope Paul VI, who, as Archbishop of Milan, had this to say in 1962 about the "internal reform" he believed necessary for the Church: "She will take care to update herself in casting off, if necessary, this or that old royal cloak resting upon her sovereign shoulders to dress herself in the simpler clothes that modern taste demands."[114] But if this is done, how will believers ever be equipped to apprehend the marvelous truth to which the medieval English mystic Julian of Norwich bore witness?

> I saw the soul as large as if it were an endless world and as if it were a holy kingdom; and from the properties in it I understood that it is a glorious city. In the center of that city sits our Lord Jesus, God and man, a handsome person and of great stature, the highest bishop, the most imposing king, the most glorious Lord; and I saw him dressed imposingly and gloriously. He sits in the soul, in the very center, in peace and rest.[115]

Indeed, Christ reigns in the soul that loves Him; He abides in that precious temple of sanctifying grace. And the liturgy, in the language of symbolism and the voice of solemn revelation proper to it, slowly opens the eyes of our mind to this dazzling but hidden reality. The rejection of Christ's kingship goes hand-in-hand with the rejection of worship fit for the King He is and the kings we are in Him. Either His royalty will be fully embodied in and expressed through our primary, fundamental, and culminating public,

---

[114] Chiron, *Paul VI,* 156. Note the language of *aggiornamento* or "updating," first introduced by John XXIII. On November 26, 1969, just before the Novus Ordo went into effect, Paul VI made a similar remark that set up a false opposition: "Understanding of prayer is worth more than the silken garments in which it is royally dressed" (see Shaw, *Latin Mass and the Intellectuals,* 250).

[115] Julian of Norwich, *Revelations of Divine Love,* ch. 67, p. 153.

political, and civic action, namely, the sacred liturgy, which will form the reference point and stable basis of Christian society; *or* His royalty will be rejected and replaced with the tyranny of man over man, the tyranny of fashion or ideology: "We have no king but Caesar." A liturgy saturated with kingliness and hierarchy protects fallen man from placing himself in the throne of Christ the King. The anti-royalism or anti-courtliness of the new liturgy reflects a "low Christology" that brings Christ down to the merely human level and neglects His kingly divinity.

Implications for the Fine Arts

Given a full-bodied understanding of the royalism or regality of the sacred liturgy in which God our King is adored in His holy court, what are the implications for the fine arts that are unavoidably called upon to aid us in offering this formal, solemn, public activity? I say "unavoidably," because, apart from emergency situations such as a secret Mass in a concentration camp, the ministers must be attired somehow, the altar must be of some shape and style, the church building must be of this or that design, the words must have one or another register, the music must have a melody and a rhythm, etc. Simply as physical beings, as rational animals who learn and communicate through the senses, our activities of worship are utterly bound up with artifacts or works of art—so much so that, as we have seen, the Book of Revelation does not even make the attempt to avoid them in depicting heaven but, if anything, pushes their use to an extreme of symbolic and gestural language. Our worship is inherently artistic, and the only relevant concern is whether the art will be good or bad, well-suited or poorly suited to the reality, done masterfully or done shabbily.

In a book on the modern composer Arvo Pärt, I read this inspiring passage:

> Under Archbishop Laud (1589–1645) there was a strong move towards greater ceremonial dignity in the church. As the house of God it was to be fitted out accordingly with the finest of human artistry, and its functions were to be conducted in a spirit of deepest reverence. The liturgy, the music, the sacred vessels, the very fabric of the building, all were to serve and make manifest *the beauty of holiness.* This

> phrase, which we find invoked time and again . . . derives from Psalm 96: "O sing unto the Lord a new song . . . O worship the Lord in the beauty of holiness."[116]

Laud was Anglican, but his devout attitude was no different from that of Catholics.[117] Do we not need "greater ceremonial dignity in the church"? Why is the procession at the start of a typical parish Mass so slapdash, casual, and quick, almost as if people are embarrassed to be engaged in divine worship, or as if they see no connection between good order and public prayer? Why are there so few processions *outside* of church? We could certainly use "a spirit of deepest reverence" in conducting our services. Less of the informal greetings, smiles, and handshakes—more of the reverential fear of the Lord that brings us to our knees in homage to the great King, begging for His mercy. We need music, vessels, and architecture that "make manifest the beauty of holiness." In particular, we have all heard music that seems neither beautiful nor holy; its mawkish sentimentality, circus-like tunes, predictably syncopated rhythms, and simpering lyrics are an appalling combination from which beauty must hide her fair head while holiness flees to the mountains to bewail her virginity.

But *why* must we seek to do such laudable things? For one simple reason: because God, the greatest and best, deserves the greatest and best from us: *date magnificentiam Deo nostro*, "give ye magnificence to our God."[118] *Deo optimo maximo*. And there is a corollary: we human beings, created in His image and likeness, need to be able to *offer* "the finest of human artistry" to Him, lifting up our minds and hearts by means of it. If only we knew ourselves, we would see that we have a longing to give the best of ourselves to Him, not what is mediocre, humdrum, worldly, or two-faced. Does not an artist who takes pride in his work wish to give his very best to a patron? Do not lovers with pure intentions long to give the best of themselves to one another? God has given us the ability and the calling to reach out to His transcendent holiness with works of beauty that carry us along with them, past the realm of the profane into the sanctuary of divinity. As St. Thomas

---

[116] Hillier and Tormis, *On Pärt*, 61.

[117] Need I mention the sincere hope of many Roman Catholics that the Anglican Ordinariates, by modeling that Laudian attitude and approach, will become a force of renewal for the rest of us?

[118] Deut. 32:3.

says, we worship God not to give Him something He does not already have, but to bring ourselves closer to Him by yielding what we owe Him. In this way, we draw nearer to His goodness and grow in likeness to Him.

This explanation will always hold true for all human beings at all times. But we can say something more specifically Catholic. The "preferential option for the beautiful" rests on the truth that the Body and Blood of Jesus, *really present*, are offered in sacrifice in *this* building, on *this* altar, enacted by *these* rituals, sung in *this* music. The elements of the liturgy are not indifferent placeholders, like paper money or coins that have value only because someone arbitrarily declares them to be valuable. Rather, as gold is precious by nature and as the king's image is honorable due to his office, liturgical signs *represent* Christ to the eyes and ears of faith and offer Him to the loving heart. Whatsoever we do to the least of His symbols and ceremonies, prayers and chants, that we do unto Him. This is not so much a fearful vision of the danger of making mistakes as it is a joyful awareness of the many ways, little and great, in which we may pay Him homage and adore Him. The traditional liturgy reminds us again and again that we are dealing with the Lord of life and death, the Alpha and the Omega, the one who is, who was, and who is to come—and (to borrow a phrase from another Anglican) He is not a tame lion.

This is why it *matters*, crucially, what we are doing, and what we are endeavoring to do, when we worship God in public prayer. If we have got the wrong idea about it, we may do that which is seriously unfitting, unworthy, and displeasing to the Lord, whom it is our great privilege to serve and to please. If we follow the lead of the Church's Tradition and the requirements or counsels of the Magisterium of the ages, we can be certain of giving glory to God and aiding, over time, the sanctification of His people.

The holy Curé of Ars, St. John Vianney, starved himself on potatoes but spared no expense for the embellishment of the church's sanctuary. He knew, like faithful Christians of every age, what comes first and what comes second. The same was true of St. Francis of Assisi, *pace* the falsification of his legacy by hippies who bow before nature instead of adoring the Blessed Sacrament. Indeed, Franciscan churches are among the most beautiful in Europe, magnificently decorated—even those built in periods when the friars themselves were dirt-poor beggars who scarcely knew where their next meal was coming from, though they trusted that the Lord would provide. They knew what comes first; they knew that when it is *God* who is to be honored, the work must call forth *everything* in us, everything great and glorious we can muster, for His sake. This is why the Catholics of old, high and low alike, never built plain, unadorned churches (if they had any choice in the matter), and, at least on special occasions if not more often, brought together the best musical forces they could find to provide the most glorious music.

St. Thomas Aquinas provides the essential rationale for the Church's longstanding practice of supplying rich vestments, splendid vessels, glorious architecture, elaborate ritual, decorous music, and so forth for the Holy Sacrifice of the Mass and the Divine Office. Here's what he writes:

> The chief purpose of the whole external worship is that man may give worship to God. Now man's tendency is to reverence *less* those things which are common, and indistinct from other things; whereas he admires and reveres those things which are distinct from others in some point of excellence. Hence too it is customary among men for kings and princes, who ought to be reverenced by their subjects, to be clothed in more precious garments, and to possess vaster and more beautiful abodes. And for this reason it was necessary that special times, a special abode, special vessels, and special ministers be appointed for the divine worship, so that thereby the soul of man might be brought to greater reverence for God.[119]

If Catholics enjoyed a proper religious formation, the trite songs infesting our hymnals would evaporate and churches would be filled with music of true artistic merit. We would *insist* that it happen; we would make it happen through personal sacrifices; we would absorb its fruits with gratitude as these heavenly harmonies penetrated and shaped our souls. The same would be true of the churches we build: their lofty architecture would captivate all who enter and move them to worship the Lord of hosts. In his final encyclical, *Ecclesia de Eucharistia*, Pope John Paul II offered theological support for this exultant and sacrificial attitude:

---

[119] *Summa Theologiæ* I–II, Q. 102, art. 4.

> Like the woman who anointed Jesus in Bethany, *the Church has feared no "extravagance,"* devoting the best of her resources to expressing her wonder and adoration before the *unsurpassable gift of the Eucharist.* No less than the first disciples charged with preparing the "large upper room," she has felt the need, down the centuries and in her encounters with different cultures, to celebrate the Eucharist in a setting worthy of so great a mystery. . . . The faith of the Church in the mystery of the Eucharist has found historical expression not only in the demand for an interior disposition of devotion, but also *in outward forms* meant to evoke and emphasize the grandeur of the event being celebrated.[120]

That the liturgy should be done with splendor and solemnity, in surroundings as magnificent as can be, evoking the transcendence, holiness, and glory of the Lord, is not a "debatable question" but a plain given, as far as Catholic tradition is concerned. This is why the Church has always striven for and sponsored the finest of human artistry—and why the poor have always contributed to the building of churches of which they and their descendants are the rightfully proud beneficiaries. Such an unequivocal dedication to the sacred liturgy does not, of course, cancel out the need for personal prayer, works of charity outside the church doors, or energetic efforts of evangelization. But neither can these things ever *replace* the liturgy, which serves as their final end from which they derive their meaning. Most simply, this is what we owe to God, and He comes first. "Glorify the Lord generously, and do not stint the first fruits of your hands."[121]

Beauty is not an extra or an add-on, a luxury, or an indulgence, but an essential and inherent dimension of truth itself, an attribute of Our Lord Jesus Christ and of His liturgy. If we abandon our pursuit of excellence in this domain, we will lose our faith, our ability to transform the world for God's sake, even our sanity. Ugliness, like ignorance, error, and sin, is a privation and a deprivation, with a peculiar *de*-evangelizing force. Beauty, like truth and goodness, calls to us, converts us, perfects us, elevates us to God. Moreover, without supernatural faith, which orders everything in life to our final destiny in God, art itself can become a pernicious and soul-destroying

[120] John Paul II, *Ecclesia de Eucharistia,* nos. 48, 49.

[121] Sir. 35:8 RSVCE.

force, as we have seen in modern times with so-called modern art and popular culture. Christianity is not only the art of salvation, it is the salvation of art.

Our Lord said to St. Margaret Mary Alacoque: "It will reign, this amiable Heart."[122] But what do we find contained in that Heart of sinless flesh, pure love, and everlasting deity? The Litany of the Sacred Heart tells us that the Heart of Jesus is *maiestatis infinitae*, of infinite Majesty—the Majesty of the One who is *rex et centrum omnium cordium*, King and center of all hearts. It is the *templum Dei sanctum, tabernaculum Altissimi, domus Dei et porta caeli*: the holy temple of God, the tabernacle of the Most High, the house of God and the gate of heaven. In like manner, the sacred liturgy of our Catholic tradition is a holy temple in which we adore the divine King, a tabernacle of the Real Presence, a dwelling-place of God with man, a portal swinging open to the sublime and blissful worship of God in the courts of heaven. And just as the Heart of Jesus is *omni laude dignissimum, fons vitae et sanctitatis, deliciae Sanctorum omnium*—most worthy of all praise, the fountain of life and holiness, the delight of all the saints—so, too, is the Holy Sacrifice of the Mass that Our Lord gave to us in His immense wisdom and love; for through it we give Him, the Father, and the Holy Ghost, perfect praise, and from it we receive the bread of angels, our food of pilgrimage and our consolation in this valley of tears—a delight for the saints who have gone before us, as it is for us today, and as it will be for our descendants.

[122] Bougaud, *Revelations of the Sacred Heart,* 267.

4

Why We Follow Inherited Rituals and Strict Rubrics

*"Everything's scripted and regimented—
no room for spontaneity or adaptation."*

Before we can understand why it is appropriate for us to follow inherited rituals and strict rubrics in the offering of the Mass, we must first grasp how liturgical worship involves receptivity, humility, subjection, submission to a truth that rules over us, and adoption of roles and language that are not natively ours. In this way, we will see that the kingliness of the liturgy defended in the last chapter implies even more profound truths about the difference between theocentric worship and egocentric activity.

What does it mean to live a "liturgical life" (*vita liturgica*) in the midst of the wasteland of secular modernity? The holy rites are our lifeline, our umbilical cord, to Holy Mother Church; they keep us nourished and safe in the valley of the shadow of death. The original Death Valley is not in California, but in hell. Hell is truly the valley of death, because one who lives there, or rather continuously dies there, is stuck down in the depths and cannot get up to the high places, up to Mount Sion and the city of the living God. Scripture calls the fallen world in which we men are living "the valley of the *shadow* of death"[123] because it is under the

[123] Ps 23:4 RSVCE. Emphasis added.

power—limited and destined to fail, but nonetheless real—of the Evil One. Hence, when we examine what is the case in Satan's kingdom, we will also acquire a better understanding of how he is attempting to undermine us here in this world.

No *Vita Liturgica* in Hell

Hell has no liturgy. The fallen angels have no common work of charity, no common work of divine worship. When the devil appeared to the desert father Abba Apollo, he had no knees, as if to say: he is incapable of kneeling.[124] His mentality is *non serviam*, and all the demons think the same way: one could call it "mindful conformism." For this reason, there is no proper hierarchy in hell.[125] They are more like bandits who stick together out of self-interest. Contrary to the prevailing democratic way of thinking, liturgy is *essentially* connected with hierarchy: Christ the High Priest is the one who leads the worship, and He deigns to allow the participation of the priest, the deacon, the subdeacon, the ministers, the cantors, the choir, the laity, each in their own place and function. One cannot demand or create a liturgical role; one rather receives it and enters into it. To be liturgical is to submit freely to an external rule, an order not of our own making, a complex whole of which we are humble parts.

Liturgy takes us beyond ourselves into roles that are not simply inborn or inherited or fashioned; into realms that are off-limits for mere creatures; into actions and passions that are *super*natural in both their source and their goal.[126] When we chant the liturgy, we are standing outside ourselves, in the heavenly places: "Our feet were standing in thy courts, O Jerusalem."[127] Given how intimately bound up are human nature, rationality, and language, our very action of placing on our lips words originated by another is a reformation of our humanity, a putting on of Christ, a renunciation of the ambitions of Babel, and a quiet welcoming of the Spirit of Pentecost.

---

124 See below, p. 220.

125 St. Thomas addresses whether either Satan or the Antichrist can be called the head of all the wicked: *Summa Theologiæ* III, Q. 8, aa. 7–8. For commentary, see Hannon, "The Politics of Hell."

126 See Kwasniewski, "Sacrifice of Praise and the Ecstatic Orientation of Man."

127 Ps. 121:1.

For all these reasons, the devil does not and cannot have liturgy. Although he is compelled to submit to the rule of the Almighty, he does not *wish* to submit, and therefore cannot enter into the joy of his Lord; he recognizes no rule but his own will, which is why there is no peace in hell; he has not the humility to allow himself to be placed as a part in a larger whole, and to take for his own the words of another. He has no desire to suffer the ecstasy of love. As Our Lord says in St. John's Gospel: "He was a murderer from the beginning, and he stood not in the truth; because truth is not in him. When he speaketh a lie, he speaketh of his own: for he is a liar, and the father thereof."[128] Jesus speaks here with metaphysical and psychological precision. The devil is a murderer because he envies God's life and takes it away from those who have it, rather than receiving God's life as a gift and promoting the reception of the same gift in others.[129] He stands not in the truth, because truth, for a creature, is always the harmony between the intellect and its object (*adaequatio rei et intellectus*), such that the intellect is measured by the reality outside itself. The created intellect *has* truth, it *contains* truth, but it cannot *be* the truth—that is God's prerogative alone. In this sense, truth can only be *in* us, but never *of* us, as if we were its origin or measure.[130]

Hence, the person who rejects the truth of God ends up evicting truth from his mind and begins a career of falsification, both in the form of self-deception (we see how the devil throughout the Gospels and indeed across all of history acts as if he could actually defeat Jesus!) and in the form of deception of others (we see how the father of lies whips people into a frenzy of lying, manipulation, and conformism). The devil, and any of his imitators, "speaketh of his own." He will speak only the shallow "worldly wisdom" that is his mental content; he will spout sophistry, banality, and cynicism. This is what comes of not being willing to take for his own the wiser, deeper, brighter, truer words of another—His Creator. Lucifer, as his very name implies (bearer of light), was created to mirror the Word and in this way to be resplendently beautiful in his own nature. He abandoned the Word and thus became ugly in spite of his wondrous nature. A lake,

---

128 John 8:44.

129 See "The Devil's War against Celibacy, Marriage, and the Eucharist" in Kwasniewski, *Treasuring the Goods of Marriage,* 183–92.

130 See Pieper, *The Silence of St. Thomas,* 45–71, especially 53–63.

when perfectly still, can take on the form of mountains against an evening sky, and in this way go beyond its nature of water to partake of the natures of earth, air, and fire. In contrast, a lake when turbulent and muddy seems in some way to lose the better virtues of water itself—its purity, transparency, ability to wash, ability to slake thirst. The clear lake in its reflection becomes more than itself; the muddy lake in its turbidity becomes less than itself. Fr. Herbert McCabe once remarked: "That is the theology behind the story of the Garden of Eden. There was no way that human beings could be simply human. They had to be either superhuman or inhuman."[131]

Upward Ascent or Downward Spiral

One of the great antiphons for Pentecost vigorously conveys this truth: *Repleti sunt omnes Spiritu Sancto, et coeperunt loqui, alleluia, alleluia*: "They were all filled with the Holy Spirit, and began to speak, alleluia, alleluia."[132] We must *first* be filled with the Spirit of God before we have anything worthwhile to say—and our first word as newborn infants will be Alleluia, that is, praise the Lord.[133] This, therefore, will be the newborn Church's first word: a word of pure praise offered to God like sweet incense. The Psalmist exclaims: *Ex ore infantium et lactentium perfecisti laudem* . . . "Out of the mouths of infants and nursing babes Thou hast perfected praise, because of Thy enemies, that Thou mayst destroy the enemy and the avenger."[134] Etymologically, the word *infans* means "the one who cannot speak," the one who must learn how to speak by constantly listening to his mother, receiving language from her mouth as he receives milk from her breast. This life of dependency thwarts the advance of the enemy, Lucifer, who, unlike the child, grasps at an impossible independence and will not praise the Lord.[135] As for the Christian, so

---

[131] McCabe, *God, Christ, and Us,* 65.

[132] In the Roman Breviary, this verse (Acts 2:4) serves as an antiphon throughout the hours of the Feast of Pentecost and a responsory: it is said or sung many times. In the postconciliar Liturgy of the Hours, its use is limited to once in Morning Prayer and once in Evening Prayer II.

[133] The same lesson is conveyed in the verses of Psalm 25 recited at every Mass: *circumdabo altare tuum, Domine, ut audiam vocem laudis et enarrem universa mirabilia tua* (Ps. 25:6–7). Note the order: first, "I will compass Thy altar, O Lord"; second, "that I may hear the voice of praise"; third, "and tell of all Thy wondrous works." One must go deeply into the liturgy, into the mystery of the altar, so that one may *hear* the voice of the Church's praise; one will then have an experience of wondrous works to talk about.

[134] Ps. 8:3 Vulgate.

[135] Cf. Is. 14:12–17.

for the Church: whenever she wishes to live in the prime of her youth,[136] she will give first place to offering up the sacrifice of praise. When we are animated by the Spirit, we speak the sacrifice of praise, we *become* the sacrifice. Conversely, when we speak "of ourselves"—this means, both *from* ourselves and *about* ourselves—we speak nothing but a lie.[137] If the Church takes as her priority anything other than the sacred liturgy worthily celebrated, she abandons her first love and starts down a path of harlotry, like ancient Israel playing the whore with the false gods of the surrounding nations.

There is a direct line connecting Babel to Canaan to Babylon to Gehenna. First, there is Babel: when we abandon sacred tradition, which unites us to one another, to the host of saints, and to the transcendent God, our penalty is a babble of vernacular tongues, a smorgasbord of options, an incoherent pluralism in the *ars celebrandi* or style of celebrating. Second, there is Canaan: our bad liturgical mentality and habits are a breeding ground for open and hidden forms of adultery, idolatry, apostasy, and atheism. Third, there is Babylon: we enter into captivity to our enemies, the world, the flesh, and the devil; we enter into exile, far from the fatherland, far from our own identity. We are dwelling in the furthest *regio dissimilitudinis*, in a condition of existential alienation accompanied by an utter lack of will-power to regain our home, to live up to sacrificial demands, or to bring our fellow men to the good. Fourth and lastly, there is Gehenna, the valley of burning garbage, image of hell. This entire downward spiral is a spiral of increasing self-indulgence and decreasing discipline. One is dispersed, wasted, spread out, thinned out, until one is a caricature of one's former substantial self. Such is what we have seen not only with the liturgy, but also with the priesthood, religious life, the missions, catechesis, the fine arts. When one gives up the supersubstantial

---

136 Cf. Ps. 42:4 Vulgate.

137 With this in mind, one might reconsider the famous claim of Paul VI that the Second Vatican Council was the Church's great opportunity to turn to herself and talk about herself: the first Council that took *self-reflection* for its primary task. Yet do we not generally suspect of vanity someone who likes to look at herself in the mirror and talk about herself? Bishop Athanasius Schneider remarks: "When one looks at photographs from that time, Vatican II as a phenomenon appeared as a huge show of clerical triumphalism. . . . The human and administrative elements were put at the center of the life of the Church and above the constant tradition of the Church. . . . Clerics, especially the bishops and the Holy See, are tasked with showing Christ to the world—not themselves" (*Christus Vincit,* 128–29).

bread of tradition with the Most Holy Eucharist at its heart, one makes a descent from nourishing food, to fast food, to starvation.

The path of ascent must take the form of positive self-denial, in imitation of Christ, and for the sake of transformation in Him. This is why any movement away from asceticism, any lessening of customary church-wide burdens of penance, is also from the Evil One. This would include the gradual reduction of the Eucharistic fast in the twentieth century, and the abolition of Septuagesima (pre-Lent) and the Lenten fast by Pope Paul VI.[138] If the smoke of Satan has emerged out of some fissure in the temple of God, as the same pope admitted, who was it who allowed that fissure to open up in the first place? Whence came the weakness of the structure? More generally, who thought it could ever be a good idea to open the windows of the Church to let in the polluted outside air? The devil normally stays away from holy places. He must have been given an invitation he couldn't refuse. The laxity of the contemporary Church and the rise in Satanic phenomena are by no means unrelated.

Given that liturgy is hierarchical, otherworldly, ecstatic, and absolute in its demands over us, it is entirely in keeping with the devil's strategy to destabilize, democratize, secularize, and relativize the liturgy here on earth. He seeks to loosen our bond with a fixed and efficacious tradition. Distinctions between sacred and profane, formal and informal, fitting and unfitting—these the devil tries to smudge and, eventually, obliterate. He seeks to darken or blot out the manifestation of the heavenly hierarchy in the earthly distinctions of sacred ministers and their complementary but non-interchangeable roles.[139] He seeks to persuade us—particularly the

---

138 Lent used to be a *fasting season*, that is, for all forty days of it (not counting Sundays). Paul VI reduced the fast to only two days (!), and that is why I say that he abolished the Lenten fast as such. There are surely cases where the rules of fasting and abstinence can be reasonably lessened for individuals. But the Catholic Church already had an intelligent flexibility in this regard, while maintaining the norm of discipline for all who could adhere to it. One might compare the Eastern Orthodox concept of *oikonomia*: the rule remains firm but its application is adjusted to circumstances.

139 As St. Thomas writes: "The Church's orders are derived from the order of the heavenly hierarchy; and so just as among the angels different actions are due to different orders, so also in the Church militant different orders are applied to different acts, just as in a body different members have different functions, which the mystical body resembles, as is clear from 1 Corinthians 12" (*Commentary on the Sentences,* Bk. IV, Dist. 13, Q. 1, art. 1, qa. 1, resp.). The darkening or blotting out of this manifestation takes place especially by the obliteration of the traditional distinctions between clergy and laity and between men and women. Outside of an emergency,

clergy—that the liturgy is *not* the font and apex of the Christian life, but only one means among many for advancing a "Christian agenda." The devil knows he cannot prevent *some* advancement of the Christian faith, but he is well aware that nothing comes close to the liturgy's power for hallowing the Name of God and establishing His kingdom in our midst, giving us our daily nourishment, and moving us to repentance of sins and the avoidance of sins. In truth, liturgy is an *end in itself* because it is *God's* peculiar possession and makes us *His* peculiar possession. If the devil can convince us that liturgy is *not* an end in itself, that it is a helpful tool we should manipulate for ulterior ends, then he has already won half the battle for souls. He has shaken our fundamental orientation to the eternal worship of God and the Lamb in the heavenly Jerusalem, the kingdom that will have no end.

If angels had bodies, the good angels would sing, dance, paint, sculpt, and build beautifully. As it is, they might view our bodily religion with a holy envy, since we have a way to externalize our interior devotion in monuments of faith, as witnesses to truth; we can give a semi-permanent being to our thoughts and feelings, shaping a "word-made-flesh" in a distant likeness to the Incarnation of the Word. With a correct instinct, Fra Angelico has depicted angels dancing circle dances with holy souls in the garden of heaven. But the evil angels would not sing.[140] They could not execute the demanding and liberating dance of the liturgy. They could not paint, sculpt, or build. If they attempted to do any of these things, it would run along the lines of atonality, abstract expressionism, primitivism, and

---

such as an enemy army about to desecrate a church, there is no possible justification for laymen handling the Blessed Sacrament; nor is there any worthwhile theological defense whatsoever for women being permitted to enter the sanctuary. Such practices are premised on the denial of the distinction between the sacred and the profane, between the supernatural and the natural, and, within the realm of the baptized, between the ordained and the non-ordained (or the ordainable and the non-ordainable). They emanate from Protestantism and lead to Modernism. For an in-depth treatment, see Kwasniewski, *Ministers of Christ.*

[140] Here is how C.S. Lewis imagines the state of affairs: "My dear Wormwood: Music and silence—how I detest them both! How thankful we should be that ever since our Father entered Hell—though longer ago than humans, reckoning in light years, could express, no square inch of infernal space and no moment of infernal time has been surrendered to either of those abominable forces, but all has been occupied by Noise—Noise, the grand dynamism, the audible expression of all that is exultant, ruthless, and virile—Noise which alone defends us from silly qualms, despairing scruples, and impossible desires. We will make the whole universe a noise in the end. We have already made great strides in this direction as regards the Earth. The melodies and silences of Heaven will be shouted down in the end. But I admit we are not yet loud enough, or anything like it. Research is in progress" (*Screwtape Letters,* Letter 22, pp. 113–14).

postmodernism—only even worse. As a modern author has said: "All the artist can produce with entire originality is disorder. It is as true in art as it is in morality, that everyone who speaks out of himself is a liar."[141]

In sharp contrast is the Son of God, who said: "I do nothing of myself, but as the Father hath taught me, these things I speak."[142] Our Lord emphasizes this point in patiently varied language: "For I have not spoken of myself; but the Father who sent me, he gave me commandment what I should say, and what I should speak. And I know that his commandment is life everlasting. The things therefore that I speak, even as the Father said unto me, so do I speak."[143] "The words that I speak to you, I speak not of myself. But the Father who abideth in me, he doth the works."[144] Our Lord goes so far as to say, in the fifth chapter of John: "I cannot do anything of myself,"[145] or, as another translation has it, "I am able to do nothing from myself."[146]

The exact instructions given under the old covenant for the priests and their worship, occupying a large part of the Pentateuch, are given for a permanent reason.[147] They are not superseded in the new covenant but fulfilled perfectly in Christ, in whom the infinite and eternal Word of God, sovereignly free, is bound permanently and singularly to *this* human flesh, this face, hands, heart, and voice, and who communicates His singularity to us in the form of liturgical traditions developed under the guidance of His Holy Spirit.[148] This is why Our Lord tells us: "He that shall break one of these least commandments, and shall so teach men, shall be called the least in the kingdom of heaven. But he that shall do and teach, he shall be called great in the kingdom of heaven."[149] The Church's liturgy applies this

[141] Berquist, *Learning and Discipleship,* 216.

[142] John 8:28. What is it that the Son declares to us? "No man hath seen God at any time: the only begotten Son who is in the bosom of the Father, he hath declared *him*" (John 1:18). Compare: "the Son cannot do any thing of himself, but *what he seeth the Father doing:* for what things soever he doth, these the Son also doth in like manner" (John 5:19), emphasis added.

[143] John 12:49–50.

[144] John 14:10.

[145] John 5:30, word order slightly modified.

[146] John 5:30 RSVCE.

[147] Note, among other examples, the emphasis placed on following "the pattern shown on the mountain" (Ex. 25:40); the care of the tent of meeting with its specific items disposed in just such a way (Num. 4; Num. 8); the consequences of Korah's rebellion (Num. 16).

[148] See Kwasniewski, *The Once and Future Roman Rite,* 33–77.

[149] Matt. 5:19.

verse to her saints, who are still doing and teaching the least of the commandments, in their Christian transposition and meaning.

As our model, let us ponder the Son of God praying the psalms of David as He grew up in the home of Mary and Joseph. What a spectacle! The New Adam, father of the world to come,[150] praying the old psalms of a child of Adam. The Word who enlightens all men and inspirits the prophets is the very author of these psalms; no less than the heavens and the earth and all the host of them,[151] the psalms are *His own creation.* Yet the Word-made-flesh submits to these words as prayers *already there*, which He planted in history for the formation of His own sacred Heart, for giving His lips and lungs and vocal chords their best exercise, for joining Him as fully as possible with the people of Israel and the human condition He assumed. He subordinated His divine freedom to liturgical tradition. Since we are all little images of the Image of the Father, the psalms are given to us, too, as the vehicle of our innermost thoughts and feelings, so that shaped by them, we may express what is deepest and truest in us, in our human nature divinized. We, in like manner, subordinate our freedom to liturgical tradition, as part of the imitation of Christ.

Humility of Service in Fixity of Form

One of the great strengths of the traditional Latin liturgy is that it leaves nothing to the will or imagination of the priest (and the same may be said of every minister in the sanctuary). It choreographs his moves, dictates his words, shapes his mind and heart to itself, to make it utterly clear that it is *Christ* who is acting in and through him.[152] Fr. Stéphane Dupré of the Priestly Fraternity of St. Peter once said: "In the traditional liturgy, I am a slave. The Church tells me where to place my hands, where to stand, when

150 See Rom. 5; 1 Cor. 15:45; Is. 9:6.

151 See Gen. 2:1.

152 A priest may choose which votive Mass to celebrate on a ferial day; again, on a feria, he may choose to celebrate, using the appropriate Common, any saint listed in the *Martyrology* for that day; certain commons offer a choice of an alternative Epistle or Gospel. Such opportunities for choice are few and well-controlled and do not introduce voluntarism into the liturgy because the choice of what to do must be made beforehand in its entirety. It is like a skier considering various trails to descend—once he commits himself to a trail, he is committed to the whole of it. The choice is pre-liturgical, so to speak, rather than intra-liturgical, unlike the multiple option-points in the Novus Ordo and the room for improvisation.

to genuflect, when to kiss the altar. In this way, I am no longer free to do my own will, and Christ's priesthood is able to act through me."[153] Or in the words of the Psalmist: "Know ye that the Lord he is God: he made us, and not we ourselves. We are his people and the sheep of his pasture."[154] Sheep are to follow the lead of their shepherd. The clergy is not and will never be the first principle of the liturgy; as St. Thomas Aquinas says with sobering humility, the priest or other cleric is an "animate instrument" of the Eternal High Priest: "Holy orders does not constitute a principal agent, but a minister and a certain instrument of divine operation."[155] Ministers are like rational hammers, chisels, or saws, by which a greater artisan will accomplish His work of sanctification, while conferring on them the dignity of resting in His hand and partaking of His action. Here is how Msgr. Ronald Knox expresses it:

> The philosopher Aristotle, in defining the position of a slave, uses the words, "A slave is a living tool." And that is what a priest is, a living tool of Jesus Christ. He lends his hands to be Christ's hands, his voice to be Christ's voice, his thoughts to be Christ's thoughts; there is, there should be, nothing of himself in it from first to last, except where the Church graciously permits him to dwell for a moment in silence on his own special intentions, for the good estate of the living and the dead. Those who are not of our religion are puzzled sometimes, or even scandalized, by witnessing the ceremonies of the Mass; it is all, they say, so mechanical. But you see, it *ought* to be mechanical. They are watching, not a man, but a living tool; it turns this way and that, bends, straightens itself, gesticulates, all in obedience to a preconceived order—Christ's order, not ours. The Mass is best said—we Catholics know it—when it is said so that you do not notice *how* it is said; we do not expect eccentricities from a tool, the tool of Christ.[156]

---

153 Quoted in Skojec, "A Priest Just Doing His Job."

154 Ps. 99:3

155 *Commentary on the Sentences,* Bk. IV, Dist. 2, Q. 1, art. 3, ad 2.

156 Knox, *The Pastoral Sermons,* 342–43. St. Thomas refers to this same line from Aristotle's *Nicomachean Ethics* 8.11 (1164b4) when explaining how a sacramental character belongs in the category of quality, a subcategory of power: "A minister is like an instrument of the one of whom he is minister: hence the Philosopher says that a slave is like an animate tool. And thus, the power [*virtus*] of a sacrament, as well as the minister and the character, are [all] instrumental" (*Commentary on the Sentences,* Bk. IV, Dist. 4, Q. 1, art. 1).

The clergy are privileged tools, to be sure, but they are still tools; and the liturgy remains the work of Christ, the High Craftsman, the carpenter of the ark of the covenant, the architect of the heavenly Jerusalem, the New Song and its cantor. In its external form, in text and music and ceremonial, the liturgy should luminously proclaim that it is the work of Christ and His Church, not the product of a charismatic individual or a grassroots community.[157]

Msgr. Robert Hugh Benson envisions a thoughtful non-Catholic reasoning about why the Mass has to be determinate, fixed, and regimented if it truly is what Catholics believe it to be—the making-present again of the supreme mystery of the Cross:

> Even to me, Protestant as I am, it did seem completely suitable that an event so stupendous could scarcely be approached by any other process than that of a sacred dramatic dance, with an accompaniment of rigid and minute Court etiquette. To leave the conduct of such a thing to the individual personality and the private taste of a simple clergyman in a surplice, would be nothing else than bathos of the worst description; human outlines must be obliterated by some overpowering uniform, personal tastes and methods of behaving must be rigidly supplanted by set movements and gestures. In fact, for such a drama as this we need not clericalism, but the most emphatic sacerdotalism. Originality in the sanctuary, as has been well observed, is the grossest vulgarity known to men.[158]

---

[157] St. Thomas even sees this as a basic difference between man under the New Law and man under the law of nature, that is, prior to the Mosaic Law. An objection against Christ's institution of the sacraments reads: "The mystery of priesthood in the New Law is not of less authority than that of the law of nature. But the ones who administered the sacraments under the law of nature, namely, priests, professed their faith as they pleased [*pro suo libito*], by means of visible sacraments. Therefore, much more should this be the case in the New Law, which is of even greater freedom" (*Commentary on the Sentences,* Dist. 2, Q. 1, art. 4, qa. 4, obj. 2). St. Thomas's response here is illuminating: "Those sacraments of the law of nature did not have any effect by the work performed [*ex opere operato*], but only by faith; and thus their determination could be done by a mere man possessing faith. However, it is not like this with the sacraments of the New Law, which confer grace by the work performed." In other words, because Christ has accomplished our salvation in a *determinate* way, this determinateness must be signified in *how* we worship God. Therefore, to avoid transmitting the error that the sacraments of the New Law are no more than personal or communal expressions of faith and to convey rather that they are *divine works containing grace* to which we respond in faith, there cannot be *ad libitum* variability.

[158] Benson, *Papers of a Pariah,* 67–68.

While still an Anglican, John Henry Newman had recognized the truth that the liturgical minister is conformed by his office to delivering, faithfully and humbly, the message of another—and in the *other's* words—without distracting personal touches or idiosyncratic variations:

> As the words in which we pray in Church are not our own, neither will our looks, or our postures, or our thoughts, be our own. We shall, in the prophet's words, not "do our own ways" there, nor "find our own pleasure," nor "speak our own words"; in imitation of all Saints before us, including the Holy Apostles, who never spoke their own words in solemn worship, but either those which Christ taught them, or which the Holy Ghost taught them, or which the Old Testament taught them. This is the reason why we always pray from a book in Church; the Apostles said to Christ, "Lord, teach us to pray," and our Lord graciously gave them the prayer called the Lord's Prayer. For the same reason we too use the Lord's Prayer, and we use the Psalms of David and of other holy men, and hymns which are given us in Scripture, thinking it better to use the words of inspired Prophets than our own.[159]

As a Catholic, Newman returned to this point, underscoring it with his usual eloquence:

> Clad in his sacerdotal vestments, he [the minister of the sacrament] sinks what is individual in himself altogether, and is but the representative of Him from whom he derives his commission. His words, his tones, his actions, his presence, lose their personality; one bishop, one priest, is like another; they all chant the same notes, and observe the same genuflexions, as they give one peace and one blessing, as they offer one and the same sacrifice. The Mass must not be said without a Missal under the priest's eye; nor in any language but that [viz., Latin] in which it has come down to us from the early hierarchs of the Western Church.[160]

---

[159] Newman, "Reverence in Worship," 9. This quotation begins: "We must in all respects act as if we saw God; that is, if we believe that God is here, we shall keep silence; we shall not laugh, or talk, or whisper during the Service, as many young persons do; we shall not gaze about us. We shall follow the example set us by the Church itself. I mean,"—and then it continues as cited above. I mention this because we can see that spontaneity or improvisation within the liturgy *always* goes with a casual and irreverent spirit: they are incestuously related.

[160] Newman, *The Idea of a University*, pt. 2, §7, pp. 425–26.

An especially earnest enforcer of this attitude of receptivity is St. Benedict of Nursia. In his *Rule*, the patriarch of cenobites presents the essence of humility as living not by one's own desires and passions but by the judgment and bidding of another: *ambulantes alieno judicio et imperio.*[161] When St. Benedict comes around to ordering the monastic liturgy, he makes continual reference to how things are done elsewhere: the psalms prayed by our fathers, the Ambrosian hymn, the canticles used by the Church of Rome. Even when fashioning his monastic cycle of prayer, he is constantly looking to the models already in existence. This is the true spirit of liturgical conservatism, piety toward elders, and the imitation of Christ. We are not the ones who determine the shape of our worship; we receive it in humility as an "alien judgment" that we make our own. To do otherwise is to put the axe to the tree of humility.[162] Liturgical prayer has always been the foremost way of inculcating submission to Christ and His Church, so that we can learn *His* ways, and assimilate *His* prayer, and drink of *His* wisdom—which will certainly not be something we ourselves could have "cooked up" in a bunch of committee meetings. We take *His* yoke upon us . . . the yoke of tradition.

Prior to the middle of the twentieth century, it was taken for granted in Catholic circles that it is a special *perfection* of the sacred liturgy to be fixed, constant, stable, an immovable rock on which to build one's spiritual life. The liturgy's numerous and exacting rubrics were understood as guiding the celebrant along a prayerful path of submissive obedience, in which he could submerge his personality into the Person of Christ and merge his individual voice with the chorus of the Church at prayer. In the words of Martin Mosebach:

> The great mystics of the past never felt rubrics to be a burden. Even the twentieth century had a great mystical saint, Padre Pio, from Apulia, who was given the stigmata and, with his five bleeding wounds,

[161] *Rule,* ch. 5. In like manner, ch. 7 warns against "doing our own will," lest we become corrupt and abominable.

[162] St. Benedict allows for a redistribution of the psalms, *as long as* monks rigorously hold to the principle of praying the full psalter in one week. Therefore it would not conflict with humility for a monastic community to make *some* adjustments to the cycle of psalms, yet it would smack of temerity to reject the most ancient and stable pillars of the office, such as the praying of the whole psalter each week, and, to take a couple of specific examples, the use of Psalms 109–112 for Sunday Vespers and Psalms 66, 50, 117, 62, and 148–150 for Sunday Lauds.

> read the Mass in iron submission to the rubrics. Formerly, seminarians learned rubrics so well they could perform them in their sleep. Just as pianists have to practice hard to acquire some technique that is initially a pure torture, but ultimately sounds like free improvisation, experienced celebrants used to move to and fro at the altar with consummate poise; the whole action poured forth as if from a single mold. These celebrants were not hemmed in by armor-plated rubrics, as it were: they floated on them as if on clouds.[163]

The formal, hieratic gestures transmitted an eternally fresh symbolism while limiting (if not eliminating) the danger of subjectivism and emotionalism. The priest or other minister was conformed to Christ the servant, who came not to do His own will but the will of Him who sent Him; the minister is commanded what to speak and what to do; he never speaks of himself.[164] As Fr. Luke Bell explains:

> Jesus does not come of His "own accord," He is "sent." For both Jesus and His followers, the struggle for true identity will be in the giving up of ownership, the readiness to receive, the acceptance of gift.... Those who do not cling to the attempt to be in control, who truly follow Jesus, are represented by Peter, who is told, "Another will dress you and carry you where you do not want to go." He learns and grows into this identity which is suffered rather than acted, received rather than grasped, given from the super-abundance of eternity rather than the constraints of time. Its essence is that it is from above.[165]

The Father who abides in the Son does the work of the Son, and the Son who abides in the priest likewise does the work of the priest. In this way, even as the Son was "emptied of glory" in taking on the form of a slave, so, too, is the priest emptied of human glory as he takes on the form of a servant, sharing the hiddenness, humiliation, passion, and death of

---

[163] Mosebach, *The Heresy of Formlessness,* 132.

[164] Except during the homily—which is why it should not be considered part of the liturgy. It pertains to the priest's office *as teacher,* yes, but it is not a liturgical offering as such. It is precisely directed *to the people* and not to God, although we do hope the preacher holds God in fear and awe as the Judge who knows whether the priest is speaking the truth in charity, or failing in truth or charity. See Kwasniewski, "The Homily Is Not Part of the Liturgy."

[165] Bell, *The Mystery of Identity,* 121.

Christ.[166] As we saw earlier, Our Lord, the great High Priest of the New Covenant, said: "I cannot do anything of myself."[167] Here we have perhaps the most radical statement of the priest's being tethered to the liturgy. It is a tethering so complete that he may truthfully say: "I *cannot* do otherwise. I am constrained from above." If he thinks or acts differently, he has not yet become a slave, in imitation of the One who assumed the likeness of a slave. Worse, if he is allowed or encouraged to do otherwise by some kind of liturgical book, that book is a smudged and fractured mirror that does not reflect the Word.

The Liturgical "Little Way"

Bishop Athanasius Schneider was once asked in an interview what lessons he had learned from celebrating the traditional form of the Mass. Here is the bishop's revealing response:

> The deepest lesson I have learned from celebrating the traditional form of the Mass is this: I am only a poor instrument of a supernatural and utmost sacred action, whose principal celebrant is Christ, the Eternal High Priest. I feel that during the celebration of the Mass I lose in some sense my individual freedom, for the words and the gestures are prescribed even in their smallest details, and I am not able to dispose of them. I feel most deeply in my heart that I am only a servant and a minister, who yet, with free will, with faith and love, fulfill not my will, but the will of Another.[168]

How much does a priest stand to gain or lose by his cooperation or lack of cooperation with the "smallest details" of the liturgical rite bequeathed to him by tradition and ecclesiastical law? To find an answer, let us turn to a great writer of the golden age of French spirituality, Catherine de Bar (1614–1698), or, in religious life, Mother Mectilde of the Blessed Sacrament. In her correspondence with the Countess of Châteauvieux, Mother Mectilde writes:

---

[166] We may even say that the priest imitates and participates in the descent of Christ into hell by offering the Holy Sacrifice for the release of souls in Purgatory, which has a certain resemblance to the limbo of the fathers.

[167] John 5:30.

[168] "Exclusive: Bishop Athanasius Schneider Interview," text slightly emended.

> The first thing I notice in you, my dearest daughter, is that you do not have enough esteem for small things. You do not envision them within the order of divine Providence; that is why you have little attention and respect for them, and in this you lose a great deal of grace. . . . God sometimes asks only for a small act of fidelity in order to make us great saints. You must always be in a state of holy and loving attention toward God, to give yourself to Him in every way. . . . If you could comprehend the waste you bring about when you act in a purely human way, you would be inconsolable. Is it not a great fault in a soul who is capable of giving glory to God and who nevertheless deprives Him of it, so as to yield to her own reasoning, which wants to convince her that life's small actions are mere nothings and do not need to be directed? O my child, if you had really understood how you are ransomed and how you belong to Jesus Christ, you would take much more care about honoring Him. If not even one beat of your heart belongs to you, then so much the more your smallest action, which always lasts longer than one heartbeat![169]

In these words, we find a striking anticipation of the better-known "little way" of St. Thérèse of Lisieux. Mother Mectilde sees that small acts of fidelity are the proving ground of our desire to be great saints, and that we should try never to act in a purely human way, out of our own creaturely resources.

Combining Mother Mectilde's spiritual doctrine, Msgr. Knox's tool comparison, and Bishop Schneider's reflection, we can arrive at a new insight into the enormous spiritual benefits of the traditional Roman liturgy for the ministers who submit to its thousand little demands, which are occasions for placing them in a state of holy and loving attention toward God. Not one word or motion is considered "a mere nothing," a trifle that does not need to be directed; all actions are governed and ordered to honoring Him.

Mother Mectilde amplifies this point in another passage from the same correspondence with the Countess of Châteauvieux:

> The Gospel tells us today briefly in what Christian holiness consists. It is a wonderful lesson, listen to this please. The law says, "You shall love the Lord your God with all your heart, with all your soul, with all

[169] Mectilde, *The "Breviary of Fire,"* 55–56, translation slightly modified.

your strength, with all your mind." Weigh these things well and you will see how much you are obliged to give God the very smallest of your actions. . . .

You will find in an endless number of places in Holy Scripture your inability to dispose of yourself—indeed, of even one of your thoughts—if you do not want to steal it from Jesus Christ. For by right you cannot. You have been purchased: the one who buys the tree, buys the fruit; hence, you are not yours at all. Ponder this truth, and repeat these words often: I am not mine, I belong to Jesus Christ. He ransomed me through love, thus I am necessarily the slave of His love. O worthy slavery! . . .

You see next how much you are obliged to give yourself to Him. That is, to consent to all the rights, powers, and authority He has over you, and to abide in Him. This means to never depart from His holy presence and to do all things by His spirit. As much as is possible for you, to never have in your ideas any other object than Him. Briefly, in everything His pure glory must be the reason you act, even in your smallest actions. Do not think that there is anything small in regard to God: all is great, all is holy. His love sanctifies all things.

Therefore be very exact in the smallest things. All is done for a great God. You must do everything with understanding, that is to say, with attention to God, and with a simple desire to glorify and please Him in all things. . . . He wants you to have this fidelity [in the smallest things], and then He will raise you to greater ones. *He who does not pay any attention to little things will soon fall into great disorders.* . . .

Do not consider little things with the perspective of your human mind. . . . You must have a prompt obedience, without considering the littleness of the action. . . . The slave has no right of choosing or refusing. She must be subject at every moment, without knowing why. Therefore, love faithfulness in little things, and remain subject to it. You can glorify God more by picking up a straw out of submission to God, than by doing fifty lashes with the discipline or other greater austerities, following your own mind. If God is pleased with these little things, you must do them purely and with the same perfection, the same love, and the same fidelity as if you were converting the whole world.[170]

---

170 Mectilde, 46–49, emphasis added.

How compelling is Mother Mectilde's doctrine of holy slavery to Christ, expressed in the constant giving over of every little thing, every small act, done for the great God, the Lord of heaven and earth! We cannot fail to be reminded of the words of Christ: "He that is faithful in that which is least, is faithful also in that which is greater: and he that is unjust in that which is little, is unjust also in that which is greater."[171] Note the emphasis on justice: the one who is unfaithful to God in little matters will prove unjust to Him in greater ones, too—not un*loving*, but un*just*. It is about justice, the "rights of God," since, as Mother Mectilde so vividly says, we belong to Him as His property. And something that is unjust is also by necessity unloving, since charity is founded on justice.

In speaking of fidelity and justice, Our Lord is making reference to the virtue of *religion*, that is, the habit of giving to God that which we owe Him, to the best of our abilities. If we do not give Him our controlled limbs, our bows, genuflections, kisses, averted eyes, and careful pronunciation of age-old syllables, why would we deceive ourselves into thinking that we shall give Him our mind and will, our love, our service to others? One might almost paraphrase St. John's First Epistle: For he that loveth not his Church's rites, which he seeth, how can he love God, whom he seeth not?[172] The school par excellence of utmost fidelity in small things as well as great ones is the sacred liturgy, wherein we obey little rubrics as we handle the Flesh and Blood of God. Prompted by Mother Mectilde's teaching, should we not say that a liturgy that offers the celebrant or the participant a greater number of opportunities to submit to the mind of another and serve His will, especially in the "smallest details," is a liturgy that will produce more abundant fruits of holiness?[173]

If I may coin a phrase, this is nothing other than the "liturgical little way"—the teaching of St. Thérèse applied to that area in which it had always been practiced without fanfare until recent decades, when the rubrics were severely curtailed, celebrant options were multiplied, a casual

---

[171] Luke 16:10.

[172] Cf. 1 John 4:20.

[173] Concerning the more intense and diversified manner of active participation possible in the traditional rite of Mass, see Kwasniewski, *Noble Beauty,* 191–213; *Reclaiming Our Roman Catholic Birthright,* 55–75; *Ministers of Christ,* 131–51.

approach was adopted, and a millennium of Western piety was dismissed as obscurantism. Whether its proponents realized it or not, this sea change reflected a paganization of liturgy, for the reasons given by the Italian historian and philosopher Giambattista Vico: "What could be more foolish and inept than to prescribe absolutely fixed ceremonies for the vague, shifting deities of Paganism? Christianity, instead, advocates unassailable dogmas bearing on the nature of God and on the mysteries of religion; hence the exactness of its rituals is fully justified."[174] As if to say: a religion of definite and unchanging truths revealed by God will necessarily be a religion of exact ritual, characterized by stability more than by change.[175] Joseph Ratzinger's famous lines comes to mind:

> The rites [of East and West] hardened into their definitive forms. . . . They elude control by any individual, local community or regional Church. Unspontaneity is their essence. In these rites I discover that something is approaching me here that I did not produce myself, which ultimately derives from divine revelation. . . .. The greatness of the liturgy depends—we shall have to repeat this frequently—on its unspontaneity (*Unbeliebigkeit*).[176]

The liturgical little way consists in appreciating and paying attention to the small things of which the liturgy consists, and doing them with great care and love. During the course of the twentieth century, many of these small things—bowing and genuflecting, kissing the altar, making the sign of the cross, covering or uncovering the head, keeping custody of the eyes, holding the fingers together—were clipped away, reduced almost to nothing. With the abandonment of this little way came an ever-increasing flood of infidelity, impiety, and depravity. "He who does not pay any attention to little things will soon fall into great disorders." Thanks be to God, the

---

174 Vico, *On the Study Methods of Our Time,* 45.

175 As I explain in *The Once and Future Roman Rite,* each traditional rite of East or West developed so gradually, over so many centuries, that it would have seemed much more *the same* to any particular generation of believers than it would have seemed to be *changing*. This is one among many reasons why the period from circa 1910 to 1970 has no parallel in Church history, in regard to the sheer nature and number of changes that occurred in public worship. Even the transition from Greek to Latin and from house-churches to basilicas would have seen fundamental continuities that were destroyed in the twentieth-century—outside of traditionalist enclaves that retained them.

176 Ratzinger, *Spirit of the Liturgy,* IV.1, in *Theology of the Liturgy,* 102–3.

growth of the traditional movement brings with it perforce a restoration of attentiveness to these little things, and this, in turn, gives us fair hope and reasonable confidence that someday we shall once again see great sanctity emerging from the liturgy.

One can imagine an objection: Doesn't this approach risk becoming a form of legalism or a preoccupation with rubrics? As far as I can tell, legalism became a danger only after 1570 when a form of Mass with a set of rubrics was promulgated for the first time by a pope. Prior to 1570, the clergy did certain things and avoided others due to strong custom and a sense of the fittingness of what might be called "best practice." The behavior stemmed more from piety and reverence than from obedience to an external law. All the same, Pope Pius V was only codifying what was already being done: the rubrics reflected time-honored custom and not the arbitrary will of a commission, as happened much later with twentieth-century rubrical reforms. Ultimately, however, we cannot but agree with Newman that if one truly believes in the dogma of transubstantiation, the dense rubricism of the old Roman missal immediately becomes comprehensible, for it serves multiple awe-inspiring ends:

> Open the Missal, read the minute directions given for the celebration of Mass,—what are the fit dispositions under which the Priest prepares for it, how he is to arrange his every action, movement, gesture, utterance, during the course of it, and what is to be done in case of a variety of supposable accidents. What a mockery would all this be, if the rite meant nothing! But if it be a fact that God the Son is there offered up in human flesh and blood by the hands of man, why, it is plain that no rite whatever, however anxious and elaborate, is equal to the depth of the overwhelming thoughts which are borne in upon the mind by such an action. Thus the usages and ordinances of the Church do not exist for their own sake . . . they protect a mystery; they defend a dogma; they represent an idea; they preach good tidings; they are the channels of grace.[177]

[177] Newman, *Certain Difficulties Felt by Anglicans,* vol. 1, lec. 7, pp. 215–16.

The Seductions of Autonomy

The foregoing observations suffice to show why we ought to find unnerving, to say the least, one of the most notable novelties in the postconciliar liturgical books, namely, that by which the celebrant is given many options among which he may choose, as well as opportunities for crafting his own speech: "in these or similar words."[178] Confronted with such a phrase, one might legitimately ask: "How similar is similar?" In reality, the word of the liturgy and the word of the minister should be *homoousios*, of one and the same substance, not *homoiousios*, of a similar substance. It makes far more than one iota of difference. In the action of selecting options and extemporizing texts, the celebrant no longer perfectly reflects the Word of God who, as the perfect Image of the Father, equal to Him, receives His words and does not originate them, who does the will of another and not His own will. The elective and extemporizing celebrant does not show forth the fundamental identity of the Christian: one who receives and bears fruit, like the Blessed Virgin Mary—one who conceives by the descent of the Spirit alone, with no help of man.[179] Instead, he adopts the posture of one who originates; he removes this sphere of action from the Master to whom he reports; he carves out for himself a zone of autonomy; he denies the Lord the privilege of commanding him and deprives himself of the guerdon of submission; for a moment he leaves the narrow way of being a tool and steps on to the broad way of being somebody. "He that speaketh of himself, seeketh his own glory."[180] He becomes not only an actor but a playwright; his *free choice* as an individual is exalted into a principle of liturgy. He joins the madding crowd that says, in the words of the Psalmist: *linguam nostram magnificabimus, labia nostra a nobis sunt; quis noster dominus est?* "We will magnify our tongue; our lips are our own; who is Lord over us?"[181]

[178] See Turner, *In These or Similar Words.*

[179] See Kwasniewski, *Noble Beauty,* 53–87. It is no serious objection to note that the early Christians did not have fully fixed and developed prayers, for the historical record indicates that as time went on, communities moved away from extemporaneity as they developed ever more definite services of prayer based on the hallowed forms they received from each generation. See Kwasniewski, "From Extemporaneity to Fixity of Form"; see also DiPippo, "Liturgical Improvisation Must End."

[180] John 7:18.

[181] Ps. 11:5.

But since free choice is antithetical to liturgy as a fixed ritual received from our forebears and handed down faithfully to our successors, choice tends to be a source of distraction, dilution, or dissolution in the liturgy rather than a contributor to its well-being. The same critique may be given of all the ways in which the new liturgy permits the celebrant an indeterminate freedom of speech, bodily bearing, and movement. Such voluntarism strikes at the essence of liturgy, which is a public, objective, formal, solemn, and common prayer, in which all Christians are equally participants, even when they are performing irreducibly distinct acts. The prayer of Christians belongs to everyone in common, which means it should not belong to anyone in particular. The moment a priest invents something that is not common, he sets himself up as a clerical overlord vis-à-vis the people; the people must then submit not to a rule of Christ and the Church, but to the arbitrary rule of this individual.[182] For these reasons, Joseph Ratzinger did not hesitate to condemn this aspect of the new missal:

> As for the Missal in current use . . . we quite often find formulae such as: *sacerdos dicit sic vel simili modo* . . . [the priest speaks thus or in a similar way . . .] or *Hic sacerdos potest dicere* . . . [Here the priest can say . . .]. These formulae of the Missal in fact give official sanction to creativity; the priest feels almost obliged to change the wording, to show that he is creative, that he is giving this liturgy immediacy, making it present for his congregation; and with this false creativity, which transforms the liturgy into a catechetical exercise for *this* congregation, liturgical unity, and the *ecclesiality* of the liturgy are being destroyed. Therefore, it seems to me, it would be an important step toward reconciliation if the Missal were simply freed from these areas of creativity, which do not correspond to the deepest level of reality, to the spirit, of the liturgy.[183]

Yet there is a better, truer, and in many ways far simpler solution: to return to a missal that has *always* been "free of false creativity" because the

---

[182] Even some progressives have recognized this fact: see the revealing admissions in "Robert Taft Acceptance Speech: Berakah Award" and in Taft's "Recovering Western Liturgical Traditions," where he writes: "The West might learn from the East to recapture a sense of tradition, and stop getting tripped up in its own clichés. *Liturgy should avoid repetition?* Repetition is of the essence of ritual behavior. *Liturgy should offer variety?* Too much variety is the enemy of popular participation. *Liturgy should be creative?* But whose creativity? It is presumptuous of those who have never manifested the least creativity in any other aspect of their lives to think they are Beethoven and Shakespeare when it comes to liturgy."

[183] Ratzinger, *Theology of the Liturgy*, 564–65.

traditional order of worship it contains *already* "corresponds to the deepest level of reality, to the spirit, of the liturgy."

Amy Welborn articulates incomparably well the thinking behind the new liturgy's "flexibility" and precisely how that quality destroys the liturgy for the ordinary faithful (and, if only they knew it, harms the ministers as well):

> God is in the here and now, and speaks to us in the here and now. To be responsive to the Spirit in this here and now means not being bound by imposed ritual or words, especially if those rituals come to us from distant times and cultures. So what needs to happen with liturgy is that it should be seen as a framework—valuable, yes—but only a framework in which the ministers and the community can respond to the Lord freely, letting Him work through the uniqueness of this particular community, this moment in time, the unique gifts of these ministers and perceived needs of this community. It [viz., the liturgical reform] was supposed to render the ritual far more accessible than any medieval, time-encrusted form ever could for Modern Man.
>
> It seemed to make sense at the time. And in the best of circumstances, saints at the helm, perhaps it does. But as I have said time and time again, one of the reasons we say that tradition possesses a sort of wisdom is that tradition has seen the strengths and weaknesses of human nature and evolved to take that—especially the weaknesses and the sinfulness—into consideration, evolving into something that discourages and inhibits those sinful tendencies.
>
> So when you have a liturgy, you have ministers. You have people in charge. And it is not shocking at all that in a context of being told that *The Spirit will work through your words and actions—trust it—* you immediately construct a huge, boundless playground for the Ego. The Ego that at one point might have been constrained by strict rules about obeying rubrics (not to speak of the use of a foreign, non-vernacular language) is unleashed, not only by the fateful "*in these or other words,*" but by his new role, in constant dialogue with the congregation, who now spend an hour or more gazing on his face, and who has been taught that, in some crucial way, the congregation's spiritual experience at this liturgy *depends on his personality*—that his personality and interaction holds a key to a fruitful spiritual moment.[184]

[184] Wellborn, "It's not the reverence; It's the ego"; see the same author's "...wishful thinking and liturgical pretense."

As we have seen, Our Lord called the devil a liar because "he speaks from himself": he vainly endeavors to pull out of his own finite mind a word that is sufficient, or we might say, self-sufficient, and he always fails. Private initiative by itself can never equal the demands of the public weal. In the liturgy *above all*, we must never speak "from ourselves," but only from Christ and His beloved Bride, the Church.

Psalm 115, which the old Roman Missal proposes as a prayer of preparation for the celebrant, elegantly sums up my entire argument to this point. *I said in my excess: Every man is a liar. What shall I render to the Lord, for all the things he hath rendered unto me?* (vv. 11–12). The Psalmist admits that fallen man, like the devil, is a liar. He asks what he should give in return for all that the Lord has already given to him—given in the traditional liturgy, spirituality, doctrine, and discipline of the Church; and he immediately continues: *I will take the chalice of salvation, and I will call upon the name of the Lord* (v. 13), as if to say: only through the liturgy itself, which does not depend on me or proceed from me, can I make an adequate return to Him. *Precious in the sight of the Lord is the death of his saints* (v. 15), namely, that cloud of witnesses who were sanctified by this liturgy, taking its yoke upon their necks. *O Lord, for I am thy servant: I am thy servant, and the son of thy handmaid* (v. 16), I am the servant of Him who became a servant for me, who serves me with His precious Body and Blood, in exchange for my rational service; I am the son of His Mother, the handmaid of the Lord. *Thou hast broken my bonds* (v. 16)—the bonds of self-will, self-determination, self-inflation, which hold me down to the earth, to prevailing fashion, to the spirit of the age, to the expectations of my social group or stratum, to the gross or subtle ideologies of my time. Being thus set free by the words and work of another, *I will sacrifice to thee the sacrifice of praise, and I will call upon the name of the Lord* (v. 17).[185] I will not make a name for myself but simply call upon His.[186]

---

185 See St. Benedict, *Rule,* ch. 7, second degree: "Self-will hath its punishment, but subjection winneth a crown."

186 See Gen. 11:4. The most subtle of all the evils unleashed by the Novus Ordo is this: it brings notoriety and applause to priests who celebrate it reverently and beautifully. See Kwasniewski, "Men Must Be Changed by Sacred Things."

Fat Sacrifices—or Thin Gruel?

We can also look to Psalm 15 for guidance. "I have said to the Lord, thou art my God, for thou hast no need of my goods. . . . *The Lord* is the portion of my inheritance and of my cup: it is thou that wilt restore my inheritance to me. The lines are fallen unto me in goodly places: for my inheritance is goodly to me."[187] The Lord truly has no need of our paltry goods that we think we can contribute; rather, we have need of the goodly inheritance and the overflowing cup He has prepared for us over the ages and now offers to us, in black lines of prayer and red lines of rubric set forth in front of our eyes and placed into our hand: "The lines are fallen unto me in goodly places."

There is a provocative line in Psalm 19: *Holocaustum tuum pingue fiat*, "may thy whole burnt offering be made fat."[188] In a number of places, Scripture goes on about "fat sacrifices." Why? The animal to be offered to the Lord should be the best that one has, not only unblemished but robustly healthy from being fed on ample quantities of the best provender. This sacrificial animal represents us. We want to give the Lord *everything*: the fat of our thoughts, volitions, passions, words, actions. No thin gruel is worthy of Him, no partial flank, no rationing in coffee spoons: He wants all of us for Himself. When we follow the path of traditional liturgy, our sacrifice is both *fat*, because the content of the rite is thick and rich and full of religion, and a *holocaust* in which all is burned up for Him in obedience, with nothing left outside the reach of the rubrics.

The fruit of this obedience to an external rule is an immense interior peace, like the peace described by Mother Mectilde:

> All happiness is contained in the divine will and . . . only a soul possessed by it is happy, and enjoys, even in this world, a foretaste of Paradise. Everything good follows from it: there is no trouble or anxiety, no inconstancy or pretension, no eagerness or sadness, no fear or darkness; all is serene in the divine will, all is light and clarity, all is immovable.[189]

---

[187] Ps. 15:2, 5–6, emphasis added.

[188] Ps. 19:4.

[189] Mectilde, *The True Spirit of the Perpetual Adorers,* ch. 14.

If everything good follows from the divine will, it is no less true that everything evil flows from the creature's abandonment of God, the root and strength of its being. Jesus tells us: "Without me you can do nothing."[190] As Jacques Maritain observes, this statement can be taken two ways: in its obvious meaning, and in a paradoxical meaning.[191] At face value, Our Lord is saying that without Him, without His grace, without the branch living from the sap of the vine, we cannot do anything supernaturally good, pleasing to God, or meritorious. But Our Lord is also telling us: "When you act without me, what you end up doing is precisely a *nothing*; when you act on your own, you are perfectly capable of doing 'nothing,' and the more you act apart from me, the more nothingness you will produce." It's as if one were to say: "The one thing I can do apart from Christ is to sin, to introduce disorder, or to render something duller, flatter, or emptier than it was or would have been."

This, too, has liturgical implications. Should we be surprised that the churches have emptied, when the new liturgy allows us to do what is in our own heads? Apart from Christ, we do nothing well, and the result is nothing good, "the improvisations of nothingness of created existents."[192] The deepest cause of the missionary collapse of the Church in the Western world is that we have lost our institutional and personal subordination to Christ the High Priest, the principal actor in the liturgy, the Word to whom we lend our mouth, our hands, our bodies, our souls. For more than half a century it has *not* been perfectly clear in our churches that ministers are in fact servants *of another*, that they are intelligent instruments wholly at His disposal. On the contrary, the opposite message has been promoted over and over again, *ad nauseam*, whether in words or in deeds: we have "come of age," *we* are shaping the world, the Church, the Mass, the entire Christian life, according to our own lights, and for our own purposes.[193] We do not kneel and receive Communion in our mouths like dependent little children; we stand up and take it in our hands like grown-ups who can do business for themselves.[194] It is not difficult to see that this "coming

[190] John 15:5.

[191] See Maritain, *Existence and the Existent,* 98–99.

[192] In Maritain's words: *God and the Permission of Evil,* 113.

[193] See Is. 59.

[194] See chapter 9.

of age" mentality is an inversion of the preaching of Christ and a repudiation of the tradition of the Church, and that it will not, *cannot*, produce renewal but rather, must generate confusion, infidelity, boredom, and desolation. We see here an exact parallel to what has happened with marriage when so-called "free love" entered the picture: out went committed love and heroic sacrifice, and in came lust, selfishness, dissatisfaction, and an unspeakable plague of loneliness. "Without me, you can do nothing." In the realm of sexual morality, as in the realm of liturgical morality, we have given a compelling demonstration of what we can accomplish without Christ and without His gift of tradition—namely, nothing.

As if the Church on earth had suddenly developed an autoimmune disease, her rulers in the twentieth century turned against her own ecclesiastical traditions, her great music, art, and architecture, her very rites and ceremonies, in what can only be seen as an inbreaking of the underworld, an influx of demonic energy and chaos.

The contradictory notions of worship discussed in this chapter and throughout this book—the one, a selfless glorification of the Father, the Son, and the Holy Spirit; the other, a self-celebration prompted by the father of lies, the son of perdition, and the spirit of the age—have far greater implications than many realize. Talking in an autobiographical sketch about the first "high-church" liturgy he had ever attended as an evangelical Protestant—which took place at Saint Mary the Virgin near Times Square, an Episcopalian Anglo-Catholic church nicknamed "Smokey Mary's" because of their liberal use of incense—Thomas Howard helps us to see what those implications are:

> I was familiar with Christian rites that were plain, and this seemed lavish. The whole business of ceremony seemed to matter here. Every gesture seemed to carry some freight of significance. One minute the priest had his hands up like this, and the next they were out like that. One minute he was facing you, and the next he was sideways, and then he had his back to you. He even changed his vestments during the hour, from a cope to a chasuble. Nothing was natural or spontaneous or unstructured. In order to get from one place to another, they processed. They never merely said anything: it was all chanted. And nothing could

be done without scattering smoke hither and thither. They walked around the altar with it, they swung it over books, shot it out at the priest, and finally waved it at us.

If everything else had put me off forever (which it hadn't), I would have gone back again for the music. All the antiphons were sung in Gregorian chant, the most pure, most austere of all musical forms, perfectly suited to the text of Scripture, since it liberates the words from the distracting style of any individual reader and sets them out, free from ornament, where there is nothing to do but listen to them. And the music of the Mass itself—the Kyrie, the Gloria, the Sanctus and Benedictus, and the Agnus Dei—was sung from a loft in the back of the church: no visible choir in robes, putting on a performance for us, but rather voices articulating these ancient canticles that utter the Church's response to the great mysteries of the gospel, and all of it sung, not by tremulous, warbling concert voices, but in that "white" tone, wholly free from vibrato, that again sets the text free from any individual's efforts to impress. . . .

What is one to make of the [formal] liturgy? I thought. It is at a polar extreme from our era's attempts at getting things unstructured and spontaneous. A chance passerby might well think it is all horribly repressive and restricting. But what he would be missing would be the way in which all this structure, lo and behold, lifts us away from the poor little tiny circumference of our own private feelings and experience and liberates us into something that is infinitely more vast than ourselves—the way any great ceremony does. It is odd, how the whole race, in all tribes and cultures and centuries, has always resorted to ceremony—in the presence of life's deepest mysteries. Birth, marriage, and death: What do we all do with these purely organic, purely functional, events? We deck them and order them and set them about with ritual. Birthday cakes, wedding solemnities, funeral obsequies. What are they all about? Well, we are clearly ritual creatures. Perhaps our own era's efforts to replace pomp and ceremony with spontaneity are a tragic betrayal of the sort of creatures we are. The stars in their courses move in solemn dance; we read of seraphim and cherubim covering their faces in adoration; we see the whole world of flora and fauna repeating its yearly rituals in exuberant obedience to the rubric. Shall we, alone in the universe, insist that our freedom is to be found in the

> random, the ad hoc, and the unstructured? Surely one way of describing the difference between hell and the City of God is to say that the former is wholly unstructured and the latter magnificently structured? I had, I thought, seen a diagram of that structured magnificence in the liturgy on that morning at Saint Mary's.[195]

Thomas Howard was set decisively on a journey to the Catholic Faith by the thoughts prompted in him at that morning's service—which (sadly and ironically) had retained many more elements of traditional Catholic worship than the same city's *Catholic* churches had done, back then and still today. A contrary kind of service may well set people on a path leading *away from* the Catholic Faith—whether it leads them literally out the door or takes them metaphorically away from orthodoxy.

Signs of Hope

We need not conclude on a dark note. We know that everything that happens is either a good willed by God because it is pleasing to Him, or an evil permitted by the One who, in His omnipotence, can bring forth some greater good from it—for example, by the testing of the saints and the purification of the Church. The case has been made that the radical changes in the liturgy cannot have been directly intended by God. But might we be in a position to see some of the goods He has drawn out of the divine permission of the liturgical revolution? I believe the answer is yes.

First, precisely because of its near extinction, the traditional liturgy has never been more loved, treasured, studied, and promoted as it is now on the part of those who are working to restore it to the place of honor it deserves. From what I can tell in my historical research, the greatness of the authentic liturgy was sometimes marred in its beauty by a complacent or compromised *ars celebrandi*, or it was taken too much for granted as an immovable piece of furniture in the rambling old Catholic mansion. One sees in the Old Testament that the Lord frequently deprives His people of goods of which they no longer strive to be worthy and for which they seldom or never thank Him. This is a *severe* mercy, to be sure, but it is mercy nonetheless, urging us to take seriously things that must be taken seriously

[195] Howard, *The Secret of New York Revealed,* 124–26.

if they are not to be taken away altogether. It is a call to repentance and recommitment. "Thou hast shewn thy people hard things; thou hast made us to drink the wine of compunction."[196]

Second, I believe that we are much more on our guard now: "the enemy of the human race"[197] has shown his cards, and we are better prepared to detect his wiles. The emergence in recent years of a rich literature on the inherent limits of papal authority, the obligation of the pope to act as servant of the servants of God rather than an oriental despot, and the inner connection between liturgy, dogma, and morality points to a reviving awareness of rights and duties, axioms and laws, that define us as Catholics.[198] As time goes on, the truth of the axiom *lex orandi, lex credendi, lex vivendi* is becoming ever more manifest in a blazing light of obviousness that swells the ranks of Catholic traditionalists and exposes the modernism of their opponents past all gainsaying.

Third, we now have a lived experience of what happens when the principles of liturgy are distorted or discarded. Never before had such a foolhardy experiment been attempted, but since the laws of nature and of grace always remain the same, the experiment was doomed to fail; the rotten fruits of the postconciliar tree are plain for all to see. This painful experience has made us more conscientious and more insistent on good liturgy—on careful celebration, appropriate adornments in the sanctuary, splendid vestments, and well-executed sacred music. One might say: Those who care, care more; and this process will only intensify as Vatican II nostalgics depart from our midst.

Each liturgically vibrant parish or chapel, each observant monastery or convent, each faithful family or school, each level-headed society or association, by putting into practice the "liturgical little way," remaining faithful to the smallest details of tradition, will have its part to play in the unexpected triumph of David, singer of psalms, over the swaggering Goliath of fabricated liturgy.

---

196 Ps. 59:5, with "compunction" replacing "sorrow" as a more literal rendering of the Vulgate.

197 As St. Leo the Great and St. Gregory the Great call the devil: see Saward, *World Invisible,* 128. In Scripture he is called our "adversary" (1 Pet. 5:8).

198 See Lanzetta, *Super Hanc Petram;* Kwasniewski, *Bound by Truth;* Kwasniewski, *Ultramontanism and Tradition*; Kwasniewski, *Unresolved Tensions.*

5

Why We Repeat Ourselves in Traditional Worship

"There's so much repetition. Do we have to say things three times or more?"

In this chapter, I'd like to suggest some ways of thinking about repetition that may help us to appreciate its positive value, over against the assumptions that stood behind the far-reaching simplification of liturgical rites in the twentieth century. First, I will look at a symptomatic text in the Second Vatican Council; second, I will explore the psychological value of repetition; third, I will examine formal repetition in a sacred context and use the Confiteor as my case study; fourth, I will consider whether there is room for improvement in the old rite of Mass; finally, I will discuss certain temptations that arise with repetition, and thus come to my conclusion.

A Weak Link in *Sacrosanctum Concilium's* Chain

Among the worst casualties of the liturgical reform were prayers and gestures in the Mass that were judged to be instances of "useless repetition," such as the tripled Confiteor, the ninefold *Kyrie*, the doubled threefold *Domine, non sum dignus*, and the genuflections and signs of the cross in the Roman Canon. Such purges were said to have been done in fulfillment of the criteria given in section 50 of the Constitution on the Sacred Liturgy *Sacrosanctum Concilium*:

> The rite of the Mass is to be revised in such a way that the intrinsic nature and purpose of its several parts, as also the connection between them, may be more clearly manifested, and that devout and active participation by the faithful may be more easily achieved. For this purpose the rites are to be simplified, due care being taken to preserve their substance; elements which, with the passage of time, came to be duplicated, or were added with but little advantage, are now to be discarded; other elements which have suffered injury through accidents of history are now to be restored to the vigor which they had in the days of the holy Fathers, as may seem useful or necessary.

The dictates in this section rest on more universal principles enunciated in section 34: "The rites should be distinguished by a noble simplicity; they should be short, clear, and unencumbered by useless repetitions; they should be within the people's powers of comprehension, and normally should not require much explanation." We might note, first, that this is a rather poor translation of section 34's Latin original,[199] which says, rendered more accurately: "The rites should shine forth with a noble simplicity; they should be clear in brevity, avoid unprofitable repetitions, and be accommodated to the faithful's capacity; nor should they generally require many explanations." While this rendering makes the text not quite so heavy-handed, it is still, regrettably, one of the weaker statements in the Constitution, as can be seen from five angles.

First, what exactly is meant by "simplicity"? The simplicity of God is actually infinite and pre-inclusive of all things; the simplicity of prime matter is potentially infinite and totally indefinite; the simplicity of a saint is bound to look strange to the world; the simplicity of a child is easily taken advantage of. Adding the qualifier "noble" helps only a little.

Second, that rites be *brevitate perspicui*, "clear in [their] brevity," raises a host of questions left unanswered: Why should we think that a ritual enactment of an unfathomable mystery could ever be transparent to the eyes of body or of soul? Why should we think that conciseness would help, rather than hinder, our assimilation of this mystery?[200] Fr. Aidan Nichols writes:

---

199 *"Ritus nobili simplicitate fulgeant, sint brevitate perspicui et repetitiones inutiles evitent, sint fidelium captui accommodati, neque generatim multis indigeant explanationibus."*

200 "Octaves are for the contemplation of mysteries that are too great for a single day, and it is

"To the sociologist, it is by no means self-evident that brief, clear rites have greater transformative potential than complex, abundant, lavish, rich, long rites, furnished with elaborate ceremonial."[201] The Eastern tradition works on the opposite assumption, namely, that leisurely length, waves of repetition, and a certain obscurity are essential to the liturgy—a fact to which Pope John Paul II bore witness when he wrote, concerning the Byzantine liturgy: "The lengthy duration of the celebrations, the repeated invocations, everything expresses gradual identification with the mystery celebrated with one's whole person"[202]—and the same may be said of the Western tradition at its best. Art historians love to speak of the *chiaroscuro* of Baroque painters, but the painters are not the inventors of this approach to light and darkness. The liturgy is the *chiaroscuro* of the divine mysteries, which shine forth with a light far too bright for our intellects to comprehend. Because of what the liturgy is about and whom it is for, it is appropriate for its very form to combine ease and difficulty, clarity and obscurity, simplicity and elaborateness (a point I shall return to in chapter 8).

Third, that rites should "avoid unprofitable repetition" leaves one scratching one's head. If we are speaking about senseless babbling, like a broken record or a scratched compact disc, who could disagree, and why would it need to be said at all? On the other hand, verbal repetition is one of the most common literary devices found in Scripture ("Amen, amen, I say to you"[203]), in the world's great poetry ("Quoth the Raven 'Nevermore'"[204]), in popular devotions (the Rosary, litanies, novenas), and in all

---

certainly true that *repetita juvant* [repetition does good], a proverb which the Roman Rite, with its habitual conservatism, historically took very much to heart" (DiPippo, "Other Readings for the Octave of Corpus Christi"). For a thorough examination of how the *usus antiquior's* calendar embodies the psychology of useful meditative repetition, see Foley, "The Reform of the Calendar and the Reduction of Liturgical Recapitulation."

201 Nichols, *Looking at the Liturgy,* 59.

202 John Paul II, *Orientale Lumen,* no. 11.

203 Examples of repeated Amens in the Bible include, in the OT, Numbers 5:22 and Nehemiah 8:6, and in the Gospel of John, 1:51, 3:3, 3:5, 3:11, 5:19, 5:24, 5:25, 6:26, 6:32, 6:47, 6:54, 8:34, 8:51, 8:58, 10:1, 10:7, 12:24, 13:16, 13:20, 13:21, 13:38, 14:12, 16:20, 16:23, 21:18. Some translations have "Truly, truly." Another example of deliberate repetition is when the Book of Numbers uses the expression "At the command of the Lord they encamped, and at the command of the Lord they set out" over and over and over, to drive home that the people rested and moved according to God's will. We can be sure that when the ancients, for whom the process of writing was expensive and laborious, repeated something, they were not doing it thoughtlessly, as we might do with the copy-and-paste function of word processing software.

204 From Poe's "The Raven," where "Nevermore" recurs as the last word of eleven stanzas in a row.

liturgies (e.g., dozens of "Lord have mercy's" in the Divine Liturgy of St. John Chrysostom), so the criterion comes across sounding uneducated or, worse, ideological. As I have explained in a previous work:

> A meaningless repetition of elements is rightly avoided as irrational. How different is the chanting of the Litany of the Saints or the Litany of Loreto, the Paters and Aves counted on the beads of a well-loved rosary, or the cascading Kyries of a Byzantine Divine Liturgy! Of such insistent pleading, it is Our Lord himself who offered the definitive example in the Garden of Gethsemane: "He left them again, and went away and prayed a third time, saying the same thing once more" (Mt 26:44; cf. Mk 14:39).[205]

The conciliar text, in its far-from-clear brevity, does not specify when repetition is useful and when it is not, nor what the criteria of utility might be. There is no hint of awareness that emphasizing the concept of usefulness might betray a utilitarianism at odds with deeper requirements of spirituality, aesthetics, and tradition.

Fourth, the statement that rites ought to be "accommodated to the faithful's capacity" is totally unhelpful. Are "the faithful" an undifferentiated homogeneous mass? Some are well-catechized, others are ignorant; some are new to the Faith, others lifelong devotees; some are inclined to contemplative prayer, others are extroverts who find it hard to quiet down and concentrate; some are avid readers of Guéranger's *Liturgical Year*, others have barely taken notice of the Liturgical Movement's existence. There is no way to succeed in creating a liturgical rite aimed at an ill-defined or indefinable "capacity of the faithful."[206] It is the *faithful* whose diverse capacities

---

[205] Kwasniewski, *Resurgent in the Midst of Crisis,* 65.

[206] Pius XII (*Mediator Dei,* no. 108) observes: "Many of the faithful are unable to use the Roman missal even though it is written in the vernacular; nor are all capable of understanding correctly the liturgical rites and formulas. So varied and diverse are men's talents and characters that it is impossible for all to be moved and attracted to the same extent by community prayers, hymns, and liturgical services. Moreover, the needs and inclinations of all are not the same, nor are they always constant in the same individual. Who, then, would say, on account of such a prejudice, that all these Christians cannot participate in the Mass nor share its fruits? On the contrary, they can adopt some other method which proves easier for certain people; for instance, they can lovingly meditate on the mysteries of Jesus Christ or perform other exercises of piety or recite prayers which, though they differ from the sacred rites, are still essentially in harmony with them."

must be accommodated to the liturgy's immense reality, not the liturgy that must be retooled and refashioned to suit an imaginary congregation. As we know, the default assumption later on was that liturgy should be accommodated to the lowest type of participant, that is, the Catholic who knows almost nothing, makes no effort to cultivate his interior life, and, consequently, needs to be constantly animated from without, spoonfed with monosyllabic banalities in magazine language.[207]

Fifth, the requirement that liturgical rites should not "generally require many explanations" is baffling in light of section 34's call for simplification. A rite is communicative to the extent that it is permeated with signs or symbols, and thus one might believe that the more densely symbolic it is, and the more numerous and pronounced its gestures, and the richer its prayers, the more powerfully will it be able to communicate to a receptive soul—and precisely without the need for many explanations.[208] But if a rite is too obvious, too brief, too straightforward, or too stripped down, it will take a huge amount of explanation to persuade people that something important, numinous, transformative, or miraculous is happening. If one wishes to avoid a lot of verbal explanations before, during, and after the liturgy, one has to protect the liturgy's own inherent language of vestments, vessels, places, postures, gestures, chants, orations, and silences.[209]

Sometimes one wonders how *Sacrosanctum Concilium* might have been written, if its authors had been altar card-carrying members of Roman Catholicism who had harnessed the insights of anthropology, psychology, and theology. Let's imagine how section 34 in particular could have sounded:

---

[207] This was the official policy behind liturgical translations into the vernacular, established in the Consilium document *Comme le Prévoit* of January 25, 1969, which was not overturned until *Liturgiam Authenticam* of March 28, 2001—so, a hegemony of over three decades; Pope Francis, in his fondness for all things Bugninian, has signaled a shift back to *Comme le Prévoit.* As part of this cretin campaign, in the United States the Bible was "translated" into "Nabbish" (that is, the language of the New American Bible), a flat-footedly prosaic, deflatingly banal, grossly paraphrastic, and frequently misleading dialect (see Esolen, "A Bumping Boxcar Language").

[208] As Joseph Shaw explains: "The presentation of truths through symbols is not simply a way of giving them greater dignity or beauty, let alone a way of hiding them from the uninitiated. It is a way, rather, of communicating a message, to those willing to enter into serious contemplation of the symbol, which transcends what could be expressed in a series of plain propositions" (*Latin Mass and the Intellectuals,* 295).

[209] On this point and all the others discussed in this chapter, see the brilliant essay by Mosebach, "Holy Routine."

> The rites should shine forth with the beauty of a unified complexity that in some way reflects the infinite simplicity of God and the ordered multiplicity of His creation. The rites should involve both clarity and obscurity, efficiency and leisure; they should cultivate meaningful repetition, accentuate symbolic objects and actions, and eschew verbal explanations. To the faithful who seek holiness, the rites should offer a lifelong apprenticeship in the Church's highest form of prayer.

In other words, the rites should be the traditional Western rites that the Church already had, most notably the Roman Rite. There was no need to "improve" them; rather, the deformations that had occurred in the decade and a half prior to Vatican II—the extensive and strange modifications to Holy Week, the abolition of octaves and vigils, the suppression of commemorations, and so forth—should have been *undone*.[210]

In any case, *Sacrosanctum Concilium*'s section 34 is what it is: a testimony to the shallowness and short-sightedness of ecclesiastical circles in the 1960s.

One must ask: Why was it even thought necessary to ask for a removal of repetitions? Where did the negative attitude come from? Let me offer, as an illustration of it, the following passage from Romano Guardini's famous and influential book *The Spirit of the Liturgy* (1918):

> The justification of methods of prayer such as, e.g., the Rosary, must not be gainsaid. They have a necessary and peculiar effect in the spiritual life. They clearly express the difference which exists between liturgical and popular prayer. The liturgy has for its fundamental principle, *Ne bis idem* [never the same thing twice]. It aims at a continuous progress of ideas, mood, and intention. Popular devotion, on the contrary, has a strongly contemplative character, and loves to linger around a few simple images, ideas, and moods without any swift changes of thought. For the people the forms of devotion are often merely a means of being with God. On this account they love repetition. The ever-renewed requests of the Our Father, Hail Mary, etc., are for them at the same time receptacles into which they can pour their hearts.[211]

---

[210] See Kwasniewski, *Once and Future Roman Rite*, 333–75.

[211] Guardini, *The Spirit of the Liturgy*, n10 of ch. 1, pp. 30–31.

What an odd thing for a man of Guardini's stature to say! Surely, he knew that *all* liturgical prayer in East and West includes *repetition* no less than popular devotions involve *progression* (as in the mysteries of the Rosary, the versicles of the Angelus, or the Stations of the Cross). Moreover, the characteristic he attributes to popular devotion, namely, that it has a "contemplative character," can just as readily be attributed to the liturgy, especially in the Western sphere. Perhaps it was this kind of dichotomous thinking that stood behind the campaign against "useless repetitions."

Members of the Liturgical Movement often praised the "objectivity" of liturgy and slighted the "subjectivism" of devotion. While there is some truth to this contrast, there is also a tendency to oversimplification if we forget the way in which the sphere of liturgy is so grand in its objectivity that it makes room for an almost endless subjective involvement of the faithful, and at the same time, that Catholic devotions at their best possess a rock-solid dogmatic core and lend themselves to, or inspire the creation of, quasi-liturgical literary and artistic forms. One might think of the many musical compositions, some of them truly great, that were inspired by the Stations of the Cross and served as food for meditation in the popular Good Friday paraliturgies that Pope Pius XII's ill-considered Holy Week reform obliterated almost overnight.

The Psychological Value of Repetition

We need to ask ourselves deeper questions than the authors of *Sacrosanctum Concilium* evidently did. What is repetition all about? When and why is it used in human life and in worship? We should seek an answer both at the natural level, that is, as regards universal human psychology, and at the supernatural level, in connection with the rituals of the Christian religion.

We repeat things for several distinct reasons, as can be seen by looking, with St. Thomas Aquinas, at the different faculties of the soul. In regard to the faculty of the intellect and our capacity for understanding, we repeat for the sake of further penetration. Since men do not have angelic intellects capable of immediately grasping a truth in its totality, we benefit from repeated encounters with a statement or an object, for each time it is possible we might catch a new glimpse of it, like an observer walking around a statue, seeing it from different angles.[212] Moreover, liturgical repetition is usually bound up with numerological symbolism, which makes an appeal to the intellect, establishing a connection between whatever it is we are saying and a larger, more encompassing mystery to which it alludes. Thus, the ninefold *Kyrie* at the start of Mass is a doubly underlined Trinitarian prayer: three petitions addressed to the Father, three to the Son, and three to the Holy Ghost.

Closely related to this intellectual aspect is the value of repetition for filling the imagination and shaping the memory. That which is repeated is more continually present to our inner sensorium, thereby making a deeper impression on our faculty of memory. It is obvious that we must repeat something if we are to memorize it, or, in that wonderful idiom, "learn it *by heart*."[213] If we want prayer to move from our intellect to our heart, it must become familiar, internalized, habitual, and connatural, so that we are not expending our energy on the more superficial activity of navigating new phrases, new sentiments, new patterns. It doesn't do me any good to be surrounded by thousands of books if I have the content of none of them in my soul.[214] It is when the Church's words given to me from without become *my* words rooted within that the liturgy becomes, in fact, the font and apex of *my* Christian life. Any amount of repetition will help in this regard, even if it is as minimal as it often is with the new Liturgy of the

---

212 Another way of showing how limited is our ability to comprehend all the meanings of a statement at once is the well-known classroom exercise that consists in taking a sentence and reading it over and over, emphasizing a different word each time, to hear the different effect it has: "*My* soul magnifies the Lord," "My *soul* magnifies the Lord," "My soul *magnifies* the Lord," "My soul magnifies *the Lord*." Each time, the mind is drawn to a different facet.

213 "Repetition and reiteration are essential elements of pedagogy for all human beings—whether the reiteration in question is the numerous side-altars in a large church, the threefold [i.e., three sets of three] repetition of the Kyrie and the *Domine, non sum dignus,* or the almost daily use of the Gloria" (Kwasniewski, *Resurgent in the Midst of Crisis,* 110). Repetition thus includes artistic and architectural repetition. The many side altars teach us about the distribution of the grace of Calvary through the many ministerial priests used by the Eternal High Priest to offer up the sacrifice of praise. Side altars did not *have* to develop, but once they existed throughout the West, their *removal* amounted to an unspoken repudiation of the doctrine that each priest is ordained to offer the true and proper sacrifice of the Mass in the name of all, in contrast to a concelebrated Mass where, no matter how many priests offer, there is but one sacramental sacrifice (see *Resurgent,* ch. 10, "The Loss of Graces: Private Masses and Concelebration").

214 This is why, if a lectionary has as one of its purposes the familiarization of the faithful with the Word of God, the old one-year lectionary, with its limited readings exquisitely chosen for their moral and Eucharistic message, will be far superior to the new multi-year lectionary when it comes to implanting the Word of God in our souls. This is my topic in chapter 6.

Hours, where some psalms are said only once a month. Far more helpful in acquiring that connaturality with prayer is daily and weekly repetition, and, in a different way, so is the straightforward verbal repetition of saying the same thing multiple times in a row.

I would add here that the very forming of words on the lips, whether we utter the words out loud or mouth them *sotto voce*, is a crucial part of this process of informing the memory. In *The Love of Learning and the Desire for God*, Jean Leclercq reminds us that medieval monks rarely read silently; they saw reading as an act of ruminating or chewing on the words, savoring their distinctive sounds, as if words were incipient music. Reading, in short, involved "muscle memory." Just as it is well known from experience and scientific studies that singing facilitates textual memorization far better than mere reciting does, and that rhymed and metered poems are easier to memorize than prose, it is also well known that making words with one's lips inscribes them more firmly on the tablet of the soul than silently passing our eyes over them. What I have said about the lips may be said about any part of the body that is subject to the control of our will, such as our head, fingers, arms, and legs. Consciously repeated bodily action produces over time a facility for doing it and a pleasure or delight in doing it. The use of the entire body in prayer, with a regimen of kneeling, genuflecting, bowing, standing, uniting of the hands, and so forth, inscribes the meaning of the words into our flesh and adds the sensible weight of our bodies to the intentions of the soul. In this way, we extend the power of memory into the whole person, while uniting what is lower and more animal to what is higher and more divine. Liturgical bodily repetition thus becomes a practical way of reintegrating our fragmentary self and reorienting it to God.

The once widespread recognition of these anthropological truths was encapsulated in the adage *repetitio est mater studiorum*, "repetition is the mother of studies." Thus, the education of children used to involve a huge amount of repetition and memorization, for there is no better way to learn the elements of language, arithmetic, geography, history, and religious doctrine. That we have so largely left behind this approach in the name of dubious pedagogical theories is one more sign of the loss of common sense for which our age is destined to be remembered—or, more likely, forgotten.

In regard to the faculty of the will and our capacity for loving, repetition both *proceeds from* and *enkindles* fervor—and this will be no less true at the level of the sensitive appetite, in our passions or emotions. Commenting on Psalm 6:9–10, "The Lord hath heard the voice of my weeping, the Lord hath heard my supplication, the Lord hath received my prayer," St. Augustine explains why the psalmist repeats himself: "The frequent repetition of the same idea does not denote the need the speaker feels to ram home his point, but the warmth of one who rejoices. Those who rejoice usually speak in such a way that it is not enough for them to give voice to their joy only once."[215] Lovers, in particular, are infamous for the repetitious nature of their chatter. With her usual charm, Jane Austen observes in *Sense and Sensibility:*

> Though a very few hours spent in the hard labor of incessant talking will despatch more subjects than can really be in common between any two rational creatures, yet with lovers it is different. Between *them* no subject is finished, no communication is even made, till it has been made at least twenty times over.[216]

Here, Jane Austen exhibits more sense and sensibility than did the drafters of *Sacrosanctum Concilium* and the liturgical reformers who took their battle axe to the liturgy, chopping away lovers' repetitions, poetic cumbrances, and verbal complexities. The reformers' rationalism, born of utilitarian thinking, could not see with a lover's eyes or hear with a lover's ears; the uselessness of leisure, of play, of contemplation, was hidden from their pedantic pride.

The Byzantine Catholic writer Adam DeVille has some pointed words on this topic:

> All Eastern liturgical traditions understand this wisdom of loving repetition. We repeat because we love. Byzantine liturgy is replete with its repetitions, usually in groups of three, both because love demands repetition (the child flung into the air by Daddy screams what? "Do it again!"), and because threefold repetition is of course a mnemonic device bearing a Trinitarian imprint. The West must therefore stop

[215] Augustine, *Expositions of the Psalms 1–32,* Psalm 6, no. 11, pp. 110–11.

[216] Chapter 49. My attention was drawn to this splendid passage by Pater Edmund Waldstein, O.Cist.

> its psychologically destructive and perverse disdain for so-called useless repetitions. Repetition is the essence of liturgy and ritual. In this light, stop assuming a three-year lectionary is better than a one-year. It isn't. One-year cycles mean more frequent repetition, which means a greater likelihood of people remembering the readings and calling them to mind later. Hatred of repetition is invariably justified by self-congratulatory talk about "noble simplicity." It is neither. "Noble simplicity" is just a sanctimonious display of bourgeois iconoclasm, with its fetishes for "cool, clean lines" and "decorative sparseness."[217]

DeVille alludes to a famous passage in G.K. Chesterton's *Orthodoxy*, which I would be remiss not to quote:

> Because children have abounding vitality, because they are in spirit fierce and free, therefore they want things repeated and unchanged. They always say, "Do it again"; and the grown-up person does it again until he is nearly dead. For grown-up people are not strong enough to exult in monotony. But perhaps God is strong enough to exult in monotony. It is possible that God says every morning, "Do it again" to the sun; and every evening, "Do it again" to the moon. It may not be automatic necessity that makes all daisies alike; it may be that God makes every daisy separately, but has never got tired of making them. It may be that He has the eternal appetite of infancy; for we have sinned and grown old, and our Father is younger than we.[218]

Repetition is not, of course, limited to the sphere of words, but extends also to gestures. A Benedictine monk gives the marvelous example of the kissing of the altar:

> We express this rich significance of the altar and impress it upon ourselves by means of certain prescribed gestures. . . . The priest and deacon kiss the altar upon arriving in the sanctuary and before leaving it. In the traditional rite of Holy Mass the priest kisses the altar

---

[217] DeVille, "When it comes to liturgy, we're all mutually-enriching mongrels." Dom Alcuin Reid agrees when he says, with more restraint: "There is no shame or heresy in asking whether or not the Council's wish to remove what it called 'useless repetitions' may in fact have taken away rites which, when prayed with devotion, in fact accentuate the mystery at hand in a manner which has ritual and indeed psychological value" ("Elements of the New Liturgical Movement").
[218] Chesterton, *Orthodoxy*, "The Ethics of Elfland," 107.

> frequently; these repeated kisses signify the desire of the priest—representing both Christ the Bridegroom and the whole bridal Body of His Church—for the fruitful consummation of their sacramental union. The suppression in the *Novus Ordo* of the repeated kissing of the altar is a cold rationalistic innovation foreign to the language of love in which one or even two kisses are not enough.[219]

Repetition, then, is for poets, for lovers, for children, and for madmen—for those who are striving to express the ineffable, those who are longing for the beloved, those who are learning from a master, and those who have lost their "wits"; these are, in the spiritual realm, the "holy fools," such as the Russian pilgrim who ceaselessly repeats the Jesus Prayer. As Dom Benedict Nivakoff observes:

> We learn from the Tradition that there is a great value in regularity and repetition. In the Rosary, we say the *Ave Maria* fifty, or a hundred and fifty, times a day, in the Holy Mass we can never make enough signs of the Cross, and according to the Greek monks, it is the very unceasing repetition of the Jesus Prayer that gives it its great power of sanctification. The examples could be multiplied indefinitely. Even the repetition of the Sunday rest and the cycle of the liturgical year seem to point to a sacredness, a divine predilection for repetition.[220]

So, if we have reached a point where we don't want or need lots of repetition anymore, it must be that we are neither children of God nor lovers of Him; we have nothing in common with holy fools; we have no poetic bone in our bodies. Without a doubt, this would be a condition to be ashamed of, not one to aspire to.

Upon consideration, it looks as though repetition plays a far more important role in intimate conversation, in our innermost thoughts, in the practice of arts and crafts, and in many other areas of life than one might have guessed at first. The beauty of poetry, no less than that of pottery, depends largely on a skillful use of repeated designs and motifs. The first principles of beautiful music are fixity of scale, constancy of beat, and the deft handling of repeated motifs. The best children's stories—of which

---

[219] Unpublished manuscript.

[220] In a newsletter dated December 6, 2019, issued by the Monks of Norcia.

there are hundreds, if not thousands—are often no more than clever variations on a small number of basic plots and morals. The very fact that a child will ask persistently to hear the same stories over and over testifies to the wonder and delight they provoke. Indeed, nature herself delights in recurrent patterns and refrains: the pulse of blood, breathing, walking. The waves of the ocean borrow much beauty from the regularity of their shape and arrival. The spider's web is a marvel of geometrical symmetry. There can be no doubt that prayer, when blended into the rhythms of daily life, will partake of the same qualities.

Having seen the natural foundations of the value of repetition, we are now in a position to address the special reasons for pre-set, formulaic reiteration in Christian worship.

Formal Repetition in a Sacred Context

Ritual, by definition, is our entry into a world that is not properly ours, but God's.[221] We are standing on holy ground; we must think, desire, act, and speak differently than we do in the everyday world to which we are proportioned by our created nature. We are in the presence of the holy, and it makes us stammer, whisper, sing, and fall silent, and then do all this over again, as if climbing a mountain by switchbacks that take us back and forth and slowly up. Ritual cannot be calculated, businesslike, logical, linear. It is, one could say, a kind of role playing, where we dare to act a part that belongs properly to someone else, and, as we saw in the last chapter, we act ceremoniously: we wear special garments and speak special words, we are formal, dignified, scripted—we hand ourselves over to the rulership of our superiors. Indeed, even the seraphim with their powerful intellects are portrayed in Scripture as crying out *Kadosh, kadosh, kadosh*, in response to the vision of God's unutterable and inexhaustible glory;[222] so too must we cry out *Sanctus, sanctus, sanctus* in our earthly sanctuary, the image of the heavenly.

---

[221] This it has in common with the experience of *eros* as Plato understands it, when man catches a momentary glimpse of Beauty itself and feels exhilarated, enthused, unsettled, unworthy. This is why lovers repeat themselves, but a cashier or clerk does not. The lover is, as Plato saw, drawing near to a divine reality (however aware of this he may be), whereas the person doing ordinary business is, so to speak, in his native environment, at a natural level, which prompts no ecstasy. See Pieper, *Divine Madness.*

[222] See Is. 6:3.

Verbal and ceremonial repetition, like many other traditional liturgical elements, perfectly and manifestly suits the sphere of the sacred, defining it and setting it apart from the ordinary and the profane. I am reminded here of an incisive remark by C.S. Lewis: "The modern habit of doing ceremonial things unceremoniously is no proof of humility; rather it proves the offender's inability to forget himself in the rite, and his readiness to spoil for everyone else the proper pleasure of ritual."[223] Lewis sees that a rite, precisely because of what it is (or rather *whom* it belongs to), demands that those who take it up or enter into it forget themselves and allow themselves to be drawn into the realm of the other. By yielding in this fundamentally passive way to another's activity and by taking part in that activity as best we can, we allow His fullness to spill over into our poverty—not once, but again and again and again, even as the all-sufficient Sacrifice of the Cross is renewed daily upon our altars.

Speaking broadly about the wealth of details in traditional liturgical rites (including their repetitions), Martin Mosebach argues that we will never be able to understand the unity and coherence of these rites until we look at them with the sensitivity and sympathy we bring to great works of art:

> The Council of Trent, in its teaching concerning the liturgy's sacred rites, said that these rites "contain nothing unnecessary or superfluous." This dictum, properly understood, again challenges us to regard the liturgy as a work of art. . . . Who would dare to pretend to find "unnecessary or superfluous" things in a great fresco or a great poem? A masterpiece may contain gaps, less felicitous parts, repetitions, things that are unintelligible or contradictory—but never things that are unnecessary and superfluous. At all times there have been people who made themselves ridiculous by trying to eliminate the "mistakes" in masterpieces, applying their half-baked scholarship to Michelangelo's frescos and Shakespeare's tragedies. Great works have a soul: we can feel it, alive and radiant, even where its body has been damaged. The liturgy must be regarded with at least as much respect as a profane masterpiece of this kind. Respect opens our eyes. Often enough, even in the case of a profane work of art, if we study conscientiously and ponder the detail, especially the apparently superfluous detail, we find

[223] Lewis, *A Preface to Paradise Lost,* 17.

> that the offending element comes unexpectedly to life; in the end it sometimes happens that we come to see it as a special quality of the work. This is always the case with the rites of the sacred liturgy. There is nothing in them that, given intensive contemplation, does not show itself to be absolutely saturated with spiritual power.[224]

An example of unprofitable repetition in the minds of liturgical reformers was the way the Confiteor was employed in the rite of Mass. First, it was "doubled" in the prayers at the foot of the altar (the same can be seen in the opening of the traditional office of Compline). Second, it was repeated by the servers or ministers after the priest's Communion and prior to the Communion of everyone else. Reformers saw both of these things as superfluous, so, already in the 1962 missal, they had suppressed the Confiteor before Communion—although this custom has tenaciously survived to the present in most places where the TLM is celebrated—and then they conflated the Confiteors at the beginning of the Novus Ordo into a single severely abbreviated text, omitting the names of all the saints except Our Lady's.

Let's take a closer look at the fittingness of these practices.

Why *shouldn't* we say the Confiteor at the beginning of Mass only once, all together? For this reason: the double Confiteor strongly brings out the dialogical nature of liturgical worship, where the celebrant acts as a mediator for the people, and where each member of the body is praying for the other. The doubling formalizes the mediation as well as the mutual assistance. It reinforces the humility needed in the celebrant, who confesses his sins alone *coram omnibus* (in the sight of all), and also exhibits the dignity of the servant who says to the master: "May almighty God have mercy on *thee*, and having forgiven *thy* sins, lead thee to eternal life." It reflects the truth of cosmic and ecclesiastical hierarchy and pushes against one of the dominant errors of our time, that of democratic egalitarianism, which lumps everyone together into an undifferentiated mass (or Mass).

---

224 Mosebach, *The Heresy of Formlessness,* 74–75. To be precise, it was not the Council of Trent as such, but the universal *Roman Catechism* edited by St. Charles Borromeo and promulgated by St. Pius V after the Council (and at its behest) that spoke as follows: "The Sacrifice [of the Mass] is celebrated with many solemn rites and ceremonies, none of which should be deemed useless or superfluous. On the contrary, all of them tend to display the majesty of this august Sacrifice, and to excite the faithful when beholding these saving mysteries, to contemplate the divine things which lie concealed in the Eucharistic Sacrifice" (*Catechism of the Council of Trent for Parish Priests,* 259).

Bishop Athanasius Schneider once told of a dialogue Mass he was offering in Africa at a large traditional Catholic school for girls. When he had confessed his sins, he heard all these little girls say to him, in perfect Latin, "Misereatur *tui* omnipotens Deus, et dimissis peccatis *tuis*, perducat *te* ad vitam aeternam."[225] He was overcome with feelings of humility, littleness, and joy. This experience of the priest—or, for that matter, the bishop, or the pope—confessing his own sins in front of the people is something we could use a great deal more of in the Church today, together with the corresponding confession of the people. And all of this in the humbling and strengthening presence of the saints invoked by name, twice: "Blessed Mary ever-virgin, St. Michael the Archangel, St. John the Baptist, the holy Apostles Peter and Paul, and all the saints"—not lumped together in an undifferentiated mass of "all the angels and saints," mentioned only once, for efficiency's sake. There are no shortcuts in penance and forgiveness.[226]

With the Confiteor before Communion, it was not only the repetition at this juncture of something that had "already been done" earlier in the Mass that the liturgical reformers objected to; it was even more the impression that the Communion rite for the faithful is "tacked on to" the Mass as a sort of extrinsic piece rather than being something intrinsic to it. Yet the old practice makes theological sense, at least from the vantage of the dogmatic teaching of the Council of Trent. The Communion of the offering priest is *essential* to the completion of the sacrifice in a way that the Communion of no one else is. In fact, the obscuring of this point by having a single Communion rite in which the priest announces "*Ecce Agnus Dei*" prior to receiving Christ and distributing Him to the faithful is among the many factors that have contributed to the obscuring of the difference *in kind* between the ministerial priesthood and the priesthood of the faithful.

Moreover, one should evaluate this practice not from a Low Mass standpoint, but from that of the Solemn High Mass, the normative Mass of the Roman Rite. Seeing the priest flanked by the deacon and the subdeacon, with the deacon chanting the Confiteor, throws into sharp relief that the sacrifice is essentially *complete* with the Communion of the priest, who

---

225 May almighty God bless thee, and having forgiven thy sins, may He lead thee to eternal life.
226 On why we mention *these* saints in particular, see Mosebach, *The Heresy of Formlessness,* 101–4.

stands in for Christ the High Priest, and that the further Communions are an *extension* of this sacrifice to the ministers and the faithful, a sacramental "rippling out" comparable to the rippling out of the Pax, the gesture of peace, passed down from on high—much as the higher angels communicate illuminations to lower angels. The one offering brings the sacrifice to completion by himself partaking of the sacrificial Victim. No other Communion is necessary for this completion, although obviously the Church rejoices in the participation of as many faithful as are in a state of grace and prepared to receive Our Lord. The scholastic distinction between intensity and extension is helpful here. For example, the separated soul in heaven fully possesses beatitude intensively, but when the body is reunited to it in the resurrection, that happiness will overflow into the flesh and so the beatitude will be greater extensively (i.e., it will have a greater extension).

The separate Communions of priest and people, with the Confiteor as a visible and audible caesura, is the liturgy's way of representing the dogmatic truth spoken of by Pope Pius XII in *Mystici Corporis Christi* when he distinguishes between the "objective redemption" that Christ accomplished in full on the Cross and the "subjective redemption" of Christians, which occurs through the application of the merits of His Passion to our souls in the sacraments of the Church.[227] This aspect of the *usus antiquior* points unambiguously to the essence of the Mass as the re-presentation of the Sacrifice of the Cross at the hands of the ordained minister, and forcefully sets aside the Protestant conflation of the Mass with the Last Supper, that is, the simple identification of the Eucharist with Communion—an error so ubiquitous in our day that Catholics not only take it for granted but are unaware that there is any other way of thinking about the matter.

---

[227] See Pius XII, *Mystici Corporis Christi,* nos. 12, 31, and 44. St. Thomas speaks of this point often, as when he explains why the faithful need not receive the chalice: "The perfection of this sacrament does not lie in the use of it by the faithful, but in the consecration of the matter. And hence there is nothing derogatory to the perfection of this sacrament, if the people receive the body without the blood, provided that the priest who consecrates receive both" (*Summa Theologiæ* III, Q. 80, art. 12, ad 2); "Our Lord's Passion is represented in the very consecration of this sacrament, in which the body ought not to be consecrated without the blood. But the body can be received by the people without the blood: nor is this detrimental to the sacrament, because the priest both offers and consumes the blood on behalf of all; and Christ is fully contained under either species, as was shown above [Q. 76, art. 2]" (*Summa Theologiæ* III, Q. 80, art. 12, ad 3).

Again, at a High Mass, the faithful are usually not able to *hear* the Confiteor of the priest and the servers at the beginning, as these preparatory prayers in the sanctuary are muffled under the soaring sound of the Introit. Thus, when the deacon sings or the servers say the Confiteor right before Communion, everyone is able to hear it and make it their own, since there is nothing else "covering over" this action.[228] Holy Mother Church offers all the faithful one final opportunity to bow low before the altar, express contrition for sins, call upon saints and angels as intercessors, and receive a minor absolution prior to receiving the *Sanctissimum*, the Most Holy One, before whom even the cherubim and seraphim veil their faces. Thus, we see that this Confiteor is both theologically appropriate and spiritually profitable.

It is worth mentioning, in passing, that the three most obvious places in the Order of Mass where the glimmering scalpels of the Consilium excised what it considered to be the fatty tissue of repetition—the Confiteor, the Kyrie, and the *Domine, non sum dignus*—all have to do with acknowledging our sins and our unworthiness to receive the Lord or even to place ourselves before Him. Is this a coincidence? No more, I would say, than the systematic removal of prayers that ask for the grace to "despise earthly things," the disappearance of "difficult" Bible verses, the cancellation of fasting, and Communion given in the hand to those who are standing rather than on the tongue to those who are kneeling. In the late sixties, Christians, it was said, had finally "come of age"; it was time for us to stand tall as the friends and brothers of Jesus, rather than kneel humbly like submissive slaves. We had matured past a medieval preoccupation with the fear of the Lord, sin, penance, detachment, asceticism; indeed, to some it seemed we had matured past the need for self-denial, reverence, and adoration.

Other examples of supposedly useless repetition would have been the nearly daily recitation of the *Gloria* thanks to the customary attachment of this hymn to every saint's feast (the old rite of Mass honors about 300 more saints in its annual calendar than the new one does[229]) as well as

---

228 Needless to say, if it is to serve a corporate purpose, the Confiteor needs to be heard at this point rather than mumbled or muttered into the acolyte's sleeve. No need for loudness; an articulate voice and a reasonable pacing will suffice to make the prayer audible even in a large church. See Kwasniewski, "Two Modest Proposals."

229 See Kwasniewski, "Sanctoral Killing Fields."

the more frequent recitation of the Creed; one might also list the Sunday Asperges, and the almost-daily repetition of Psalm 42 at the start of Mass and the Prologue of John at the end of it. All these instances of repetition, however, can be explained, justified, and defended by arguments analogous to those given above for the Confiteor, the Kyrie, and the *Domine, non sum dignus*. The same might be said for the immemorial practice of using the *full* conclusion for the Secret and Postcommunion prayers and various other prayers in the Order of Mass (that is, ending with "through Our Lord Jesus Christ, Thy Son, who liveth and reigneth with Thee in the unity of the Holy Ghost, God, for ever and ever" or something similar, instead of merely "through Christ our Lord"). The full conclusion was evidently judged to be yet another "useless repetition," but its purging contributed to an overall de-trinitarianization, a de-doxologizing of the liturgy that is absolutely foreign to the mature (post-Arian) liturgical tradition.[230] Phenomenologically, it demotes the prayer over the offerings and the prayer after Communion to second-class orations.

The arguments I have made in favor of repetition in the Mass (and against the ideological removal of it) can be made likewise for the other traditional sacramental rites, the blessings and pontifical ceremonies, the Divine Office—the entire realm of formal, solemn, public prayer. To take a formidable example, consider just how much repetition in prayer St. Benedict of Nursia enjoined in his *Rule*, which played a pivotal role in the rise and flourishing of Christendom. I refer not only to the singing of the *entire* psalter *each week* (a program that Benedict considered just a bit lazy compared to those desert fathers who prayed the whole psalter daily!), but also the manifold repetition of particular psalms over the course of the week: Lauds daily repeats Psalms 148–150, the "Laudate psalms" from which that hour takes its name; Terce, Sext, and None consist of the same "gradual" psalms from Tuesday through Saturday; Compline features the same three psalms every night. Our predecessors in the Faith were not only not worried about excessive repetition, they seemed to *thrive* on it. A modern Benedictine monk formed in this tradition comments:

[230] See "Offspring of Arius in the Holy of Holies" in Kwasniewski, *Illusions of Reform,* 93–113.

> Generations of monks in the cloisters, in the nooks and crannies of their monasteries and choirs, alone or maybe in groups (since copies of the Scriptures may have been hard to come by), muttering over the words of the psalms and the readings, often enough quite painfully and slowly, committed them to memory. The slowness and the repetition of the work, its necessary patience, is its point. It was not in itself an arcane or complicated process. It was just learning by heart. For [the monks], as for the Desert Fathers before them, the practice had an effect, almost certainly not self-conscious or deliberate. It was at a deeper level than the conscious. Reading became meditation (in the sense of murmuring, repeating, learning, chewing over) became prayer became contemplation: these are the traditional stages of *lectio divina*: *lectio*, *meditatio*, *oratio*, *contemplatio*. It was perhaps a bit too simple and apparently undramatic for later ages, who sought to make it more deliberate and conscious and to systematise it more, but the practice had an effect, which was to shape a culture.[231]

Nor was it only Benedictines who defended liturgical repetition. The Jesuit Alfonso Salmerón (1515–1585) wrote, in his exegesis of Christ's repetitious prayer in Gethsemane:

> You should not feel aversion toward the reading of the same Psalter every week, nor the repetition of the same prayer, as the Church does in the Litanies and in some responsories, and in the Rosary, which is recited to the honor of the Blessed Virgin. The Jews without good reason disdained eating the same manna (Num. 11:6), but Christians should seek the spirit and the taste when they say the same prayers, rather than new text or doctrine.[232]

---

[231] Everitt, "Let them learn some of the Psalter." This Christian practice itself had notable pagan precedents: "There existed in the Greek schools of philosophy, in addition to abstract academic studies, a course of methodical training in the ways of living according to the principles of these schools. . . . 'Soliloquy' is defined as a method of training oneself by the spoken word or by writing. It includes elements of 'meditation' in the more restricted sense of the term, but primarily it consists in saying over and over to oneself, either quietly or more loudly, certain sentences which the student wishes to engrave on his memory. In the process the thoughts sink not only into his memory but into the depths of his psyche as well, with the result that they cause reactions and reflexes in him which are in conformity with the principles of wisdom taught by the masters. They had discovered the pedagogical, or rather the 'psychological,' power of repeated verbalization. For example, Thrasea, the Roman Stoic, repeated incessantly the words, 'Nero may kill me but he cannot harm me.' This is based on a saying of Socrates" (Hausherr, *The Name of Jesus,* 175).

[232] Salmerón, *Comentarii in Evangelicam Historiam,* vol. 10, p. 125.

As anyone who peruses spiritual literature is aware, this attitude was unceasingly inculcated in clergy and religious on whom the duty of singing or reciting the Divine Office chiefly fell, and it survived every upheaval of Church history until it met its match in the impatient rationalism and pastoral utilitarianism of the last century.

Improvements to the Old Rite?

I have a confession to make: I used to think about certain things the way modern liturgists do. I have found notes in my drawer from decades ago in which I argued that the Confiteors and other aspects of the Latin Mass should be simplified. Fortunately, these notes were never published! What I lacked was *long and patient experience.* As time went on, I came to appreciate, even to relish, every detail of the old Roman Rite; things that had once struck me as superfluous or "useless" came to acquire a meaning in my eyes—perhaps an idiosyncratic meaning, but so what? The liturgy is like a vast epic poem, an *Iliad* or an *Odyssey*, in which every age, every generation, finds and latches onto the characters, scenes, and turns of phrase that mean the most to it. Every element in the liturgy is like spiritual scaffolding or ladders or handholds by which we can lift ourselves up to God—or rather, be drawn up by Him. Why would we remove any such occasion of grace? We don't need to add things randomly to the liturgy, in fact we should hesitate seriously before introducing anything; but for a like reason, we should not remove what is *already there*, even if it came about "by accident."[233] There's a marvelous passage in Ratzinger's memoirs where he describes his gradual apprenticeship to the Roman Rite:

> It was a riveting adventure to move by degrees into the mysterious world of the liturgy, which was enacted before us and for us on the altar. It was becoming more and more clear to me that here I was encountering a reality that no one had simply thought up, a reality that no official authority or great individual had created. . . . Not everything was logical. Things sometimes got complicated, and it was not always easy to find one's way. But precisely this is what made the whole edifice wonderful, like one's own home.[234]

[233] See Kwasniewski, "The Chop-Chop Reform."

[234] Ratzinger, *Milestones,* 19–20.

Now, do these comments indicate that I think the old Roman liturgy is "perfect" in every way and could never benefit from any further change? To be honest, I reject the validity of the question, for three reasons.

First, no human liturgy could ever be "perfect" in comparison to the worship of the heavenly Jerusalem; but each of the authentic rites of Christendom—be it Roman, Ambrosian, Mozarabic, Greek, Slavic, Georgian, Coptic, Syrian, Syro-Malabar, or what have you—has its own identity, integrity, and coherence, its *relative* perfection within the tradition in which it developed, and should be treasured as such. It is not our business to construct a liturgy according to our own bright ideas; it is our privilege to receive a rite of apostolic heritage, to venerate it as a given, to embrace it, and to bear fruit by it. Not even the pope is the maker or manager of liturgy; he is only its servant. We have had quite enough of tinkeritis.

Second, the question of improvements usually betrays a progressivist mentality, as if change can take place in only one direction, namely, that of "modernization," which generally means accommodation to the secular world's standards (or lack thereof). When people ask me what I think the "future development" of the 1962 Missal will look like, and whether it will continue to be "frozen in time" like a fly in amber, my answer is simple: we have *already* gone beyond the 1962 Missal, but in the direction of reclaiming things that were unwisely abolished in the period between 1948 and 1962, such as the old Holy Week, abundant octaves, multiple orations, doubled readings, folded chasubles, proper last Gospels, and the three-hour Eucharistic fast. There will be development in the sense of unshackling the old rite from its simultaneously antiquarianist and modernizing redactors who, in the wake of World War II, were busily reconfiguring its wardrobe and coiffure in preparation for the extreme makeover they dreamt of and eventually performed. I agree with Catherine Pickstock that any good liturgical reform would have to be *anti*-modern, not *ne plus ultra* modern. She writes: the reform "failed to challenge those structures of the modern secular world which are wholly inimical to liturgical purpose"; indeed, it surrendered to them.[235] In truth, we have far more to learn from the Middle Ages

[235] See Pickstock, *After Writing,* 169–273, where she maintains that the liturgical reform failed because it did not question the false philosophical suppositions of modernity but instead adopted them as guiding principles.

and the Baroque than we have to learn from the twentieth century, for we are still wading in the shallows compared with the deep sea diving of our distant predecessors. Rather than flexing our engineering muscles, we ought to cultivate the virtue of attentive receptivity to the great gift that has come down to us. Reading medieval commentators on liturgy, such as the *Jewel of the Soul* by the twelfth-century writer Honorius of Autun or Pope Innocent III's *The Mysteries of the Mass*, is one of the best ways we can push forward liturgical renewal in our times.

Third, the question is highly ambiguous. There are changes, and then there are changes. The Church Father St. Vincent of Lérins distinguished between *profectus* and *permutatio*. *Profectus* means growth according to kind, as when a child puts on height and weight in becoming a man, but remains the same person; *permutatio* means a change away from a thing's original identity, as when an animal dies and thereby ceases to be an animal, or when a heresy takes a certain partial truth, rips it from its larger context, and erects a new version of Christianity upon it. So, yes, the liturgy should welcome and has always welcomed *profectus*, growth by augmentation, even if the pace of change slows down over time, and the additions are minor ones like new feasts. But a *permutatio* of the liturgy would be its demise, as experience has all too clearly demonstrated.

Temptation Associated with Repetition

I would be remiss not to mention a problem that confronts us fallen human beings: repetition, for all its advantages, also makes it easier for people to zone out and lose focus. One does not have to be immersed for long in traditional prayer forms to experience the temptation to speed up in order to get through a lengthy liturgical text, particularly when it involves repetitious phrases. The lightning speed at which some priests say *Domine, non sum dignus ut intres sub tectum meum, sed tantum dic verbo et sanabitur anima mea* before receiving the Most Holy Sacrament of the Altar might prompt one to wonder just how unworthy they feel and whether they see themselves as directly addressing the Lord of heaven and earth, really present a few inches away, or how sincerely they are asking Him to heal their souls. We would want St. Thomas's observation on why custom has the force of law to be applicable to ourselves whenever we are repeating liturgical words or actions: "By repeated external actions, the inward movement of the will and concepts of reason are most effectually declared; for when a thing is done again and again, it seems to proceed from a deliberate judgment of reason."[236]

The worst thing that can happen with repetitions is to rush through them so speedily that they lose the density of their meaning, the benefit of their insistence, and the merit of their humble pleading. Rote and thoughtless repetition is more fitting to parrots than to persons. *Domine, non sum dignus* is worth saying three times because it is worth saying *well once*, and therefore three times as weighty when repeated. As a friend of mine wrote: "The threefold *Domine, non sum dignus* is no vain repetition; it is a trirhythmic grace of compunction that batters the door of even the most hardened heart."[237] And yet, if this exclamation is to bring the grace of compunction, it must be done deliberately and attentively. If we are to rejoice in repetition, we must always strive to attend to the meaning of our words and gestures as well as we can, and thus avoid becoming susceptible to Our Lord's warning against "vain repetition." Was it not St. Francis de Sales who said that haste is the great enemy of devotion?[238]

---

[236] *Summa Theologiæ* I–II, Q. 97, art. 3.

[237] He went on to say: "The single recitation of the centurion's heartfelt prayer sounds pathetically and artificially truncated." (All this in a private communication.) This feeling of awkward incompleteness is keenly felt on those rare occasions—which do occur, especially in a college chaplaincy—when a congregation accustomed to the old Latin Mass attends a Novus Ordo Mass in Latin. They all say *"Domine, non sum dignus . . ."* once—and then everyone wants to continue but has to pull up short.

[238] *The Beauties of St. Francis de Sales,* 103.

6

Why We Use a One-Year Lectionary of Readings

"We read a lot more of the Bible in the Novus Ordo, so it's clearly better."

While almost every other aspect of the liturgical reform following Vatican II has been the target of serious and sustained criticism, the revamped multi-year lectionary is the one element consistently put forward as a notable success, an instance of genuine progress. A popular Catholic author opined:

> I believe . . . that the most significant change [in the liturgy] came about in 1969, with the introduction of the revised lectionary. The media missed this one because there was so little controversy. Almost everyone agreed that the finished product was a remarkable achievement. And there can be no doubt that it was a major development in the life of the church. The lectionary was designed specifically for the purpose of highlighting the essential relationship between scripture and liturgy.[239]

Another well-respected theologian concurs:

> It seems likely that, whatever future developments occur in the Roman Rite, this extended use and emphasis on Sacred Scripture in Catholic worship may prove to be Pope Paul's most lasting contribution, and, arguably, even the most important long-term gift of his pontificate to the life of the Church.[240]

---

[239] Hahn, *Letter and Spirit,* 2–3. Subsequently, Hahn has drawn closer in sympathy to the traditional lectionary.

[240] Harrison, "Biblical Dimension of Paul VI's Liturgical Vision," 6.

No less a figure than Pope Benedict XVI, though an outspoken critic of many postconciliar changes, praised the gains of the new lectionary:

> In the first place I wish to mention the importance of the Lectionary. The reform called for by the Second Vatican Council[241] has borne fruit in a richer access to sacred Scripture, which is now offered in abundance, especially at Sunday Mass. The present structure of the Lectionary not only presents the more important texts of Scripture with some frequency, but also helps us to understand the unity of God's plan thanks to the interplay of the Old and New Testament readings, an interplay "in which Christ is the central figure, commemorated in his paschal mystery."[242]

And yet, it is no secret that knowledge of the Bible among Catholics today has reached an abysmal level, with surveys showing that most cannot say anything intelligent about any of the major figures of salvation history, especially from the Old Testament, and with awareness of the actual teaching of Christ in the Gospels at an all-time low. The first thing we have to note, therefore, is that without adequate catechesis and well-prepared preaching, no amount of Bible reading is going to be able to penetrate into the minds and hearts of the faithful. Sacred Scripture is an ancient collection of many different types of writing, most of which seem very remote to us, and some of which are downright impenetrable without help. Just hearing Scripture read aloud, all by itself, is probably not going to do much for most people. We can therefore say, with certainty, that the new lectionary has not yielded the harvest of biblical literacy that was promised by the ivory-tower intellectuals who designed it, just as the liturgical reform in general has not lived up to the utopian prophecies of Pope Paul VI about churches packed with eager and joyful Catholics of all ages, actively participating better than ever (or maybe even for the first time!). This much is clear: the vast postconciliar simplification of the liturgy, together with the vast increase in Bible reading, has not achieved the overarching goal that was given as their justification, namely, that by such means Catholics would become more liturgically conscientious and more committed to their Faith.

---

241 See Constitution on the Sacred Liturgy *Sacrosanctum Concilium,* nos. 107–8.

242 Benedict XVI, *Verbum Domini,* no. 57, quoting *Ordo Lectionum Missae,* no. 66.

At the same time, we have seen a slow but steady increase in the number of Catholics who have found their way to the traditional Latin Mass, which has its own much more compact lectionary contained within the missal, and, of course, reproduced in the daily hand missals used by many of the faithful. Traditionalists take Scripture very seriously: they are practically the only ones, among Catholics, who still believe that the Bible is the very Word of God, inspired and inerrant in every jot and tittle.[243] And because they believe in catechizing their children (and do so with older resources), there is often a reasonably good outline of salvation history in their minds. This revival of the Latin Mass, in spite of its powerful enemies, prompts us to ask a controversial question: Are there reasons to believe that the ancient lectionary—and, in general, the ancient approach to Scripture in the Mass—has more to be said on its behalf than we've been led to think? Could it be that here, too, the Church knew what she was doing for centuries and even millennia? We may find that we are once again "turned around" to see things a different way from how the slogans have persuaded us to think.

A Little Background

We need just a little historical background to understand our subject. The Roman Rite of Mass, like every other traditional Christian rite Eastern or Western, had always had a one-year cycle of readings. This means the same selection of Epistles and Gospels are read from year to year on any day that has a fixed Mass formulary, either from the temporal cycle or from the sanctoral cycle, although of course the shifting of calendar dates might mean that a certain Epistle or Gospel happens not to be read in a given year (say, if a saint's feast falls on a Sunday). There are other readings attached to Votive Masses that can be chosen under certain conditions.

However, the oldest lectionaries of the Roman Rite (seventh and eighth centuries) did contain more readings than the 1570 Tridentine Missal: in particular, we find (albeit inconsistently) that Mondays, Wednesdays, and Fridays outside of Lent had ferial readings that could be used when there was no clash with a feast. Because of the increasing number of

---

[243] See Crean, *"Letters from that City."*

saints' feasts and the increasing popularity of Votive Masses, and because of a desire to make the one-volume missal as compact as possible—it was the itinerant Franciscans who, more than anyone else, popularized the liturgical use of the papal court that was eventually codified in 1570 as "the Tridentine Mass"—these ferial readings dropped away in the later Middle Ages.

So, one thing we can say, even up front, is that *if* there is good reason to introduce more readings or a greater variety of readings, there were already *precedents* within our tradition by reference to which the number of readings could have been gently and intelligently increased without having done violence to the many positive features of the existing one-year lectionary. For example, some ferial readings could have been provided for Advent and for Easter.

In any case, by 1951, liturgists were already talking about creating a three- or four-year lectionary, and in 1956, Pope Pius XII's liturgical commission had prepared a draft of a three-year cycle. Seven years later, in 1963, the vast majority of the Fathers of the Second Vatican Council voted in favor of a Constitution, *Sacrosanctum Concilium*, that contained the following provisions: "In sacred celebrations a more abundant, more varied, and more suitable reading from Sacred Scripture should be restored [*instauretur*]"—that's a key term, because it suggests not inventing something whole-cloth—and "The treasures of the Bible are to be opened up more lavishly, so that richer fare may be provided for the faithful at the table of God's word. In this way a more representative portion of the Holy Scriptures will be read to the people in the course of a prescribed number of years."[244]

The Council threw its weight behind a multi-year lectionary but said nothing about getting rid of the existing lectionary.[245] As with every other

[244] *Sacrosanctum Concilium,* no. 35 §1 and no. 51.

[245] *Sacrosanctum Concilium* in any case forbade such a step, saying "There must be no innovations unless the good of the Church genuinely and certainly requires them; and care must be taken that any new forms adopted should in some way *grow organically from forms already existing*" (no. 23); "elements which have suffered injury through accidents of history are now to be restored to the vigor which they had in the days of the holy Fathers" (no. 50); and, as just quoted above, "In sacred celebrations a more abundant, more varied, and more suitable reading from Sacred Scripture should be restored [*instauretur*]" (no. 35, accurately translated from the Latin). Taking these three lines together, one sees clearly that the Council Fathers approved a restoration of earlier Roman practice in accord with the genius of the rite (which, in this case, would have meant restoring lessons that once actually belonged to the rite), *not* a wholesale

aspect of the reform, there was plenty of debate among the members of the body, called "the Consilium," charged with executing the liturgical reform. Pretty early on, the members of Coetus XI, the sub-group in charge of the lectionary, decided to throw out the existing lectionary—which was born in the first millennium, in the golden age of the Church Fathers, and had reached its classic form by the eighth century, when St. John Damascene was writing the first "summa" to sum up the achievements of the Fathers. In that sense, the traditional Roman lectionary has a clout that can be compared to that of the Roman Canon, the Roman calendar, and the corpus of Gregorian chant. The Fathers of the Second Vatican Council never debated the question of discarding *any* of these things because it would have been unthinkable to them to treat our inherited liturgy this way—as a laboratory experiment whose parts could be removed and replaced, fabricated *ad libitum.*

Coetus XI's work resulted in the Novus Ordo lectionary in use today: a three-year cycle of Sunday readings, a two-year cycle of weekday readings, and a veritable mountain of reading options for feasts, sacramental rites, and other special occasions. It is therefore not correct to call it a "revised" or "reformed" lectionary; it is simply a *new* one, having very little overlap with the cycle used, in one form or another, for over 1,300 years.

Amidst the cork-popping celebrations that surrounded the release of the new lectionary in 1969, lone voices began to point out various problems with it, ranging from the selection, length, and sheer number of readings to the academic structuring of the cycles, to worrying omissions, to incidental problems that have arisen in practice.

In the remainder of this chapter, I will first try to define the purpose of Scripture in the Mass. Second, I will re-examine several guiding principles of the lectionary revision, namely: the lengthening of readings; their arrangement as a multi-year cycle; the general preference for *lectio continua* or continuity of readings; and the decision to omit "difficult" readings. Third, I will consider how the new lectionary was implemented in the flesh, namely the *ars celebrandi* it inaugurated. Then I will draw some conclusions.

---

reinvention. But here as elsewhere, Paul VI opted to ignore more than 2,000 Council Fathers in an act of unpredecented papal absolutism.

The Purpose of Scripture in the Mass

The question that must be asked first and foremost is this: What is the *purpose* of the reading of Scripture in the Mass? Is it a moment of instruction for the people or is it an element of the worship offered by Christ and His Mystical Body to the Most Holy Trinity? We can say, on historical, liturgical, and theological grounds, that the proclamation of the readings at Mass has *both* of these purposes, but in a certain order.

First, the readings are undoubtedly instructional for the faithful. This is rather obvious: they are words chosen to impart to us a certain "lesson," to show us the life, miracles, parables, and teaching of the Lord, and thus to prepare our minds and hearts for receiving Christ Himself when He comes, even as the Old Testament prophets culminating in John the Baptist prepared the way for the coming of the Messiah. In a way, we could say that the Mass of the Catechumens stands to the Mass of the Faithful as John the Baptist to his cousin Jesus: the first points to the second, saying: "Behold, the Lamb of God, who takes away the sin of the world!"[246] The readings in the traditional missal were chosen for their universal moral, dogmatic, and Eucharistic content, and for their connection with individual saints or classes of saints. The saints themselves are presented to us as living icons to which the letter of the Bible points us, and in which its message is fulfilled. The readings hold up great examples of virtue and prepare the congregation for communion with the Lord in adoration and in the heavenly banquet.

Second—and this point is less obvious to modern Catholics, though I suspect it was obvious in centuries past—the readings are themselves an offering of worship to Almighty God: they are proclaimed for His glory and honor, and to obtain His blessing. The clergy chant the divine words in the presence of their Author as part of the *logikē latreia* or rational/verbal worship we owe to our Creator and Redeemer. These words are a making-present of the covenant with God, an enactment of their meaning in the sacramental context for which they were intended, a grateful and humble recitation in the sight of God of the truths He has spoken and the good things He has promised. In Scripture itself, we often see this manner of praying to God ("Remember, Lord, the promises Thou hast made!")—not

[246] John 1:29 RSVCE.

that He will forget, but He wants *us* not to forget His promises, and He lovingly wants us to "hold Him to them," so to speak.[247] A striking passage in the Book of Wisdom presents exactly this picture of the minister's function in the liturgy:

> The experience of death touched also the righteous, and a plague came upon the multitude in the desert, but the wrath did not long continue. For a blameless man was quick to act as their champion; he brought forward the shield of his ministry, prayer and propitiation by incense; he withstood the anger and put an end to the disaster, showing that he was thy servant. He conquered the wrath not by strength of body, and not by force of arms, but by his word he subdued the punisher, appealing to the oaths and covenants given to our fathers.[248]

The solemn and formal style of the readings as done in the TLM, directed elsewhere than the people immediately present—the Epistle is read toward the east, and the Gospel toward the north[249]—makes it clear that we are acknowledging that the God whom these texts mention is really here in our midst, or rather, we are come into *His* presence with thanksgiving; thus, the readings turn into gifts that, having been placed in our hands by God, we turn around and offer back to Him, even as we do with the bread and wine. Or to use a different metaphor, the readings are a form of verbal incense by which we raise our hands to His commandments.[250]

When we take seriously the traditional view of the divine inspiration of Scripture, we can see that the loving care, the reverential homage paid to the Word of God in the first part of the Mass—everything from praying that one might be worthy to speak its content, accompanying the book with candles, making the sign of the cross on it, incensing it, kissing it, and singing the readings to dignified and penetrating chant tones—is very much like the worship paid to the cross on Good Friday, or the veneration given

---

247 Thus, we read in the Epistle (2 Mach. 1:1–5) for the traditional Votive Mass for Peace: "May God be gracious to you, and remember His covenant that He made with Abraham and Isaac and Jacob, His faithful servants. . . ."

248 Wis. 18:21–22 RSVCE.

249 For an explanation of this, see my lecture "Escaping the Closed Circle: Why in the TLM the Epistle Is Read Eastwards and the Gospel Northwards."

250 See Ps. 118:48, *et levavi manus meas ad mandata tua,* sung in the great Gregorian chant *Meditabor* on the Second Sunday of Lent.

to Byzantine icons: in a real way, we are coming into contact with God Himself. He is the one whose truth is made present when the reading is proclaimed: it is not a past memory but a present power for conversion and illumination. Surely, Scripture is not the Real Presence of the Holy Eucharist, but it is divine in a way that no other human words are divine. This is why the rich ceremonial in which the ancient Roman Rite wraps the reading or chanting of the Word of God makes so much sense: the liturgy wants to accentuate the fact that in *this* scenario, the word on paper, the word floating through the air, is superior to our minds, determinative of our wills. In short: it is *God in verbal mode*, and we enter into His verbal presence with signs of veneration. We glorify Him by the liturgical enactment of His revelation.

It is, needless to say, a minority view nowadays that the chanting of the readings at Mass is an act of worship directed to God as well as a time of instruction for the people. In fact, there is something counterintuitive about this idea. After all, it would seem obvious that the reason Scripture is read in the Mass is to educate the faithful. But it is not so simple as a binary "either/or." The traditional Roman liturgy tends, over the centuries, to make *everything* a prayer directed to God, as if there should be no place in the liturgy for something that is exclusively "for the people." A great example of this is how the Creed is recited or sung in the *usus antiquior*. We all know that the Creed is a confession of faith, that it is basically a list of dogmas held by Christians. It has no obvious characteristics of being a prayer directed to God; rather, it looks like a badge of orthodoxy we hold up in the sight of the Church. And yet, in the *usus antiquior*, the priest recites the Creed *ad orientem* at the high altar, bowing the head at the mention of God the Father, the Holy Name of Jesus, and the divinity of the Holy Ghost, genuflecting at the *Et incarnatus est*, and making the sign of the cross at the *Et vitam venturi saeculi*, concluding with an "Amen." In this way, the profession of orthodoxy has been turned into a prayer to the Triune God, a manner of communing with the One who has graciously revealed His mysteries to man. How appropriately, then, does St. Ambrose say: "This Creed is the spiritual seal, our heart's meditation and an ever-present guardian; it is, unquestionably, the treasure of our soul."[251]

---

[251] *CCC* 197, quoting St. Ambrose, *Expl. symb.* 1, PL 17:1193.

What we see with the *Credo* is what we see with every element in the Mass, the Office, and the other sacramental rites. The *whole liturgy* is for God, and in fact its highest educational value consists precisely in communicating to the people the primacy and ultimacy of God—that He is the Alpha and Omega of all our exterior and interior acts, including the act of listening to readings and comprehending them. In a sense, the readings are offered up to God so that we may be offered up to Him in our understanding of the Word and the affections stirred up by it. This is why it does not matter so much whether or not every word is intelligible; what matters far more is that we see that this Word is divine, and that in its midst we are standing on holy ground. The verbal comprehension can follow in due time, but we will never grasp the Word rightly if we do not first venerate it *as divine* and worship the God from whom it emanates and in whose presence it comes alive. The traditional Roman Rite does not treat "the apostolic letters and the Holy Gospel" as mere "books," "documents," or "instructions," but as "moments of liturgical action, deriving from the liturgy, where they do not have a simply narrative or purely edifying meaning, but one even more important—precisely an active, sacramental meaning."[252]

Therefore, the goal of divine worship is not to make us familiar with Scripture in the manner of a Bible study or catechism class (which, of course, ought to be taking place at some other time) but to give us the right formation of mind and heart with regard to the *realities* of our faith so that we may worship God in spirit and in truth. In the traditional rites of East and West, Scripture serves as a *support* to the liturgical action; it illustrates or magnifies something *else* that the worship is *principally* about.[253] A poignant indication that this is exactly how the old rite understands Scripture's role is the rubric that has the priest *genuflect* (upon which everyone present also genuflects) during the reading of certain Gospels. This happens at the verse "*Et verbum caro factum est*" of the Prologue of John, read at the end of almost every Mass; on the Feast of the Epiphany

[252] The quotation is from Pavel Florensky, quoted in Kwasniewski, "'Moments of Liturgical Action.'"

[253] For a penetrating treatment of this important point together with a trenchant critique of the equation "more = better," see Miller, "Bible by the Pound," in Kwasniewski, *Illusions of Reform*, 180–97.

at the verse "And entering into the house, they found the Child with Mary His mother, and falling down they adored Him";[254] on Palm Sunday at the verse "For which cause God also hath exalted Him, and hath given Him a name which is above all names: that at the name of Jesus every knee should bend . . .";[255] and several others times in the liturgical year. In these instances, the Gospel comes vividly alive as we physically perform the adoration described in the text.

The Length of Readings

Now, as we saw, the Council Fathers desired that there be more Scripture in the Church's liturgies. The first way to pursue this goal is to put *more* Scripture into *each individual* liturgy. This was done both by adding a reading to Masses on Sundays and feasts and by lengthening the readings on average in all Masses. In light of Scripture's purpose within the Mass, however, I believe we should reconsider the wisdom of increasing the readings *within* a given Mass. It is a truism that more is not necessarily better, but there are specific reasons to be concerned about what one might call the ecology of the Mass, the delicate balance of its interacting parts.

The generally longer readings of the revised lectionary, together with a new emphasis on the homily as an integral part of the liturgy, have contributed to what one might call "verbal imperialism," that is, the tendency of words and wordiness to take over at many Masses, suffocating silence and meditation, and obscuring the centrality of the Eucharistic sacrifice.

We must keep in mind that, in the Novus Ordo, nearly everything is said aloud from start to finish. From the greeting to the Collect to the readings to the homily to the Eucharistic prayer and so on until the end, everything is placed on the same level phenomenologically; it can be like going point by point through the items on a meeting agenda, and we all know how thrilling it is to sit through a long meeting. Because of this monotony, sheer length translates inevitably into emphasis. In this approach, the Eucharistic Prayer tends to be the loser; it simply does not have enough prominence to hold its own. In the *usus antiquior*, the silent Roman Canon provides a center of gravity that no text or talking can

---

[254] Matt. 2:11.

[255] Phil. 2:9–10, with "at the name" instead of "in the name," as most translations render it.

outshine. It was and will always be the great counterbalance to lengthy sermons or sub-optimal music—or even sumptuous music.

The total size of the Sunday Liturgy of the Word, if one takes into account the two readings, a responsorial psalm, the Gospel, a homily, the Creed, and the prayer of the faithful, when followed by a diminished Liturgy of the Eucharist, has left far too many Catholics with a false impression of what the Mass primarily *is*. It seems like the main thing we do together is read Scripture and talk about it. A reenactment of the Last Supper is then added on so that everyone gets to receive something before going home. As we know, Catholics like to get something at Mass, whether ashes or palms or bulletins, and, in a way, the lamentable phenomenon of *everyone* lining up to receive Communion, regardless of the last time they darkened a confessional's door, fits in with this pattern.[256] The Mass as a true and proper sacrifice has therefore been almost entirely eclipsed by the Mass as "a table of the Word and a table of the Eucharist from which we are fed," to use the language of official documents.[257] Obviously, there is some truth in this language, but when it becomes the central way of understanding the Mass, we are looking at a profound distortion.

If the purpose of the readings at Mass is to prepare people for and lead into the great Eucharistic sacrifice, then the harm caused by verbal imperialism is obvious: by unduly prolonging the readings, the words have broken off and become their own thing, a center of gravity that *dominates* the liturgy. At this point, the readings are no longer in harmony with their purpose at Mass but are militating against it. Here we see, for the first time, the possibility of Scripture *in tension with* the Eucharist rather than serving it as a handmaid. The lengthening of the readings and the overemphasis on the homily, coming together with other liturgical changes made after Vatican II (more often than not, abridgements or simplifications), has disturbed the balance of the Mass, as excessive farming can lead to soil erosion and the destruction of an ecosystem.

---

[256] It is the solemn teaching of the Church that one must confess mortal sins in kind and number in order to be minimally worthy to receive the Holy Eucharist; receiving the Eucharist in a state of separation from God is itself a further mortal sin. The Church requires, moreover, that every Catholic over the age of reason must confess at least once a year. On these points and on the lamentable phenomenon of unworthy reception, see my book *The Holy Bread of Eternal Life.*

[257] See, e.g., the *Catechism of the Catholic Church,* no. 1346.

Fittingness of an Annual Cycle

We have considered some of the problems of increasing the readings *within* a Mass. A second way of putting more Scripture into the Mass would be to extend the readings over a greater *number* of Masses. While this could be done even within the scope of one year, it seems that everyone involved in liturgical reform quickly favored the approach of a multi-year cycle. With multiple years at its disposal, the new lectionary is able to present the whole arc of salvation history and offer a remarkable array of important biblical passages. If we compare statistics for Sundays, vigils, and major feasts, the new lectionary has 58% of the Gospels, 25% of the Epistles, and 3.7% of the Old Testament; while the old missal has 22% of the Gospels, 11% of the Epistles, and 0.8% of the Old Testament (not counting the Psalms, which play a prominent role in both).[258]

However, quite apart from the fact that even the new lectionary, as bulky as it is, can present only a small portion of the Old Testament and not quite three-quarters of the New Testament, leading to a total of 27.5% of the Bible read across the cycle (12.7% for those who attend only on Sundays)—hardly "reading the whole Bible at Mass!" as some overexcited new lectionary enthusiasts can be found to say—I would like to urge caution in regard to the underlying assumption that "more = better."

A one-year cycle of readings can be considered not only with regard to the *quantity* of Scripture it presents but also with regard to the *way* in which it presents the Scripture it contains. One year is a natural unit of time, with a satisfying completeness, like that of a circle. As mentioned before, Western and Eastern rites have always had a one-year cycle of readings, as does synagogue worship. Indeed, every culture has linked the rhythms of human life to the combined rhythms of the sun and the moon, joining the human to the cosmological. *Sacrosanctum Concilium* itself furnishes a convincing account of why the liturgical year is just that—a *year*:

> Holy Mother Church is conscious that she must celebrate the saving work of her divine Spouse by devoutly recalling it on certain days throughout *the course of the year*. Every week, on the day which she

[258] See The Catholic Lectionary Website compiled by Felix Just, S.J., https://catholic-resources.org/Lectionary/.

> has called the Lord's day, she keeps the memory of the Lord's resurrection, which she also celebrates *once in the year*, together with His blessed passion, in the most solemn festival of Easter. *Within the cycle of a year*, moreover, she unfolds the whole mystery of Christ, from the Incarnation and birth until the Ascension, the day of Pentecost, and the expectation of blessed hope and of the coming of the Lord. . . . In celebrating this *annual cycle* of Christ's mysteries, holy Church honors with especial love the Blessed Mary, Mother of God, who is joined by an inseparable bond to the saving work of her Son. . . . The Church has also included in the *annual cycle* days devoted to the memory of the martyrs and the other saints.[259]

With the one-year cycle comes repetition and its fruit of familiarity, which leads to internalization—the planting of the seed of the word deep in the soil of the soul. One who immerses himself in the traditional liturgy becomes aware that its annual readings, over time, are becoming bone of one's bone, flesh of one's flesh. One begins to think of certain days, months, seasons of the year, or categories of saints in tandem with their particular readings, which open up their meaning more and more as one meets them again and again. If the Word of God has an infinite depth to it, the traditional liturgy bids us stand beside the same well year by year, dropping down our bucket into it, and in that way *awakening* us to an inexhaustible depth that may not be so clear to someone who is dipping his bucket into different places of a flooding stream over the course of two or three years. Joseph Shaw points out:

> The [traditional] Lectionary's limited size allows the Faithful to attain a thorough familiarity with the cycle, particularly in the context of the use of hand-missals and commentaries on the liturgy, which expound the passages and their connection with the season, and the proper prayers and chants of the day. The association of feasts and particular Sundays with particular Gospel or Epistle passages echoes the practice of the Eastern churches, where Sundays are often named after the Gospel of the day.[260]

---

259 *Sacrosanctum Concilium* nos. 102–4.

260 Shaw, *The Case for Liturgical Restoration,* 103.

The fundamental elements of faith and habits of prayer need to be inculcated week after week, day after day; and thus it is pedagogically most appropriate to have a well-chosen selection of readings repeated annually: the age-old Epistle and Gospel assigned for the various Sundays after Pentecost, the readings for the Easter Octave, the readings for certain categories of saints—martyrs, apostles, Doctors of the Church, bishops, confessors, virgins. In this way, the Christian people are strongly *formed* by a set of "core texts" throughout the cycle of the year, rather than being carried off each day into new regions of text—especially some of the lengthier historical narratives and prophetic passages from which it may be hard to benefit except by extra-liturgical study. As Gregory DiPippo observes:

> People generally need to be *reminded* more than they need to be *taught*. This is the wisdom behind the one-year lectionary cycle (a universal custom of all historical Christian rites before 1969), and the annual recurrence of the same Tract on First Lent [i.e., the First Sunday of Lent], the same Epistle on the feast of St Thomas, etc.: a liturgical tradition in which we can live, rather than a classroom we visit. . . . The post-Conciliar rite is extremely didactic, but not very pedagogical.[261]

The faithful need more Scripture in their *lives*—no one will dispute this point. But it does not follow that we must cover as much Scriptural ground as possible *at Mass*. Consider the matter from a psychological point of view. The reading at Mass is a "feature of an event": the mind does not easily connect yesterday's reading to today's, or today's with tomorrow's. A number of things are happening in the course of the liturgy and in the rest of our day, and unless the priest very deliberately connects the readings, each day is an entity unto itself. The daily Mass is the discrete unit, and so the readings should be proportioned to *it*, not to a larger time sequence (apart from the general character of the liturgical year and its seasons). The result is that, with an expanded lectionary, people will hear and *forget* more Scripture than they did before; whereas, on the old one-year cycle, people hear things repeatedly and have the opportunity to become familiar with them. We stand to gain more, spiritually, out of *one* inspired passage that becomes familiar to us than from a long-term cycle attempting to "get through" a lot

[261] DiPippo, "The Unfunded Mandate," emphasis added.

of Scripture. There's a reason we have the expression "to learn something *by heart*." What you have in your heart is really a part of *you.* What exists only in a book or on the internet is not really part of you. That's why it's silly when people say things like: "We moderns are so much better off than the medievals, because we can access millions of texts online instantly at any time!" The medievals memorized huge swaths of Scripture and it therefore shaped their inmost selves. A modern person has memorized very little except his social security number, some phone numbers, and maybe a couple of poorly-understood scientific laws, so having every library of the world at his fingertips means almost nothing—he doesn't know what to look for, he doesn't know what wisdom tastes like, and he isn't carrying a library of truth within himself. As Fr. Thomas Dubay says: "Mere verbal information is no substitute for what we might call tasted insight."[262]

The practice of *lectio divina*, or praying with Scripture, where each day one is focusing exclusively on the Bible, makes it easier to connect days to each other. This is why the most sensible way to increase Catholic knowledge of Scripture is to teach it in religion/catechism class and to encourage *lectio divina.* The Catholic biblical renewal in recent years is largely owing to scripturally literate Protestant converts who have moved mountains to introduce salvation history ("The Great Adventure") and *lectio divina* into parish programs and schools. This suggests that the work we need to be doing is more at home *outside* the Mass than *inside.*[263]

Thus, although it is common to praise the new lectionary for containing much more Scripture than its predecessor, experience with both could lead one to quite the opposite conclusion—namely, that the multi-year lectionary is unwieldy and hard to absorb, whereas the old cycle of readings is beautifully proportioned to the rhythm of the natural cycle of time and the fullness of the ecclesiastical year of grace that builds upon nature. And we can say, in general, that an annual cycle of well-chosen readings is more suited to the morally propaedeutic, iconic, and worship-oriented purpose of Scripture in the Mass.

---

262 Dubay, *Fire Within,* 300.

263 My personal theory is that we find enthusiasts for the new lectionary mostly among the clergy because, if they take their work seriously, they end up using the lectionary as a kind of *lectio divina* for preparing their homilies, so they stand to benefit much more from it than those who merely attend Mass—particularly as the congregation at daily Mass is not the same from day to day, even if there are some "regulars."

Primacy of the Sanctoral Cycle

Having looked at the extension of the readings both within a given Mass and over many Masses, I turn now to a third guiding principle of the new lectionary, namely, the preference for continuous reading or *lectio semi-continua*; in other words, that we read sequentially from a certain book or letter or Gospel over a period of time, and that maintaining this continuity for the most part trumps the sanctoral cycle. This is a distinct and important principle.

Everything I said above about the impracticality of connecting readings from day to day could be repeated here, but I want to draw attention to the special relationship the saints have to Scripture and to the Mass. Since the goal of Christian faith is not a *material* knowledge of Scripture but personal sanctification and conversion—after all, this is the *formal* content and aim of Scripture itself!—the saints are rightly put forward in the liturgy as our examples of how to live, how to believe, how to love. The TLM rightly presses Scripture into service of this goal by correlating specific readings with specific saints or classes of saints. On account of both their more limited number and their memorable (and mandated) alignment with particular saints, the sanctoral Epistles and Gospels facilitate *familiarity* with the Word of God as it illustrates or teaches us about the triumph of God's holy ones.

The saints are, one could say, the message of Scripture in flesh and blood, and that is why the written word is appropriately called upon to minister to *them* and reflect their existential primacy. It bears mentioning that scholarship on the history of the liturgy has established that, apart from Easter, the earliest liturgical commemorations were not always those of the great mysteries of Our Lord and His Mother, but rather those of the martyrs, like St. Stephen and St. Lawrence. For example, the feast of St. Stephen is so ancient and authoritative that its celebration on December 26 predates that of Christmas on December 25. The special feastdays that ornamented the primitive Eucharistic liturgies with proper readings, prayers, and antiphons were nearly always those of the saints; the sanctoral cycle enjoyed a *de facto* pride of place for many centuries. On the basis of respect for tradition, therefore, this cycle deserves at very least to be allotted a place of honor within the framework of the later emphasis on Sundays and holy days honoring the mysteries of Christ. This the Novus Ordo calendar and rubrics have, regrettably, failed to do.[264]

Scripture, by itself, is a dead letter. It is the saints who are the ultimate proof and most glorious manifestation of the truth of the Christian faith. The saints demonstrate that Scripture is not a lifeless book but a living paradigm. We must understand the role of Scripture at Mass in reference to its embodiment in the lives of the saints and its continual directing of our gaze to the supreme reality of Jesus Christ, Eternal and Incarnate Wisdom. Fr Roberto Spataro exults in this quality of the old rite:

> The *communio sanctorum* is powerfully tangible in the Tridentine Mass! The saints, the most eminent members of the Mystical Body, are united around the sanctifying act *par excellence* that is the Sacrifice of Calvary ritualized upon the altar, sharing with us in the holy realities of the faith. The faith we profess today in our liturgy is knit together with that of the martyrs, confessors, virgins, and the innumerable crowds of the saints, projecting itself toward the beatific vision of the coming eternity of heaven.[265]

Let's take a concrete example. On May 4, the traditional feastday of St. Monica,[266] the Epistle of the Mass is St. Paul speaking of the honor due to pious widows—a reading Monica shares with several other holy women—but the specially chosen Gospel recounts when Jesus raised the weeping widow's son from the dead and restored him to his mother. What more perfect Gospel could there be for the mother of St. Augustine! What could better impress both the Gospel *and* Monica's life on our minds than this striking juxtaposition! Each year, throughout her sojourn on earth, no matter how many thousands of years will pass by, Holy Mother Church thus commemorates the mother who never lost faith in God and eventually regained her son, dead in sin and error, risen

---

[264] The 1962 missal also fails to do this, to some extent, by omitting the commemoration of saints when they fall on Sundays, already a step on the way to the Novus Ordo concept that each Mass must have only a single "theme." To read about an egregious example of what can result from this rationalistic axiom, see Kwasniewski, "Why 1962 Must Eventually Perish."

[265] Spataro, *In Praise of the Tridentine Mass*, 103-4.

[266] See Foley, "The Feasts of Saint Monica."

in the life of grace. With the new lectionary's insistence on the preferability of *lectio continua*, it is highly likely that no special readings will take place on Monica's feastday, and instead we will hear whatever other readings happen to be in the lectionary that day. In tension with Scripture's inner purpose, the readings are extrinsic and accidental to the saint commemorated.

The traditional Mass treats each day as a coherent whole unto itself. When we are celebrating the feast of a saint, all the variable parts of the Mass—the Propers (Introit, Gradual, Tract, Alleluia, Offertory, Communion), the Readings (Epistle and Gospel), the Orations (Collect, Secret, Postcommunion), sometimes the Preface and the Sequence—all of these coalesce around the saint of the day. This has the effect of knitting an entire liturgy together as a seamless garment: the prayers honor and invoke the saint; the readings and antiphons extol the virtues of the saint, who is put forward as our example and teacher; the Eucharistic sacrifice links the Church Triumphant, represented by the lists of saints in the Roman Canon, to all of us pilgrims in the Church Militant. The whole liturgy acquires a unity of sanctification, showing us both the primordial Way of sanctity—Jesus in the Holy Eucharist—and the models of sanctity achieved. The elements of the Mass connect with one another like links in a chain, providing the worshiper with a focused spiritual formation and a powerful incentive to prayer (see Exhibit A, p. 162). It could be due to my own limitations, but the same number of years of immersion in the new lectionary and the new Mass—even at a time in my life when I was taking my faith quite seriously—never produced in me the same depth of remembrance, association, resonance, and penetration into the texts of the liturgy as my immersion in the old Mass has done.

If we take a step further back and look at the changing antiphons, prayers, and readings against the backdrop of the stable presence of the Scripture quotations and allusions that permeate the Order of Mass, we can see just how impressive is the result (see Exhibit B, p. 164). This biblical permeation or scriptural suffusion is supported by the unchangingness of the Order of Mass: because the rite is not subject to a plethora of options, it is much easier to connect the variable parts to the invariable. For example, the characteristic use of Old Testament texts in the antiphons strongly harmonizes with the Roman Canon's express mention of Abel, Abraham, and Melchizedek and with its hieratic language of sacrifice, so reminiscent of the Mosaic Law. The solidity and stability of the Canon is like a massive foundation of rock on which the carefully hewn stones of the Propers are built up into a spacious edifice for prayer. As the diagram shows, Scripture permeates the *usus antiquior* at every level. Even though many of the prayers are said silently, Catholics who assist at the old rite often follow along in their missals and make these rich prayers their own. This has certainly been my experience: I have come to cherish not only the changing Propers but also the fixed verses from Psalm 42, Psalm 25, Psalm 115, and the Prologue of John's Gospel.

In the new liturgy, by contrast, the prayers, readings, and Eucharist are awkwardly situated vis-à-vis one another: they no longer fit together into a single flow of action but follow in sequence like independent blocks. There is a reason for that: each part of the New Mass was designed by a separate subcommittee, and the subcommittees seldom communicated with one another. At the end, all the separate pieces were glued together by papal decree, so what you are really getting is a compilation of independent projects. The end result is a liturgy in which the Propers, the Orations, the biblical lessons, and the Order of Mass simply do not cohere with one another; sometimes a component may not even *exist* if its use is optional. The general problem here is the overall *integrity* of the liturgical service. To evaluate Scripture in the Mass, we must go beyond the formal "readings" and look at how the Word of God is present throughout the *rest* of the liturgy. How "saturated with Scripture" is the liturgy *as a whole*? Do the proper antiphons, prayers, and readings cohere with one another and with the Order of Mass? Accordingly, while there is obviously a vastly greater *extension* of Scripture in the new rite's Liturgy of the Word, one may still raise a question about the *intensity* of its presence throughout the Mass. Is the modern missal of Pope Paul VI as deeply imbued with the language, imagery, and spirit of Scripture as the old *Missale Romanum*?

Omission or Dilution of "Difficult" Passages

To this point, I have called into question those guiding principles behind the reform of the lectionary that concerned the quantity of Scripture in the Mass. I want to look briefly at one of the *non*-quantitative aspects of the reform, namely, the decision to omit or marginalize "difficult" passages.

It might be assumed that once the reformers allowed themselves three years of Sundays and two years of weekdays, they would certainly not fail to include in their new lectionary *all* the readings that are found in the traditional Roman liturgy, and that in their march through various books of the Bible they would not omit any key passages. Instead, they made a programmatic decision to avoid what they considered "difficult" biblical texts. What kind of texts did they have in mind? I will offer a couple of examples.

In the vast new Lectionary, the following three verses from 1 Corinthians 11 *never appear*, not even once: "Therefore whosoever shall eat this bread, or drink of the chalice of the Lord unworthily, shall be guilty of the Body and of the Blood of the Lord. But let a man prove himself; and so let him eat of that bread, and drink of the chalice. For he that eateth and drinketh unworthily, eateth and drinketh judgment to himself, not discerning the Body of the Lord."[267] St. Paul's warning against receiving the Body and Blood of the Lord unworthily, that is, unto one's damnation, has not been read at *any* Novus Ordo Mass for more than half a century. And yet, in the traditional Latin Mass, these verses are heard at least *three times every year*, once on Holy Thursday (where the Epistle is 1 Cor. 11:20–32), and twice on Corpus Christi (where both the Epistle and the Communion antiphon repeat them). If, moreover, the faithful happen to attend a votive Mass of the Blessed Sacrament—a popular choice among votive Masses—they will encounter them yet again. Catholics who attend the *usus antiquior* will never fail to have these challenging words placed before their consciences. Let me be frank: the concept of an unworthy Communion has simply disappeared from the general Catholic consciousness, and the new lectionary obviously shares some of the blame.

---

[267] 1 Cor. 11:27–29.

It is well known that the cursing or imprecatory psalms were removed from the Liturgy of the Hours,[268] but it is less known that selective psalm suppression affected the Mass as well. There are a surprising number of psalm verses *prominent* in the old Missal that are either *absent* in the new lectionary or much more rarely found. For example, the moving lines of Psalm 42 with which every celebration of the *usus antiquior* begins—"I will go in unto the altar of God, to God who giveth joy to my youth," and so forth—were, in the new lectionary, exiled to a lonesome Friday of the 25th week of Ordinary Time in Year 1, and a couple of verses in the Easter Vigil. That's it. Psalm 34, so beloved to our ancestors for its Passiontide language and ascetical images, was whittled down from eight appearances in the traditional Mass to a single appearance in the Novus Ordo—and only *if* the Introit is said or sung, which is optional (see Exhibit C, p. 166).

What is happening in such examples (and they are numerous) seems, regrettably, to be this: embarrassed by a divinely revealed doctrine or spiritual attitude, certain members of the Church do what they can to ensure that it is never mentioned, or only very rarely.[269] The men of Coetus XI knew what the traditional lections were, and it appears that they deliberately suppressed some of them. The novelty of the multi-year cycles and the monumental fact of "more Scripture" distracted attention from the subtler question of what was *lost* in the transition. A similar process of doctrinal attenuation can be seen in the Consilium's editing of the Collects, whose postconciliar versions frequently omit or downplay mention of things regarded as incompatible with modern ideas or offensive to modern ears.[270] That is why we should not hesitate to say openly that Archbishop Arthur Roche is telling fibs (that's putting it politely) when he says that "the *Missale Romanum* of Pope Saint Paul VI is the richest Missal that the Church has ever produced" and that it "retains . . . ninety percent of the texts of that [Tridentine] Missal."[271] No, in actual fact, it *removes* many of the riches of the old missal, and fills in the gaping space with modern watered-down, dumbed-down content, "lest anyone" (to

---

268 See Kwasniewski, "The Omission of 'Difficult' Psalms."

269 For abundant examples, see Pristas, *Collects of the Roman Missals.*

270 For many examples, see Kwasniewski, "Christian Militancy in the Prayer of the Church."

271 Roche, "In the earthly liturgy," 3; "The Roman Missal," 251.

use Annibale Bugnini's words) "find reason for spiritual discomfort in the prayer of the Church."[272] But why shouldn't we want Christians to experience *some* spiritual discomfort during the liturgy? It is in wrestling with these "difficult" passages and coming to understand them that the faithful advance in the spiritual life. It is for analogous reasons that we should be asked to embrace some asceticism, such as fasting for a longer time before Communion and kneeling throughout Mass, instead of avoiding physical discomfort by eating till an hour before, then sitting in the cushioned pews of an air-conditioned church.

The *Ars Celebrandi*

Everything I have said to this point has to do with the lectionary itself: what led to its creation, what principles guided its formation, and how particular readings were selected or excluded. But how Scripture is *treated*, how it is reverenced by the ministers, how it is integrated into the entire liturgy, is arguably no less important than the selection and quantity of readings. A metaphor would be the contrast between the modern printed book and the medieval illuminated manuscript. A Bible that has been written out by hand in a beautiful script, ennobled with an elaborate initial and surrounded by lavish ornamentation, is a certain way of *viewing and treating* the Word of God, no less than a cheap modern paperback that crams the words onto thin sheets with a drab, uniform layout and no special images. In this final section, I will turn to the domain of what is called the *ars celebrandi*.

One sign of whether we are grasping the Eucharistic nobility and finality of the readings is whether the lections are proclaimed with due solemnity. They should be surrounded by a rich ceremonial, including the *chanting* of the sacred texts, candles, and incense. At a High Mass or *Missa cantata*, the priest's chanting of the readings elevates them in a manner fitting to the depth and beauty of God's own words and fitting, also, to the public act of transmitting divine revelation. The chant is like musical incense. At a solemn Mass, the hierarchical chanting, first by the

272 Bugnini made these remarks concerning 1965 revisions to the solemn orations of Pius XII's Good Friday service. See Shaw, *The Case for Liturgical Restoration,* 285–86.

subdeacon, then by the deacon, wonderfully expresses the relationship of the elements: the lowest major minister sings the Epistle, the mid-level major minister sings the Gospel, and the highest major minister, the one who directly represents Christ the High Priest, whispers the words of consecration that infinitely exceed any song on earth. In such ways, the classical Roman Rite brings out forcefully the fact that when we are handling Scripture, we are handling not mere human verbiage but precious secrets proceeding from the mouth of God. The Latin Mass treats the Word of God with tremendous veneration and yet, at the same time, decisively subordinates that written Word to the *Mysterium Fidei*, the Word-made-flesh.

At a High Mass, the chanting of the Epistle and Gospel and the slow-moving elaborate beauty of the interlectional chants—the Gradual and the Alleluia throughout the year, the Gradual and the Tract in Septuagesima and Lent, or the pair of Alleluias in Paschaltide—prompt us to receive the Word as *God's Word* and to meditate on it. While theoretically available in the Novus Ordo, chanted readings and the chants between the readings are encountered extremely rarely. Rather, the delivery of the Sunday readings—up to four of them in a row if we count the responsorial psalm, read out from the same exact place, and all too often with monotonous delivery—treats these words as merely human, not divine, and discourages meditation.[273] The traditional Low Mass, where the readings are recited rather than sung, avoids these problems for a number of reasons: the brevity and fewness of the readings themselves (with rare exceptions); their being read *at the altar* and *only by the priest*, which underlines their link to the sacrifice and to the ordained ministry that hands down God's gifts to men; the controlled environment of reverent ritual, which opens up a space for meditative engagement with the texts of the liturgy on the part of the faithful, including also the orations and antiphons that complement the readings so well; the prayerful silence in which many other parts of Mass are enveloped, an atmosphere that greatly promotes the receiving of the word.

[273] Nearly all musical settings of the responsorial psalms leave much to be desired; certainly they have none of the outstanding qualities of the Gregorian Graduals.

We saw earlier that the Council had stated, in words that warmed the hearts of Fr. Louis Bouyer and others of their generation: "To achieve the restoration, progress, and adaptation of the sacred liturgy, it is essential to promote that warm and living love for Scripture to which the venerable tradition of both Eastern and Western rites gives testimony."[274] How, in a manner proper to liturgy, do we best promote a *warm and living love for Scripture*? The answer is not hard to figure out. We treat Scripture in a special ceremonial way: we enclose it in a silver or gold case (this is more common in the East); we chant the readings; we incense the Gospel, flank it with candles, and carry it back to the priest at the altar to be kissed. With its simultaneous introduction of a multitude of readings and of lay lectors, the Novus Ordo has ironically rendered a sung and solemn Liturgy of the Word vanishingly rare, and, as we know too well, the spoken version tends to be rather dull and easy to ignore, when it is not positively annoying due to well-intentioned attempts to declaim the readings with dramatic flair. While there are plenty more verses from the Bible, they seem so much less the pearl of great price handed down from on high.

Finally, we can ask ourselves: Does there *need* to be a homily at a weekday Mass? Cannot the Word of God, or better yet, the liturgy as a whole, sometimes be allowed to "speak for itself"? We need to find ways to make our liturgies less centered on human opinions and personalities and more centered on Jesus Christ, on His Word and His Sacrifice. Indeed, it was a normal practice for a very long time to have no preaching at daily Mass—a custom still followed today in many parishes that offer the TLM—and it even happened that Sunday's preaching was not part of Mass but either done in between Masses (so that those about to leave an earlier Mass and those just arriving for a later Mass could both hear the same sermon) or incorporated into the well-attended Vespers and Benediction service in the evening.

[274] *Sacrosanctum Concilium,* no. 24.

Conclusions

Fr. Spataro elegantly ties together many of the points I have made in this chapter when he writes:

> The first part [of the TLM, that is, the Mass of the Catechumens] has its own inner coherence: it humbly leads us into the presence of God through the prayers at the foot of the altar, with their sublime penitential orientation. Out of this humility, which is the proper basis of the relationship between creature and Creator, sinner and Redeemer, springs the supplication of the Kyrie and the prayer of the Collect. At this point, we are ready to be instructed by the Wisdom of God that is revealed in salvation history and unfolds the truth that leads us to heaven, for only the humble will "hear" and be glad, as the Psalm says (Ps 33:3). We find a copious sprinkling of Scripture passages and Psalm verses—a *prayed* Bible!—that make up the text of the Introit, Gradual, Tract, Alleluia, and then the pericopes of the Epistle and the Holy Gospel. In every place we find the proportion that is the intrinsic property of beauty: texts that, except on a few special occasions, are neither too long nor too many, as is the case with the biennial or triennial cycle of the *Novus Ordo*.[275]

The criteria we have looked at—the function of Scripture in the Eucharistic sacrifice, the internal cohesion of the Mass as an ecosystem, the psychology of memory, the natural unit of the year, the due place of the sanctoral cycle, the spiritual role of difficult passages, the aesthetic and ceremonial treatment given to the divine Word, and, not least of all, the authority inherent in traditional practice—permit us to draw some general conclusions.

First, like much else in the liturgical reform conducted under Pope Paul VI, the new lectionary exhibits signs of unseemly haste, overweening ambition, and disregard of principles approved by the Council Fathers.[276] The Council's call for "more Scripture" was open to different and even conflicting realizations. The revised lectionary, while it does represent one possible implementation of numbers 35 and 51 of *Sacrosanctum Concilium*, ends

[275] Spataro, *In Praise of the Tridentine Mass,* 113–14.
[276] See Kwasniewski, "Who Was Captain of the Ship in the Liturgical Reform?"

up contradicting outright numbers 23 and 50 of the same Constitution, which enunciate the controlling principle of continuity with tradition as well as the request that elements already present in our tradition be *restored.* It is worth noting that the bulk of the readings in the preconciliar *Missale Romanum* represent a venerable inheritance from the early centuries of Catholic worship, a stable body of lessons on which generations of pastors, preachers, theologians, and laity had been nurtured, a tradition deserving of immense respect for its venerable antiquity. It is, to speak plainly, outrageous that this unbroken tradition, which had withstood all the ravages of time, fell victim to the scalpels of academic specialists. The result has been an obvious rupture and discontinuity at the very heart of the Roman Rite.

Second, quite apart from whether or not it can be seen as faithful to the Council's desiderata, the Novus Ordo lectionary is gravely flawed because of its overall conception, its unwieldy bulk, its omission of "difficult" texts, and its watering down of key spiritual goods emphasized in the old readings.[277] No human mind can relate to so great a quantity of biblical text spread over multiple years: it is out of proportion to the natural cycle of the year and its seasons; it is out of proportion to the supernatural cycle of the liturgical year.[278] The revised lectionary does not lend itself readily to the sacrificial finality of the Mass but, inasmuch as it appears to serve a didactic function, sets up a different goal, quasi-independent of the offering of the Sacrifice. The use of the names "Liturgy of the Word" and "Liturgy of the Eucharist" underlines the problem: it is as if there are two liturgies glued together.[279] They are seldom joined by the obvious connection of being

[277] See, for examples and commentary, Miller, "Bible by the Pound."

[278] Fr. Spataro observes: "Though it had the laudable intention of offering a semi-continuous reading of the entirety [*sic*] of Sacred Scripture, this cycle ends up 'wasting' a great number of texts that the average layman cannot remember and, sometimes, cannot even hear, not only because of the length and difficulty of certain passages, but also because they are read by lectors insufficiently prepared for their task, chosen in obedience to the equality called for by an erroneous understanding of *actuosa participatio.* Length and bad diction are signs of vulgarity, not beauty" (*In Praise of the Tridentine Mass,* 114).

[279] Indeed, the Eucharistic orientation of Scriptural proclamation, so far from being "renewed" by means of the liturgical reform, has been inverted; the Holy Eucharist itself is all too often viewed as a mere sign—a collective symbol of being "gathered together in God's name." It is as if the Liturgy of the Eucharist has fallen into the gravitational field of the Liturgy of the Word, with the flesh-and-blood reality of Christ reduced to the conceptual status of a sign of identity and belonging. The proliferation of "celebrations of the Word of God," i.e., liturgies in

related to one and the same *feast*, since the new lectionary prefers to ignore the saints in its march through the books of Scripture. Nor has it often been the custom to join the two liturgies by means of ceremonial practices that show the chanting of Scripture to be one phase of the journey toward Jerusalem and the hill of Calvary.[280]

Third, in light of this critique, we are in a better position to acknowledge that the traditional Latin Mass possesses what is, in many ways, a superior lectionary. Catholics who love the Roman Rite should be unafraid to maintain and argue this advantage. We have a magnificent treasure to preserve and to share generously with our fellow Catholics, in spite of the scandal of coreligionists who persecute us.

Fourth, the current Latin Mass readings are less varied and numerous than they have been at different points in the Roman Rite's history, and there is no inherent reason why the annual cycle could not be judiciously enriched with daily readings for certain seasons and by the selection of appropriate new readings for certain saints' feasts or commons, all the while scrupulously respecting and maintaining the readings already in place.[281] In this way, the primacy of the liturgical year and the coherence of the sanctoral cycle would be maintained, and neither sound tradition nor valuable spiritual goods would have to be compromised. Yet *now* hardly seems the best time to undertake such a task. Those who love the classical Roman liturgy appreciate the stability and serenity of the old missal and quite reasonably wish to avoid further upheaval, while those who are in charge of liturgical matters in the Church seem doggedly committed to the defense, at all costs, of the novelties of the 1960s and 1970s. In short: ours is a situation favorable neither to the preservation

---

the absence of a priest that end up looking somewhat *like* Masses to the untrained faithful (because there is Scripture reading followed by Communion), only furthers this process of inverse gravitation. If there is to be a priestless celebration, it should rather take the form of the Divine Office, the original and authentic "Liturgy of the Word."

280 See Luke 9:51.

281 It is only fair to acknowledge the gains in the new lectionary: the splendid selection of prophetic readings for the ferias of Advent, the selection of readings for ferias of Paschaltide, and the felicitous pairing of certain Old Testament and New Testament pericopes. But these gains are marred by all the other problems noted in this chapter and cannot be said to "win the day." In truth, the opportunity for a judicious enrichment of the old missal was squandered by the destructive mindset of the Consilium and it may be a very long time before sufficient peace exists in the Church to allow the question even to be broached again.

of tradition nor to its legitimate and prudent development. I sympathize with those who say we need a breathing space, a season of refreshment, in which we rediscover and rejoice in the Church's traditional liturgy, with the notion of change far from our minds. A sort of practical "work-around" is Sophia Institute Press's *Benedictus,* a liturgical aid that includes not only all the Mass texts one would need for a given month, but also scripturally saturated meditations on the feasts and the liturgy. By such means, one can gently expand one's biblical literacy in conjunction with the missal as it stands.[282]

Fifth, pastors in charge of *usus antiquior* communities ought to promote *lectio divina* and Bible studies and not be afraid to base their preaching on Sacred Scripture, while not neglecting texts from the missal, approved catechisms, and other classic homiletic sources. The tight integration of the Propers of the Mass often makes it easy to fulfill the Council's request that "the sermon . . . should draw its content mainly from scriptural *and liturgical* sources."[283] How rare it is to hear homilies or sermons that comment at any length on the texts of the Mass, whether proper to the day or from the *Ordo Missae*! Is it not strange that, apart from baptisms, First Communions, and other special events, priests so rarely draw their themes from the immense treasury of the liturgy itself?

Lastly, the Catholic parish, like the life of every Catholic, should feature a variety of prayer forms and a breadth of education. The vast increase in the quantity of Scripture at Mass reflects a mentality that sees Mass as the *only* time when Catholics are ever going to be in church or anywhere near a Bible, so one feels compelled to pack everything one can into that time. This mentality obviously neglects the role of the Divine Office, which is and has always been a dedicated liturgy of the Word of God and deserves an important place—for example, in publicly celebrated Vespers. Moreover, nothing can substitute for extra-liturgical formation in catechism classes, prayer groups, and Bible studies, through pamphlets, books, and

---

[282] If ever there were to be a commission appointed to recommend an expanded selection of readings for ferias and feastdays, it should consist of contemplative traditionalist monks who live, breathe, eat, and sleep Scripture, and who will take a long time to make their recommendations, instead of ramming huge innovations through in a few breakneck years, as occurred in the late 1960s.

[283] *Sacrosanctum Concilium,* no. 35.2, emphasis added.

DVDs distributed to the faithful, and even through well-written bulletins. As Pope Benedict XVI reminded us, *lectio divina* should be taught and encouraged. The biblical education and piety of the faithful is not a burden that the Mass, as such, was ever meant to carry, or is even well-suited to carry. Its purpose is something far greater: the glorification of God in the supreme sacrifice of Christ and the sanctification of the people in their communion with Him, the Word-made-flesh.

Exhibit A

Proper of the Mass for the Feast of St. Thérèse of Lisieux (MR *1962, October* 3)

Introit **Song 4:8–9; Psalm 112:1**	Veni de Líbano, sponsa mea, veni de Líbano, veni: vulnerásti cor meum, soror mea sponsa, vulnerásti cor meum. Laudáte, púeri, Dóminum: laudáte nomen Dómini. Gloria Patri, et Filio, et Spiritui Sancto… Veni de Líbano…	Come from Libanus, my spouse, come from Libanus, come: thou hast wounded my heart, my sister, my spouse, thou hast wounded my heart. Praise the Lord, ye children: praise ye the name of the Lord. Glory be to the Father … Come…
Collect	Oremus. Dómine, qui dixísti: Nisi efficiámini sicut párvuli, non intrábitis in regnum cælórum: da nobis, quæsumus; ita sanctæ Terésiæ vírginis in humilitáte et simplicitáte cordis vestígia sectári, ut præmia consequámur ætérna. Qui vivis et regnas…	Let us pray. O Lord, Who hast said: Unless ye become as little children, ye shall not enter into the kingdom of Heaven, grant unto us, we beseech Thee, so to follow the footsteps of saint Teresa, virgin, in lowliness and simplicity of heart that we may gain everlasting rewards. Who livest ...
Epistle **Isaiah 66:12–14**	Léctio Isaíæ Prophétæ. Hæc dicit Dóminus: Ecce ego declinábo super eam quasi flúvium pacis, et quasi torréntem inundántem glóriam géntium, quam sugétis: ad úbera portabímini, et super génua blandiéntur vobis. Quómodo si cui mater blandiátur, ita ego consolábor vos, et in Jerusalem consolabímini. Vidébitis, et gaudébit cor vestrum, et ossa vestra quasi herba germinábunt, et cognoscétur manus Dómini servi ejus.	Lesson from Isaias the Prophet. Thus saith the Lord: Behold I will bring upon her as it were a river of peace, and as an overflowing torrent the glory of the gentiles, which you shall suck; you shall be carried at the breasts, and upon the knees they shall caress you. As one whom the mother caresseth, so will I comfort you, and you shall be comforted in Jerusalem. You shall see and your heart shall rejoice, and your bones shall flourish like an herb, and the hand of the Lord shall be known to His servants.
Gradual **Matthew 11:25; Psalm 70:5**	Confíteor tibi, Pater, Dómine cæli et terra: quia abscondísti hæc a sapiéntibus, et prudéntibus, et revelasti ea párvulis. Dómine, spes mea a juventúte mea.	I confess to Thee, O Father, Lord of heaven and earth, because Thou hast hid these things from the wise and prudent and hast revealed them to little ones. My hope, O Lord, from my youth.

Alleluia **Sirach 39:17–19**	Allelúia, allelúia. Quasi rosa plantáta super rivos aquárum fructificáte: quasi Líbanus odórem suavitátis habéte: floréte flores, quasi lílium, et date odórem, et frondéte in gratiam, et collaudáte cánticum, et benedícite Dóminum in opéribus suis. Allelúia.	Alleluia, alleluia. Bud forth as the rose planted by the brooks of waters. Give ye a sweet odor as Libanus. Send forth flowers, as the lily, and yield a smell, and bring forth leaves in grace, and praise with canticles, and bless the Lord in His works. Alleluia.
Gospel **Matthew 18:1–5**	In illo témpore: Accessérunt discípuli ad Jesum, dicéntes: "Quis, putas, major est in regno cælórum?" Et ádvocans Jesus párvulum, státuit eum in médio eórum, et dixit: "Amen dico vobis, nisi convérsi fuéritis, et efficiámini sicut párvuli, non intrábitis in regnum cælórum. Quicúmque ergo humiliáverit se sicut párvulus iste, hic est major in regno cælórum."	At that time, the disciples came to Jesus saying: "Who, thinkest Thou, is the greater in the kingdom of Heaven?" And Jesus calling unto Him a little child, set him in the midst of them and said: "Amen I say to you, unless you be converted and become as little children, you shall not enter into the kingdom of Heaven. Whosoever therefore shall humble himself as this little child, he is the greater in the kingdom of Heaven."
Offertory **Luke 1:46–49**	Magníficat ánima mea Dóminum: et exsultávit spíritus meus in Deo salutári meo: quia respéxit humilitátem ancíllæ suæ: fecit mihi magna qui potens est.	My soul doth magnify the Lord. And my spirit hath rejoiced in God my Savior. Because He hath regarded the humility of His handmaid: He that is mighty hath done great things to me.
Secret	Sacrifícium nostrum tibi, Dómine, quæsumus, sanctæ Terésiæ vírginis tuæ precátio sancta concíliet: ut in cujus honóre solémniter exhibétur, ejus méritis efficiátur accéptum. Per Dominum…	We beseech Thee, O Lord, that the holy intercession of saint Teresa, Thy virgin, may make our sacrifice agreeable to Thee, so that it may be made acceptable by the merits of her in whose honor it is solemnly offered. Through our Lord…
Communion **Deuteronomy 32:10–12**	Circumdúxit eam, et dócuit: et custodívit quasi pupíllam óculi sui. Sicut áquila expándit alas suas, et assúmpsit eam, atque portávit in húmeris suis. Dóminus solus dux ejus fuit.	He led her about and taught her: and He kept her as the apple of His eye. As the eagle, He spread His wings and hath taken her, and carried her on His shoulders. The Lord alone was her leader.
Postcommunion	Illo nos, Dómine, amóris igne cæléste mystérium inflámmet quo sancta Terésia vírgo tua se tibi pro homínibus caritátis víctimam devóvit. Per Dóminum…	May the heavenly mystery, O Lord, enkindle in us that fire of love, whereby the saint Teresa, Thy virgin, offered herself to Thee as a victim of charity for men. Through our Lord…

Exhibit B

Biblical Permeation in the Mass (MR *1962,* Laetare *Sunday, Solemn Mass)*

	Order of Mass / Proper of Mass
Asperges	Psalm 50:9, 1 (Asperges me) Psalm 84:8 (Ostende nobis) Psalm 101:2 (Domine, exaudi)
Prayers at the Foot of the Altar	**Psalm 42** (Judica me) Psalm 123:8 (Adiutorium nostrum) Psalm 84:7 (Deus tu conversus) Psalm 84:8 (Ostende nobis) Psalm 101:2 (Domine, exaudi) Ezekiel 42:13; Hebrews 9:3 [sancta sanctorum]
Entrance antiphon	Isaiah 66:10–11 (Laetare, Jerusalem) Psalm 121:1 (Laetatus sum)
Kyrie	Psalm 122:3; Isaiah 33:2; Matthew 20:30-31; Luke 17:13; Judith 7:20; Esther 13:15; Tobit 8:10
Epistle	Galatians 4:22–31 (Scriptum est)
Gradual	Psalm 121:1, 7 (Laetatus sum)
Tract	Psalm 124:1–2 (Qui confidunt)
Prayer before the Gospel	Isaiah 6:6–7 [tetigit os meum]
Gospel	John 6:1–15 (Abiit Jesus trans mare)
Offertory antiphon	Psalm 134:3, 6 (Laudate Dominum)
Offertory of the Mass	Psalm 115:4 [calicem salutaris] Exodus 29:41, Leviticus 2:9, 8:28, 17:16, Numbers 15:7, Ephesians 5:2, Philippians 4:18, etc. [odorem suavitatis] **Daniel 3:39–40** (In spiritu humilitatis) Luke 1:11 (a dextris altaris incensi) Revelation 8:3–4 [angelus venit] Psalm 32:22 (misericordia tua super nos) **Psalm 140:2–4** (Dirigatur, Domine, oratio mea) **Psalm 25:6–12** (Lavabo inter innocentes)
Sanctus	Isaiah 6:3 (Sanctus) Mark 11:10 (Hosanna in excelsis) Psalm 117:26, John 12:13 (Benedictus qui venit)

Roman Canon	*{Of the elaborate tapestry of biblical allusions, here are a few threads}* Tobit 8:9, Psalm 49:14, 49:23, 106:22 (sacrificium laudis) Psalm 49:14, 55:12, 60:9, 65:13, 115:5 [redde vota/reddam vota] Luke 6:20, John 11:41 (elevatis oculis) Matthew 26:26, 1 Corinthians 11:25, etc. {institution/consecration} Genesis 4:4, 22:7–13, 14:18 {Abel, Abraham, Melchisedech} Ephesians 1:3 [omni benedictione spiritali in caelestibus in Christo] Psalm 50:3, 68:17 (multitudinem miserationum tuarum)
The Lord's Prayer	Matthew 6:9–13
Agnus Dei	John 1:29 (Agnus Dei, qui tollit)
Prayers before communion	John 14:27 (Pacem relinquo vobis) Matthew 16:16 [Filius Dei vivi] Galatians 1:4 [secundum voluntatem … Patris] 1 Corinthians 11:29 [indigne … iudicium]
Prayers at communion	Psalm 77:4, John 6:31, etc. [panem de caelo] Psalm 115:4 (nomen Domini invocabo) Matthew 8:8 (Domine, non sum dignus) Psalm 115:3–4 (Quid retribuam… Calicem salutaris accipiam) Psalm 17:4 (Laudans invocabo)
People's communion	John 1:29 (Ecce, Agnus Dei) Matthew 8:8 (Domine, non sum dignus)
Communion antiphon	Psalm 121:3–4 (Jerusalem, quae aedificatur ut civitas)
Placeat tibi	Daniel 3:40 (Placeat tibi)
Blessing	Genesis 28:3 [Deus omnipotens benedicat tibi]
Last Gospel	**John 1:1–14** (In principio erat Verbum)

On days that call for a Gloria, one might note the following Scriptural allusions:

Gloria	Luke 2:14 (cp. 19:38); 1 Chronicles 29:13; Tobit 8:17; John 4:22; Revelation 11:17; Romans 8:34; Ephesians 1:20; Hebrews 1:3; Psalm 82:19; Philippians 2:11

Exhibit C

Psalm 34 [35] in the Mass of the Roman Rite

In the *usus antiquior* (*MR* 1962)

Friday in Passion Week	Gradual (Ps 34:20, 22)	Mine enemies spoke peaceably to me: and in anger they were troublesome to me. Thou hast seen, O Lord, be not Thou silent: depart not from me.
Saturday in Passion Week	Gradual (Ps 34:20, 22)	Mine enemies spoke peaceably to me: and in anger they were troublesome to me. Thou hast seen, O Lord, be not Thou silent: depart not from me.
Monday in Holy Week	Introit (Ps 34:1–3)	Judge Thou, O Lord, them that wrong me, overthrow them that fight against me; take hold of arms and shield, and rise up to help me, O Lord, the strength of my salvation. Bring out the sword, and shut up the way against them that persecute me; say to my soul: I am thy salvation.
	Gradual (Ps 34:3, 23)	Arise, O Lord, and be attentive to my judgment, my God and my Lord, [be attentive] to my cause. Bring out the sword, and shut up the way against them that persecute me.
	Communion (Ps 34:26)	Let them blush and be ashamed together, who rejoice at my evils: let them be clothed with shame and fear, who speak malignant things against me.
Tuesday in Holy Week	Gradual (Ps 34: 13, 1-2)	But as for me, when they were troublesome to me, I was clothed with sackcloth, and I humbled my soul with fasting, and my prayer shall be turned into my bosom. Judge Thou, O Lord, them that wrong me, overthrow them that fight against me; take hold of arms and shield, and rise up to help me.
September 15 (Seven Sorrows of BVM)	Gradual (Ps 34:20, 22)	Mine enemies spoke peaceably to me: and in anger they were troublesome to me. Thou hast seen, O Lord, be not Thou silent: depart not from me.
September 18 (Joseph of Cupertino)	Offertory (Ps 34:13)	But as for me, when they were troublesome to me, I was clothed with sackcloth, and I humbled my soul with fasting, and my prayer shall be turned into my bosom.

In the *usus recentior* (*MR* 1970/2008)

Monday in Holy Week	Introit (Ps 34:1–2)	Contend, O Lord, with my contenders; fight those who fight me. Take up your buckler and shield; arise in my defense, Lord, my mighty help.

7

Why We Pray in Latin

"The Mass is in a foreign language. I can't follow it."

The question of the language in which a Christian liturgy should be conducted is a question more complicated than most people realize at first glance. To the extent that we have been brainwashed by rationalism, we tend to assume that the only purpose of speaking, of using words at all, is to communicate ideas between people. Language has a utilitarian function; this is its only justification.

Of course, it is true that we use words to convey ideas and information. But language has loftier functions. Poetry, to take a prime example, pays attention to the beauty, sound, associations, and intricate inner meanings of language; it is meant as a testimony to and a revelation of something of the mystery of being. That is why it is often harder to grasp but more rewarding when understood, and why, at its best, poetry reaches toward the ineffable or inexpressible—a thought or vision or experience that cannot be captured in words. Or consider nursery rhymes, lullabies, and nonsense songs that we sing to little children to entertain them or to help them fall asleep. The communication of a definite meaning is not the point; it is about togetherness, comfort, reassurance, simple delight. Language here becomes more a vehicle of sentiment and feeling. Prayer, at least formal public prayer, shares some of these trans-communicative properties, particularly in the realm of so-called sacred languages that I will be exploring in this chapter. As Michael Fiedrowicz explains:

> In order to understand the essence and meaning of a sacred language, it is important to be aware that language has multiple functions. First, it is a medium of communication that allows for the transmission

> of thoughts or information. Here intelligibility is vital. Beyond this, however, language is a form of expression. By means of language, man can give expression to his feelings and experiences, even his entire being. Thus, for example, singing a song does not convey information, but rather expresses sentiments, creates an atmosphere, and brings about fellowship. Considered from the standpoint of linguistics, prayer belongs more to the realm of expression than to that of communication. This applies not only to personal prayer, but also to collective prayer. Insofar as the sacred language in the liturgy is primarily directed toward God, it does not especially aim at imparting information in the sense of human communication. Here the language serves rather as a bridge between the profane world and the transcendent God. The sacred language, as a simultaneously human and stylized speech, seeks to create an atmosphere that both reflects and evokes a certain religious attitude in those who pray.[284]

It is obviously a good thing for the minister offering a liturgical prayer to understand what he is saying. However, when we consider it as a prayer *of the Church* presented *to Almighty God*, we can confidently say that its principal purpose is not human comprehension—as if the goal of the uttering of the prayer is the grasping of it by either the reciter or the audience—but rather, the humble and efficacious supplication of God: *He*, or His grace and blessing, is the purpose of the prayer. From this vantage, what matters the most is manifestly the objective content, the goodness, the orthodoxy, the traditional credentials (so to speak) of the prayer itself, and not so much whether the speaker or the hearers fully grasp its meaning. This radically theocentric conception of prayer matches the eastward stance, the separation of the priest from the people as their mediator, the kingly and courtly ceremonial with its fixed ritual, and the favoring of repetition. In other words, given all that we have seen so far, it is absolutely to be expected that the liturgy would also have a special elevated language proper to it.

To the extent, moreover, that there *is* definite content to be communicated, the use of Latin is by no means an insuperable barrier to comprehension. As Dr. Joseph Shaw explains:

---

[284] Fiedrowicz, *The Traditional Mass,* 155.

> Neither the inaudibility nor the use of Latin in practice creates a barrier of understanding between the worshipper and the liturgy, since members of the congregation can consult a hand missal, printout, or smartphone, to see exactly what is being said, translated into a wide variety of languages. What it does do is to mark off the liturgy as something special and distinct from ordinary life. When we enter into the Latin zone, so to speak, we are entering into a spiritual space. In this way Latin powerfully reinforces the atmosphere created by the architecture and fittings of a church building, the special vestments worn by the clergy, the distinct type of music appropriate to the Mass, and so on. . . . The Latin of the Mass was never, in truth, the language of the street, or of the public speaker. Not only is it often flowery and poetic, but it is strongly marked by the influence of Greek and Hebrew, and makes extensive use of repetition and deliberate archaism. It was always intended to be what it is: a distinct, holy language, to be used only in the liturgy.
>
> One does not have to understand the Latin text word by word as it is spoken to perceive the solemn character with which it clothes the liturgy, and to be moved by that. The meaning of the text can be immediately available to the worshipper in a book or leaflet, but the impact of the *form* that the text takes, the fact that it is proclaimed in an ancient, sacred language, of unique grandeur and gravity, is also of considerable value.[285]

This should, after all, be a matter of common sense. There is much about solemn liturgy that can lift the mind and draw the heart even where verbal and rational understanding is limited. As Joseph Shaw writes elsewhere: "An ounce of devotion is worth a ton of intellectual comprehension. And that statement could stand as a summary of the traditionalist case for the preservation of our ancient liturgy."[286] The history of the missions affords

---

[285] Shaw, *Sacred and Great,* 29–30, 32. On the interconnectedness of the sense of incomprehensible mystery, the use of ancient languages, the irregularity of old rituals, and the involvement of the subconscious, see the insightful commentary in Otto, *The Idea of the Holy,* 64–65. For further arguments against the claim that Christian Latin was simply "the vernacular of the day" (and, accordingly, that liturgy should always be in the vernacular of a given place and time), see "Was Liturgical Latin Introduced As—and Because It Was—the Vernacular?," in Kwasniewski, *Illusions of Reform,* 114–22.

[286] Shaw, *Latin Mass and the Intellectuals,* 47.

many examples of how non-Latin-speaking native peoples were drawn to Christianity in part through the impressiveness of the liturgical services they witnessed. I will return to this point in a moment.

Preaching with Words and Signs

The Feast of Pentecost is so great in the eyes of the Church that it was celebrated as an octave (for eight consecutive days) in the Latin rite from the sixth century on—a custom that continues today wherever the ancient Roman Rite is used—and, what is more, gave its name to the longest season in the year, the "Sundays after Pentecost," which may number as many as twenty-eight and are notable for vestments in green, a symbol of abounding life and fecundity.

A friend once told me of a situation in which he had expressed his love of the traditional Latin Mass to a deacon of a certain generation, who then countered in a huff: "Pentecost shows that the apostles spoke to everyone in their *own* language—and it wasn't Latin." This statement contains an elementary misinterpretation of Pentecost and the gift of tongues. What the Acts of the Apostles shows is that the Apostles *preached* to the people in many languages. There is nothing in the Pentecost story about worship in the temple or synagogue, or the Eucharistic liturgy and the Divine Office that developed out of them and supplanted them. And as far as I know, it's always been the custom to preach in the vernacular at Latin Masses, except in highly specialized academic contexts. The gift of tongues is a gift for the sake of evangelization, apologetics, and catechesis—not specifically for liturgical worship.

Moreover, it's worthwhile to point out that as useful as preaching is, the Church over the centuries developed many other modes of expression that proved to be as effective or even more effective in evangelizing. Having explained how missionaries made use of pagan vernacular languages in the sixteenth-century Spanish empire, historian Daniel Wasserman-Soler observes:

> We must leave behind a widespread modern assumption . . . made famous in the Protestant Reformation . . . that the written and spoken word constitute the fundamental and best way for people to learn about religion. . . . The first bishops of Mexico City, Guatemala, and

> Oaxaca indicated to King Charles I that sermons may not have been the key to the conversion of the American natives: "We confirm, Your Majesty, that the Natives are edified very much by devoted service, ceremonies, and ornate artwork, perhaps even more than by sermons." Thus in the minds of many clerics, the combination of vivid artwork, the fragrant smell of incense, the sense of inclusion in a community, and the example of a pious, Christ-like cleric together could prove a more powerful force for religious conversion than preaching alone.[287]

In a way, it is perfectly obvious once you state it, but there are so many people today who, in the grip of an unconscious rationalism, do not recognize how much is conveyed through non-verbal language, as well as through the emotional and supra-rational elements of language itself.

Language is never "merely" language; its cultural history, its traits and associations, the very *sound* of it falling on the ear—all of this is borne along *with* the language and often delivers as much impact as, or even a greater impact than, its conceptual content. The moment we hear "*In nomine Patris, et Filii, et Spiritus Sancti, Amen. Introibo ad altare Dei,*" we are placed in a different zone; it's almost like when the angel takes up the prophet Habakuk by the hair of his head and carries him off to Babylon, except that it's in the opposite direction: the worshiper is carried from Babylon to the Promised Land, from the valley of tears to the holy of holies.[288] Observes Fiedrowicz:

---

[287] Wasserman-Soler, *Truth in Many Tongues,* 166–67. Carolina Arminteros, an expert on the thought of Joseph de Maistre, notes that for de Maistre "evangelization is less an informative activity than a mission accomplished through 'preaching accompanied by music, painting, solemn rites, and all the demonstration of faith without discussion.' The Christian spirit is best nurtured with the values and traditions that ecclesiastical institutions encode, and that Latin transmits. That the *vulgus* does not fully understand them does not matter too much, since moral and spiritual development proceeds not so much through intellective understanding of spiritual things . . . as through the living, feeling, and acting out of spiritual truths" (quoted in Shaw, *Latin Mass and the Intellectuals,* 26n20); again, this time in Sebastian Morello's words: "In the face of the rationalist assumption that evangelization takes place when all is understood, formulated, explicitly comprehended, and vernacularized, Maistre sees evangelization arising out of habit, devotion, pious feeling, sacral culture, mystery, and awe" (Shaw, 27).

[288] In terms of the "sacred atmosphere," one might add that the concentration, discipline, and seriousness of the congregation at a traditional Latin Mass is supported by, and in turn supports, the ambiance created by and within the liturgy, in a classic "feedback loop." As with the chicken and the egg, there *is* an answer to what comes first: it is the objective nature of the liturgy, in its ceremonies, language, music, and silences, which then calls forth behavior suitable to itself. If a stable and imposing objectivity is lacking, the behavioral response will be haphazard and flaccid (which people will call "creative" and "relaxed").

> Here the Church also proves to possess a thorough understanding of human nature, as in this way she helps her faithful to detach themselves from their everyday language, where each word recalls profane realities, and to feel, even sensibly, that "wholly Other" sought by all piety. . . . The sacred language spreads a delicate veil over the truths of the Faith, which protects the holy mystery and eludes hasty comprehensibility. . . . A language that is not commonly understood suggests to the faithful that they stand before a mystery that eludes total transparency. In contrast, vernacular language counterfeits an understanding that is absolutely not real.[289]

In the past sixty years of wayward liturgical reform and abuse, far too much emphasis has been placed on the vernacular (a particular language spoken by a group of people), as if it is somehow the magic key to participation. But it is not. For one thing, any vernacular excludes everyone who does not speak it—and that includes people who speak a lower register of the language, as well as that forgotten group whose education equips them to grasp higher registers as more appropriate in worship, and who will be vexed by translations into flat, dull, gray modern tones.[290]

What the reformers seemed to have forgotten is that there is a universal non-verbal "vernacular" accessible to all mankind: the language of symbols. Be they colors, actions, sounds, smells, or other religious signs, this vocabulary has an immediate (although at times perplexing) effect on the consciousness. It *shows* us reverence without talking about it; it *shows* us mourning or rejoicing without spelling it out in trite or laborious words. A black chasuble, unbleached candles, a catafalque, and the repeated refrain "*Requiem aeternam*" instantly tell us more about the meaning of a liturgy for the dead than a hundred books written on the subject.

Liturgical Latin is "strange" in the sense that it is not something of the everyday, familiar, easy, at our level or at our disposal; it evokes the transcendence and majesty of God, the universality of His kingdom, the age-old depths of the Faith. Over time, we identify this set-apart language as a sign of honor, we experience it as a promoter of reverence, and we find in it an invitation to prayer. When we dive into a pool, the moment we hit

[289] Fiedrowicz, *The Traditional Mass,* 163, 164, 165.

[290] This group is quite naturally attracted to the Anglican Ordinariate liturgy, if they can find it.

the water, we know—not just rationally, but viscerally—that we are in a new medium and we must swim. So too, when we hear chanted or recited Latin, we know we are in a new medium and we must pray. Sometimes we will do so in those Latin words themselves, once we are familiar with them; sometimes we will pray by means of a translation; and sometimes we will use our own words that rise up in our hearts. All are equally legitimate, for what matters is *that we pray*; "where the Spirit of the Lord is, there is freedom."[291]

"Sacred Language" as a Universal Phenomenon

Far from being a peculiar custom of the Western Church, the custom of employing a sacred language in religious rites is already prominent in salvation history, as Shaw points out:

> The tradition of Gregorian chant goes back to the Temple in Jerusalem, where we are told professional singers were employed (2 Chron 5:15); the use of Latin recalls the use of Hebrew as a sacred language, when the [everyday] language of the Jewish people had become Aramaic; the traditional liturgy's emphasis on priest, altar, and sacrifice is redolent of the atmosphere of ancient Jewish worship, something sometimes noted by Jewish converts . . .
>
> As Jews, they [the Apostles] were brought up to pray and sing the Psalms in Hebrew, as well as in their mother tongue. No word of criticism of sacred languages is to be found in Scripture, and the earliest liturgies were by no means composed in the language of the street. In Greek-speaking areas, the Church was able to employ the sacred register created by the Septuagint translation of the Bible: a distinct form of Greek already two centuries old and filled with Hebraisms. Latin liturgy did not emerge until Latin translations of the Bible had created something equivalent, and, when it did, we find a liturgy in a sacred Latin with a specialized vocabulary, replete with archaisms, loan-words, and other peculiarities; similarly, liturgical Coptic is an archaic language larded with Greek terms and written in Greek letters. As for Church Slavonic and the language of the Glagolitic Missal, their origins and history are not reducible to the simple idea of the

[291] 2 Cor 3:17 RSVCE.

> "language in use at the time," and, in any case, they quickly become liturgical languages for people not able to understand them. They remain culturally connected to the peoples they serve, but not readily comprehensible by them.[292]

We see, in fact, that every ancient Christian church developed a sacral language and idiom for worship: the Greek Orthodox Church still uses koine Greek, the Russians use Church Slavonic, the Ethiopians use Ge'ez, the Copts use literary Coptic, etc. The fact that some Eastern Christians have adopted a modern vernacular is an historical anomaly that should by no means be taken as normative, even if we do not need to condemn it either. The Eastern Christian sphere has always seen far more linguistic diversity than the Western sphere, which remained stalwartly committed to Latin for over 1,600 years—a longer time with a single language for worship than can be found in any other religious tradition except for the use of Hebrew by the Jews and the use of Greek by the Greek Orthodox.[293] It is hardly surprising that a belief grew up that the three great sacred languages are Hebrew, Greek, and Latin, on the basis of the threefold inscription that Pontius Pilate placed on the Cross of Our Lord Jesus Christ.

Indeed, the use of a special set-apart sacred language for religious rites goes well beyond the borders of Judaism and apostolic Christianity, as Fiedrowicz explains:

> The phenomenon of a sacred language is found in all religions. Such a language was used by the Greek oracles of ancient times and can be found in ancient Roman pagan prayers, whose formulas date back to distant antiquity, occasionally having become unintelligible even to the priest himself, though still used in order to remain true to ancestral

[292] Shaw, "The Novus Ordo at 50: Loss or Gain?"

[293] Apart from the fact that not all Eastern Christians utilize vernacular languages, the far-flung diversity of the Eastern churches seems to call for a plurality of languages in a way that was never seen as true in the "Latin West." With few exceptions such as the Glagolitic rite in Dalmatia, Roman Catholics offered their public worship in one universal, venerable language, unbroken for over a millennium and a half. To break the unity of this language was to break its symbolism and to transmit the message that the liturgy is simply a human artifact, subject to the whims of a free-thinking council, a monarchical pope, or an agitating committee. The sudden and universal transition to the vernacular in Roman Catholic worship is not a concession to modern needs but an expression of modern autonomy or self-determination, the spirit of democracy, and the refusal to submit to tradition.

> tradition. At the time of Christ, the Jews used the language of Old Hebraic for their services, though it was incomprehensible to the people. In the synagogues, only the readings and a few prayers relating to them were written in the mother tongue of Aramaic; the great, established prayer texts were recited in Hebrew. Although Christ adamantly attacked the formalism of the Pharisees in other respects, He never questioned this practice. Insofar as the Passover Meal was primarily celebrated with Hebrew prayers, the Last Supper was also characterized by elements of a sacred language. It is therefore possible that Christ spoke the words of Eucharistic consecration in the Hebrew *lingua sacra*. Other world religions also recognize sacred languages that differ from everyday idioms. The Muslims use classical Arabic for their prayers. The Buddhists employ Pali, and the Hindus Sanskrit.
>
> Even within Christianity various dedicated languages of worship have developed. Thus the Orthodox Greeks celebrate their liturgy in ancient Greek and the Russians in Church Slavonic. In addition, there is the use of Armenian, Coptic, and Syrian. Though originally these were certainly the living, vernacular language, over the course of time they grew ever more distant from everyday speech and finally assumed the character of a proper language of worship. Even Anglican services use the melodious Elizabethan English found in the *Book of Common Prayer*.[294]

This remarkable unanimity of practice across thousands of years and across every continent and culture—even those furthest removed from one another with no contact until fairly recently in history—indicates a profound common awareness, rooted in human nature, that we must relate to the ultimate divine source or the invisible spiritual dimension of reality differently than we relate to the business or pleasures of ordinary everyday life. Fiedrowicz puts his finger on the underlying reason:

> If sacred languages existed in numerous cultures and almost all epochs of history, and still continue to exist, this fact is an expression of a fundamental human need. In the background stands a particular religious experience that shapes and changes speech and language. It is the experience of something supernatural, divine, transcendent, and

[294] Fiedrowicz, *The Traditional Mass,* 153–54.

> wholly other, to which man seeks to respond by using a language that differentiates itself from the form of everyday speech by means of a sacred stylization. Here lies the origin of the so-called hieratic or "priestly" languages. Far from creating a language barrier, the sacred language calls to mind that religion has "something else" to say to man. The sacred language prevents man from dragging the divine down to his own level, and instead lifts man up to the divine, which it does not, however, reveal and expose completely to the human understanding, but instead indicates as a mystery.[295]

The same author goes on to identify "the characteristics of a sacred language":

> (1) a conscious distancing from the words of colloquial language, which makes the "complete otherness" of the divine felt; (2) an archaizing or at least conservative tendency to favor antiquated expressions and adhere to certain speech forms from centuries ago, as is well-suited for the worship of an eternal and unchanging God; (3) the use of foreign words that evoke religious associations, as, for example, the Hebrew and Aramaic forms of the words *alleluia*, *Sabaoth*, *hosanna*, *amen*, *maranatha* in the Greek books of the New Testament; and finally, (4) syntactic and phonetic stylizations (e.g., parallelisms, alliterations, rhymes, and rhythmic sentence endings) that clearly structure the train of thought, are memorable and allow for easy recollection, and strive for tonal beauty.[296]

Levels of Language

We will understand better why Latin is the correct and fitting language of the Roman Catholic liturgy if we begin with a truth everyone knows from experience. Any time a language is spoken, it is spoken in what linguists call a "register," which refers to its level of formality, polish, and sophistication—ranging from rough, casual, or slangish at the lower end, to intricately-wrought poetic diction at the higher. Depending on circumstance and education, individuals can speak their native language in various registers.

[295] Fiedrowicz, 154.
[296] Fiedrowicz, 154–55.

Analogously, we may say that languages *as such* present themselves in different registers. *Slang and pidgins* occupy the lowest rank,[297] while *ordinary vernaculars* stand at a higher level, reflecting significantly higher linguistic expectations in regard to usage, pronunciation, grammar, style, and so on. What people get away with in slang is not allowed, so to speak, in many everyday contexts, especially in writing and in professional interactions. Higher up still are so-called *prestige languages.* Of course, these are native languages for some people, but they are chosen as second or third languages by many others due to their reputation. French has been a prestige language for over a thousand years. For many centuries, Latin was a prestige language in Europe, as Classical Greek was for the Romans. Note that linguistic expectations here are even higher, as these languages are supposed to be a sign of education, culture, urbanity. A nineteenth-century Russian spoke French to show that he was cosmopolitan and upper-crust. Higher up still, and with the highest level of expectations, are *reserved languages.* The examples that come to mind were all at one time prestige languages, and now their use is often limited to religious purposes: Biblical Hebrew, Classical Greek, Christian Latin, Syriac, Old Church Slavonic, and, outside of Christianity, Sanskrit and Quranic Arabic. These languages are revered because they are languages in which we express our reverence; they have become reserved to (or at any rate specially associated with) sacred contexts.

One may also distinguish between a *lingua franca* and a prestige language. A *lingua franca* is adopted by speakers of other languages as a common means of communication for *practical* reasons, as when an Italian and a Japanese do business in English. But a prestige language is studied *in addition* for reasons of culture. One might, in other words, choose to study a prestige language even when there is no practical need to do so. Since reserved languages always come from the ranks of prestige languages, they are not used simply for reasons of practicality. In short: the lower registers of language tend to be more practical in nature, while the higher registers are more cultural, ceremonial, and numinous.

---

[297] A pidgin is defined as a "grammatically simplified means of communication that develops between two or more groups that do not have a language in common: typically, its vocabulary and grammar are limited and often drawn from several languages." https://en.wikipedia.org/wiki/Pidgin.

To reiterate: language is not merely a matter of practical communication; it is *also* an embodiment of thought and a work of art, a very high expression of our rationality, spirituality, and transcendence. People do not write poetry, for example, just for practical reasons. Part of what makes a prestige language prestigious is the depth, subtlety, and amplitude of expression found in it, owing to its rich history; and this is even more true of reserved languages, which, having been prayed with for centuries or even millennia, are saturated with sacral associations. The language has, in a sense, fused with the action, the rite, the content. It has itself become a symbol supporting and adorning other symbols.

Having grasped these distinctions, we see that the transition of Latin from being a vernacular to being a prestige language to becoming finally a reserved language is a natural one, paralleled by other languages, in a phenomenon seen throughout the world and throughout history.

Now, when a sacred liturgy is already conducted in a reserved language, any change from it is necessarily going to be a step down, linguistically speaking—perhaps a big step down, as we would normally be looking at "vernacularization," which is a lower register. Not only will a great deal of the conceptual content of the reserved language be lost, but its entire ethos, atmosphere, resonance, symbolic association, and consecrated status will be lost as well. One ends up losing far more than a language; one loses a culture, a psychological space, a spiritual environment, an entire world that has its own historical rootedness, unique qualities, and powerful assets.

Respecting God's Liturgical Providence

It is striking to consider what the Roman Pontiffs have taught on the subject of Latin. In 1922, Pope Pius XI wrote: "The Church . . . of its very nature requires a language which is universal, immutable, and non-vernacular."[298] In 1947, Pope Pius XII stated in his encyclical *Mediator Dei*: "The use of the Latin language, customary in a considerable portion of the Church, is a manifest and beautiful sign of unity, as well as an effective antidote for any corruption of doctrinal truth." In 1962, right on the eve of the Second Vatican Council, Pope John XXIII solemnly promulgated an Apostolic

[298] Pius XI, *Officiorum Omnium,* August 1, 1922, cited in John XXIII's *Veterum Sapientia.*

Constitution *Veterum Sapientia* in defense of Latin as the proper language for studies, documents, and liturgy in the Latin-rite Church. He says:

> The Church's language must be not only universal but also immutable. Modern languages are liable to change, and no single one of them is superior to the others in authority. Thus if the truths of the Catholic Church were entrusted to an unspecified number of them, the meaning of these truths, varied as they are, would not be manifested to everyone with sufficient clarity and precision. There would, moreover, be no language which could serve as a common and constant norm by which to gauge the exact meaning of other renderings. But Latin is indeed such a language. It is set and unchanging. It has long since ceased to be affected by those alterations in the meaning of words which are the normal result of daily, popular use . . .
>
> The Catholic Church has a dignity far surpassing that of every merely human society, for it was founded by Christ the Lord. It is altogether fitting, therefore, that the language it uses should be noble, majestic, and non-vernacular. In addition, the Latin language "can be called truly catholic." It has been consecrated through constant use by the Apostolic See, the mother and teacher of all Churches, and must be esteemed "a treasure . . . of incomparable worth."
>
> The employment of Latin has recently been contested in many quarters, and many are asking what the mind of the Apostolic See is in this matter. We have therefore decided to issue the timely directives contained in this document, so as to ensure that the ancient and uninterrupted use of Latin be maintained and, where necessary, restored.[299]

It deserves mention that this Constitution, although ignored by progressives and modernists and, after a while, even by conservatives, was never rescinded or contradicted by later popes in any document of comparable status. The universal truths it contains remain no less true in spite of the unwillingness of churchmen to implement its policies—just as the universal truths contained in the motu proprio *Summorum Pontificum* remain true regardless of the efforts of Pope Francis or Cardinal Roche to suppress the traditional liturgy of the Roman Church.

---

[299] John XXIII, *Veterum Sapientia,* with internal quotations from Pius XI and Pius XII.

We might be tempted to rush past the claim made by Popes Pius XII and John XXIII that the use of Latin safeguards orthodoxy, but it deserves a moment's attention. They are referring, of course, to the traditional Latin formulas used in the liturgy, in the Vulgate, in the Western Fathers of the Church, in the canons and decrees of ecumenical councils, in canon law and in other magisterial documents. This body of Latin teaching is astonishingly unified and consistent across centuries. Anyone who knows Latin well can pick up almost any Latin text from a period of over two thousand years and understand it. This record of continuous worldwide use of a single stable language is practically unique in human history and supports what the popes are claiming on its behalf.

The adaptation of liturgical books into the vernacular has, on the other hand, demonstrated the claim negatively: we are drowning in examples of dumbed-down, erroneous, and theologically problematic renderings, and quarrels over the register of language to be used in official translations are always brewing. The version of the Bible inflicted on American Catholics—the New American Bible—isn't even written in proper English; it's written in "Nabbish."[300] Whether one is talking about doctrinal texts or liturgical texts, the vernacular tends to be a non-stop headache, earache, and heartache.[301]

Latin is a crucial part of Catholic Tradition—not alongside it, but *within* it; indeed, it is that by which Tradition was transmitted in the Western world. It is part of the way God has provided for His Church. Even if modern people all agreed that Latin should be abolished completely, it would not cease to be part of Tradition: this is an unarguable and unchangeable fact. We might compare it to celibacy. The ecclesiastical law that a priest

---

300 See p. 113, n. 207 above.

301 The war opened with *Traditionis Custodes* is about so much more than the TLM. Francis is attempting to eliminate a whole way of being Catholic—even for people who never go to the TLM. By this, I mean a commitment to perennial truth, unchanging doctrine, moral absolutes, reverence for tradition, all of which attitudes are embodied in the immemorial Roman Rite, and which are, not surprisingly, under attack from the same people who stand against the traditional liturgy. Put it this way: without *Summorum Pontificum,* there can be no *Veritatis Splendor, Fides et Ratio,* or *Ecclesia de Eucharistia.* The English liturgist Clifford Howell was wont to say that the use of vernacular in the liturgy was pointing toward a new world order that couldn't otherwise be expressed coterminously with Latin; in other words, the new liturgy is a social movement based on a rejection of the traditional Catholic worldview. The Old Mass is too "off-message" now to be allowed to continue; that is what the "prison-guards of treachery" believe.

cannot marry derives from Tradition. Nowadays many "experts" say they know that celibacy is responsible for low numbers of priests. Next to the all-male priesthood and diaconate, celibacy is a favorite target for modernists, and sophisticated Catholics are supposed to be opposed to its retention. Yet it is part of Tradition, and as such irreversible.[302] Latin is similar to celibacy in this regard. While it is used in the liturgy not by divine law but by Church law, it is nevertheless part of Tradition (as are Greek, Slavonic, Syriac, Armenian, etc., for the Eastern churches) and should therefore be preserved, regardless of our personal modern opinions.

The error that led to the abolition of Latin was neoscholastic and Cartesian in nature—namely, the belief that the content of the Catholic Faith is not embodied or incarnate but somehow abstracted from matter. Thus, many Catholics think that Tradition means only some conceptual content that is passed down, irrespective of the *way* in which it is passed down. But this is not true. Latin itself is one of the things passed down, together with the content of all that is written or chanted in Latin. Moreover, as we have seen, the Church herself recognized this point on numerous occasions by singling out Latin for special praise, recognizing in it an efficacious sign of the unity, catholicity, antiquity, and permanence of the Latin Church. Latin thus possesses a quasi-sacramental function: just as Gregorian chant is "the musical icon of Roman Catholicism" (in Joseph Swain's phrase), so is Latin its "linguistic icon." Liturgical reformers in the grip of rationalism treated Latin like a mere accident, as if it were the dispensable packaging of a product. In reality, it is more like a person's skin: superficial, yet necessary for the body's structure and vitality.

Vatican II and the Latin *Novus Ordo*

Many Catholics throughout the world—including, apparently, bishops and cardinals—seem to be unaware that the teaching of Popes Pius XI, Pius XII, John XXIII, and other popes was deliberately echoed and confirmed by the Second Vatican Council's Constitution on the Sacred Liturgy *Sacrosanctum Concilium*: "The use of the Latin language is to be preserved

---

302 See Kwasniewski, *Treasuring the Goods of Marriage*, 164–75.

in the Latin rites"[303]; "steps should be taken so that the faithful may also be able to say or to sing together in Latin those parts of the Ordinary of the Mass which pertain to them"[304]; "in accordance with the centuries-old tradition of the Latin rite, the Latin language is to be retained by clerics in the Divine Office."[305] Contrary to the claims of Pope Francis, most of the bishops at the Second Vatican Council, if you study their speeches, actually supported the retention of Latin, which is why they voted for it in the final document.[306] The Council did open the door to a greater use of vernacular, but it did not *mandate* the vernacular, and in fact mandated *Latin*. The constitution was passed by a huge majority only because the bishops had been reassured that there would be a moderate reform, not a revolution.[307]

Thanks to the careful research of historians like Yves Chiron, we now know that Annibale Bugnini, who spearheaded the writing of *Sacrosanctum Concilium*, had—already before the Council began—successfully colluded with his teammates to execute such a revolution once the Council had ended, and in a Machiavellian manner, counseled the use of vague, ambiguous, and open-ended language with plenty of loopholes that could be exploited later on.[308] So, while Vatican II officially reaffirmed Latin in the liturgy and made a cautious opening to some use of the vernacular, what came afterward, with Pope Paul VI's support, neutralized or neutered it, and that pope's departure from both Tradition and the Council has never been opposed by any of his successors. This is one of the reasons why Latin will never reappear in any significant way in the Novus Ordo: Paul VI waved goodbye to it, and only traditionalists, who adhere to the preconciliar liturgy, have dared to question his good judgment in undertaking a wholesale reinvention of the Catholic Church's divine worship.

The Novus Ordo was created for maximum intelligibility, maximum ease of understanding. It was supposed to remove every possible barrier

---

303 *Sacrosanctum Concilium,* no. 36 §1.

304 *Sacrosanctum Concilium,* no. 54.

305 *Sacrosanctum Concilium,* no. 101 §1.

306 See Kwasniewski, "The Council Fathers in Support of Latin" and "What They Requested, What They Expected, and What Happened."

307 For the evidence that this was, in fact, exactly what transpired at the Council, see Shaw, *Latin Mass and the Intellectuals,* 114–18, and Kwasniewski, "The Lie That Was Told."

308 See Chiron, *Annibale Bugnini,* 61–82, especially 82.

to the comprehension of the faithful: they are supposed to see, hear, and know everything that is being said and done at every moment, instantly and without preparation or reflection. I shall explain in the next chapter what is wrong with this model and the presumption behind it. Let it suffice here to say that never in the entire history of apostolic Christianity, Eastern or Western, and never in the history of world religions, has this been the way anyone has ever thought about divine worship. In any case, if such immediate and total transparency is the goal aimed at, *everything* will have to be simplified, put into the most common language, and made visible and audible. Thus, the priest will be turned to face the people, he will have a microphone, there will not be much silence, only one thing will happen at a time, etc. If this is your paradigm for worship, then it's rather obvious that Latin—and Gregorian chant, too—will have no place in it, at least for 99% of congregations. This is why the "Latin Novus Ordo" necessarily "falls between two stools": it has neither the instant accessibility for which it was designed, nor the grandeur, solemnity, symbolic richness, and ceremonial depth of the Tridentine rite—that panoply of qualities that augments our awareness of mystery and our receptivity to truths that cannot be put into simple linguistic packages. In short, Latin befits the old Mass as stained glass befits a Gothic church, or gold befits a chalice, or silence befits the Roman Canon; it doesn't work with the design principles of the new Mass.[309]

The accessibility of the Novus Ordo is, however, illusory and deceptive in two ways. First, its verbal approach tricks us into thinking that we have understood or that we are capable of comprehending divine worship and the mysteries of Christ. Because its mode of active participation is very much on the surface, about voices and bodies in motion, we can easily pass through an entire such liturgy without having once pondered or interiorly prayed, without having suffered wonder, bewilderment, or awe. This is not a problem the Latin Mass has, in which there are frequent and diverse provocations to the acts of prayer, and where the intended participation is more of the heart and mind. Second, the Novus Ordo is accessible only to those who speak a given vernacular language, and who can hear it and follow it.

[309] See Kwasniewski, "The 'Latin Novus Ordo' Is Not the Solution."

In a multicultural world, and with factors like inadequate elocution, poor sound systems, or ambiant noise, the curse of Babel can quickly fall down on us. I would like to focus on this point for a moment.

Reversing the Curse of Babel

Fr. Louis Bouyer pointed out: "Every religious tradition represents language as a gift of the gods that makes society possible and continues to hold it together like a thread. Conversely, Genesis sees in the fragmentation of speech into mutually incomprehensible languages a curse from heaven upon a sinful society."[310]

The first Christian Pentecost, ten days after Our Lord ascended into heaven, is presented in the Acts of the Apostles as a reversal of the tower of Babel. The original curse upon ambitious man was to divide his progeny into a thousand tongues. Even if the rich poetic fruits of multiple languages can be counted a blessing willed by God, the difficulty and often impossibility of common discourse among rational animals is unquestionably a curse. This curse is renewed whenever we are confronted with a liturgy in which the use of some vernacular that is foreign to us effectively says: "This is not for you; it's only *for them*, for *that* demographic."

When particular apostolic churches such as those of Rome, Antioch, and Alexandria developed a common language of public worship within their spheres, it was a symbolic return to the prelapsarian condition of the Garden of Eden, when human beings would have spoken only one language. In the Latin of the Western liturgy, we are not confronted with a foreign vernacular that excludes us; rather, we hear the sound of a single voice that belongs to the Church at prayer, welcoming all nations and peoples into one celebration, united across countries and across centuries. In some dioceses, the Novus Ordo Mass can be found celebrated in fifteen different languages, and each language group is an island unto itself, hardly mixing with the other groups. But there are multi-ethnic and multilingual Latin Mass parishes where the Mass itself is truly the unifying force for all the subgroups, bringing them together in fraternal relations, and allowing them to mingle socially as well. How many of us have been to a Latin Mass and seen people

---

[310] Bouyer, *The Invisible Father,* 46–47.

of various ethnicities and nationalities, white, black, Asian, Hispanic, all gathered in one act of Catholic (that is, universal) worship? As Pope John XXIII pointed out, Latin belongs equally to everyone in general and to no one in particular. The Latin liturgy in history has always been an ethnically and culturally integrating force; it continues to build those bridges today.[311]

I had a potent experience of this a few years ago when visiting Poland for a conference. In spite of my surname, which is as Polish as pierogi and kielbasa, I hardly speak a word of Polish, which is widely considered a very difficult language to learn. For days, I had been surrounded with unintelligible noises to which everyone else could respond and I could not (thankfully the conference organizer provided me with earphones broadcasting a simultaneous English translation). One morning on my visit, I walked with a group of friends to Wawel Castle, one of the most beautiful and historic places in the city of Kraków, to reach a side chapel where Low Mass would be offered by a priest of the Priestly Fraternity of St. Peter.

We arrived just as Mass was starting. The comforting words of the Latin fell like a refreshing rain on my ears, or like a ray of light piercing the impenetrable fog of the foreign language of the country outside. We were in *God's* country now. The priest said the Mass deliberately and with an easily audible voice, so that I missed not a single word. Sadly, in response to the clumsy and illicit provisions of *Traditionis Custodes*, the Epistle and Gospel were given only in Polish, which suddenly plunged me into the fog of unintelligibility again and reminded me of how the vernacular not only

---

[311] Writing in praise of the education she received at Wyoming Catholic College—a four-year, integrated liberal arts program—Veronica Clarke describes the uniting power of the Western (Catholic) tradition with words that can be applied, *mutatis mutandis,* to the international, indeed supranational language that stood at the core of this tradition and served as its primary vehicle of transmission: "Insofar as the Church tells us that we are pilgrims in this world, it seems to anticipate those who have no nation, or have too many. The Church offers an antidote to the shortcomings of globalism: the fruits and riches of a Catholic tradition, larger than any national heritage, spanning continents and centuries, and the promise of a new kingdom. My classmates and I had different backgrounds and came from different places, but we were bound together through our shared faith, our liberal arts education, and our common goal: to be together in heaven. The riches of the Western tradition—the literature, the art, the music—were our common heritage. We were all part of one, holy, catholic, and apostolic Church" ("Why I Went to a Catholic College"). For profound arguments in defense of normative Latin, see Sebastian Morello, "Maistre, Latin, and the Conserving of Christendom" and Joseph Shaw, "Tito Casini on Latin," in Shaw, *Latin Mass and the Intellectuals,* 18–30 and 43–47; see also "Understanding Liturgical Participation" in Shaw, *Liturgy, Family, and Crisis,* 57–85.

includes the locals but excludes the stranger. It was the only part of the Mass that lost its world-embracing catholicity in favor of a narrow localization. At the conclusion of the Gospel, the server said: "*Laus tibi Christe*," and all was well again. The remainder of Mass alternated between moments of Latin that surfaced above the silence and the enveloping quiet in which the Word became flesh anew, as it were, upon the altar, in the power of His incarnation, passion, death, resurrection, and ascension.

That Mass in the Wawel side chapel was a perfect experience of the liturgy as synchronic and diachronic: synchronic, because I felt instantly at home in the very same liturgy said all across the world, wherever tradition is treasured—an experience I've now had dozens of times on my travels; diachronic, because it was substantially the same liturgy that had been prayed at most of the altars of Christendom in the West for centuries. Alcuin of Charlemagne's court, St. Anselm of Canterbury, St. Gertrude the Great, St. Thomas Aquinas, St. Ignatius of Loyola, St. Edmund Campion, St. Vincent de Paul, St. Thérèse of Lisieux, St. Padre Pio, St. Charles de Foucauld—all would have been at home, together with thousands of saints who worshiped the same way. With the traditional Latin Mass, across the ages and around the world, one is always at home. The miracle that undoes, for some sacred moments at least, the chaos of Babel demands the strong stability and inner coherence of the great Roman liturgy whose language gives to Latin-rite Catholics their very name.

Latin, Like Faith, Comes "From Without"

Our native language, our "mother tongue," comes from our earthly mother: when we are living inside her womb, her voice is the first we hear, and when we come forth into the world, we hear the same voice as we nestle in her arms. Our everyday vernacular is something we are, in a sense, equipped with by nature, by effortless immersion in the family culture. This language represents the *natural* order in which we live and move and have our natural being.

As Joseph Ratzinger writes, "nobody is born a Christian, not even in a Christian world and of Christian parents. Being Christian can only ever happen as a new birth. Being a Christian begins with baptism, which is death and resurrection, not with biological birth."[312] Even as baptism or rebirth comes to the Christian from outside, so, too, the sacral language in which we worship comes to us from outside, from Holy Mother Church, who teaches us a new Christian language—our *spiritual* "mother tongue" that represents the *supernatural* order in which we live and move and have our supernatural being. Latin-rite Catholics have a *sacral* language that comes to them "from outside," just as baptismal rebirth does.

The Christian liturgy should somehow convey to us that, when we enter the Lord's temple, we are speaking not with a merely natural speech, but with a supernatural speech, a language of saints, of angels, and of God. Obviously, Latin is not the only language that qualifies—as noted above, there are many reserved sacral languages used in traditional apostolic rites—but the language used in the liturgy should *not* be the everyday vernacular of the hearth and the marketplace, or even the technical speech of academic disciplines. It should be set apart by centuries of use consecrated to divine worship; in this way, it helps worshipers to set aside earthly cares and consecrate symbolic portions of our time to God alone. A traditional liturgical language is a reminder that our supernatural adoption into the family of God is more fundamental and more ultimate than any earthly family, citizenship, nation, or race.

Most importantly, something the Catholic Church in the West has practiced for over 1,600 years—something that nearly all of our thousands of canonized Western saints personally practiced—cannot be condemned without blasphemously denying that the Holy Spirit has been guiding the Church into the fullness of truth.[313] The Holy Spirit who gave linguistic utterance to the Apostles as they preached to all the nations also gave liturgical Latin to the Western Church as her inheritance, handed down from century to century with ever-increasing veneration. What was established by choice was confirmed by custom and preserved by piety. The forms of worship developed over centuries with a richness of content and texture that made it increasingly unlikely that such richness could ever be readily duplicated in or adapted to a foreign idiom; this made it all the more precious and worthy of assiduous

---

312 Ratzinger, *Truth and Tolerance,* 87.

313 See John 16:13; cf. Kwasniewski, *Once and Future Roman Rite*, 33–77, et passim.

retention.[314] Against the backdrop of experiments in vernacularization from the mid-twentieth century onward—experiments that could be called, with more justice, Babelization—an ever-increasing number of Catholics are coming to see that this unique and unitive Latin heritage remains precious and worthy of cultivation today.

Nor should we overlook the crucial fact that no modern vernacular is capable of conveying all that is contained in the traditional Latin prayers. Every translation is a betrayal; all the more so when we are looking at the vast treasury of liturgical Latin spanning centuries. A hand missal can give the gist of the content fairly well, but the Latin prayer says *more*, says it *better*, more subtly and fully and strikingly.[315] Does this make a difference? By all means. The one we are principally addressing is *God*, and how we speak to *Him* matters. When we offer Him solemn, beautiful, densely packed, highly-valued, saint-spoken prayer, it is pleasing in the way that an unblemished lamb is pleasing—in the way that the unblemished Logos offered on the Cross was pleasing. The very fact that countless holy men and women had the very same words on their lips over the centuries endows them with a special efficacy. According to St. Mectilde of Hackeborn, the court of heaven rejoices whenever it hears the same words its members prayed while on earth.[316]

---

314 John Lamont has made this argument forcefully: "Christianity was from the first a civilized religion—that is, a religion that used and incorporated the resources of civilization in its belief and practice, that was aimed at civilized people (among others), and that was intended to be suited to civilized people and to be capable of functioning as the religious part of their civilization. This was dictated by the logic of Christian theology: the human nature redeemed by Christ should be shown to reach its highest potential; the divinely revealed message should be expressed with the greatest power and majesty possible; the worship of God should be carried on using the highest forms of human culture. . . . The character of Christianity as a civilized religion includes its liturgy. The development of Christian liturgy as a form of civilization was hindered by the legal persecution of the religion by the Roman Empire in its first three centuries, but after Christianity was legalized by the emperor Constantine in 313 AD, this development was rapidly undertaken. The TLM is the civilized liturgy produced by Latin Christian civilization, as the Byzantine Rite is the civilized liturgy produced by Greek Christian civilization. The TLM, together with the music and architecture developed to accompany it, is indeed the central part of Latin Christian civilization, which would not exist if these things were removed from it. . . . The idea that a pope could replace the TLM by a new rite composed of texts of even more eloquent orthodoxy and piercing beauty is absurd. The richness of the TLM is the product of an entire civilization, and required a civilization to produce it; an entirely new rite would have to emerge from an entirely new Christian civilization. . . . An equivalent Christian civilization cannot be produced at will, and we cannot expect that another one will come into existence" (Lamont, "Dominican Theologian Attacks Catholic Tradition: Defending Kwasniewski against Donneaud's Positivist Reductionism").

315 See Foley, *Lost in Translation*.

316 Mectilde, *Liber Specialis Gratiae* 3.11, cited in Kwasniewski, "Praying in the Same Words."

Losing and Regaining Catholic Identity

Beyond its liturgical fallout, the abandonment of Latin has massive intellectual and theological consequences. The vast majority of Western Christian writing in all areas—theology, exegesis, canon law, liturgy, hagiography, etc.—was composed in Latin, and the vast majority of this literature has not been translated into modern languages. The radical progressives who waged war against Latin in the mid-twentieth century knew very well what they were doing: they wanted to blow up the bridge that connected Catholics with their heritage, their tradition, their collective memory. The vaunted "modernization" of the Church could be carried out only if the past were forgotten, sealed inaccessibly behind a wall of incomprehensibility. The loss of Latin has therefore had ramifications far beyond the sanctuaries of our churches, even if that is where we most notice its presence or absence. Heresy thrives on a combination of amnesia, anarchy, and novelty. The liturgical crisis is only one part of the larger crisis of Catholic identity in the West, which has more to do with language than most people realize.[317]

Following on this point, I think it's important for Catholics to realize that *all of us* should learn some Latin. When I understand the Latin of the liturgy, it doesn't lose its special character and sacred function or become any less wonderful; on the contrary, one's appreciation grows because one can savor its meaning and beauty. This is not *necessary* for fruitful worship, but it is a real advantage, and one that we should care to acquire. Latin was once a standard subject for Catholic students and many individuals

---

[317] The move away from Latin, as Robert W. Keim explains, has contributed to the shattering of the Faith, the loss of commonality in belief, practice, and vision: "In the Western Church, Latin was once the ideal complement to the plurality of tongues: a shared, sacred language that uplifted and united without encroaching upon local customs, folk culture, ethnic identity, and the judicious distribution of political and spiritual authority. But Latin is increasingly *persona non grata* in the postconciliar Church, and the Babelian tongue has returned with a vengeance: the language now spoken at the Vatican, a fusion of bureaucratese and Newspeak, has infiltrated every diocese on earth. Proclaimed *ad nauseam* from the high tower of papal authority, it promises to amalgamate the peoples of God into a formless mass of mediocrity and ambiguity. Having buried Christendom under six feet of vacuous teachings, sentimental palaver, and appallingly prosaic liturgies, Vaticanspeak has become the official language of the *civitas pontificis,* the vast ecclesiastical city built around the decadent postmodern papacy. Let us pray that the language of the Church regain its commitment to conviction, reality, beauty, and Truth. Let us pray that the good God will scatter the neo-Babelian empire of dissimulation, sophistry, and insufferable prolixity. *Let your speech be yea, yea: no, no: and that which is over and above these, is of evil*" (Keim, "The Tower, and the City, of Babel," in Kwasniewski, *Ultramontanism and Tradition,* 252).

learned it to a high degree. Practically speaking, it is not difficult to acquire some basic facility with the Latin language used in the liturgy. Simply by assisting at Mass and other ceremonies on a regular basis and using a hand missal, we will begin to pick up a rough-and-ready knowledge of the Latin vocabulary. Let's be honest: the *Gloria* and the *Credo* are not hard to follow! The more zealous could pick up a good Latin instructional book or enroll in an online course. Happily, there are already many people out there who are reviving the language, including in its *spoken* form. (Recall that Hebrew was considered a dead language until the Zionist movement and the State of Israel revived it as a spoken language; today, millions are fluent in it. Moslems study classical Arabic because they value their heritage. How embarrassing, how shameful it is that we Catholics care far less for our own heritage than Jews and Moslems do for theirs!) It should go without saying that children above all ought to learn Latin, since language acquisition is much easier for children than it is for adults. Singing Gregorian chant, whether informally at home or as part of a choir, is an important and enjoyable way to gain some acquaintance with the treasury of ecclesiastical Latin. I recommend, for example, singing the seasonal Marian antiphons at home as part of evening devotions: the *Alma Redemptoris Mater*, the *Ave Regina Caelorum*, the *Regina Caeli*, and the *Salve Regina*.

We must not be afraid to assert boldly that it is good and fitting and optimal to use Latin for the sacred liturgy—the solemn, public, formal, official worship of the Roman Catholic Church. The reasons for its use are so numerous and overwhelming, the substance and authority of tradition are so unanswerable, that there is no way to escape the conclusion that retaining Latin is a serious obligation before God, and abandoning it is an ungrateful repudiation of His liturgical Providence. In the midst of cultural diversity, the Catholic Church had the wisdom to recognize the spiritual power of central elements of unity that bring us together in confessing the one true Faith and paying homage to the Most Holy Trinity. May our Church leaders receive once again the spirit of wisdom and take steps to recover what was foolishly squandered in shortsighted reforms. We, for our part, are able to show our gratitude to God by maintaining and promoting the sound traditions of the Latin Church.

8

Why It Is Better Not to Understand Everything Immediately

"The new Mass is so clear, easy, accessible. The old Mass is obscure and demanding."

I enjoy keeping my finger on the pulse of how the Catholic and secular media are reporting on the resurgence of traditional forms of Catholic life and worship. You can learn a lot by considering how other people see you from the outside. Often enough, they make mistakes, even occasional howling blunders, but I also find that they seldom fail to perceive, with a mingled respect and curiosity, something different, special, intriguing—something that is perceived as countercultural, in a good way. I think there's more to it than "everyone roots for an underdog." It seems that everywhere there is a thirst for meaning, for contact with reality, for self-transcendence, and it also seems that the modern world—especially thanks to the stranglehold of technology, the internet, constant communication, and social media—continuously thwarts that vital contact with original reality, that possibility of escaping from the prison of the self, that quest for ultimate meaning rather than ephemeral information. So, whenever a newspaper, magazine, or website runs a major story on the traditional Latin Mass, I sit up and take note.

Just such an article appeared on October 26, 2023, in (of all places) *National Geographic*: "These devout young Catholics are embracing the old ways." The subtitle brought a smile: "The movement embraces some

Old World traditions that even the Church has referred to as backwards." For cultural anthropologists, this must be like stumbling across Tutankhamun's inviolate tomb! An observation by the author, Matthew Teague, caught my eye:

> Each week traditionalists gather at more than 1,200 sites, mostly in the United States. They embrace a version of religious life that had drifted out of fashion—the "smells and bells" of previous generations—and reach for symbols and language that bewilder the outside world, and which the congregants themselves may not fully understand.

Is this last observation—that even folks in the pews (and perhaps—shall we admit it?—some clergy as well) don't fully understand what they are seeing, hearing, saying, singing—meant as a criticism, or as a compliment? Or perhaps neither; could it be an implicit question about whether there might be a *positive* role for not understanding things fully? I can't help thinking of the remarkable words in the Byzantine Divine Liturgy of St. John Chrysostom, when the priest, right before consecrating the bread and the wine, prays:

> You brought us forth from non-existence into being, and raised us up again when we had fallen, and left nothing undone, until You brought us to heaven and bestowed upon us Your future kingdom. For all this we give thanks to You, and to Your only-begotten Son, and to Your Holy Spirit, for all that we know and all that we do not know, the manifest and the hidden benefits bestowed upon us.

Let's shift gears and look at this from another angle. Nowadays, the "slow movement" has really taken off. The reader has probably encountered phrases like slow food, slow wine, slow travel, slow reading, slow art, slow cinema, slow fashion, and even slow conversation (meaning, one in which each person is given the floor to say all that he or she wishes to say, without being interrupted—a technique that would be useful in many seminars at Great Books colleges!). The basic idea is "a cultural shift towards slowing down life's pace," letting things take the time they need in order to be good, optimal, fulfilling, or even, quite simply, human in scale. There are many ideas and personalities involved in this diffuse worldwide movement—many of them plainly contradictory—but I think it would be fair to say that, as a whole, it's a reaction against the rationalism and utilitarianism of the modern industrial age. The ubiquitous model of mass-production—"delivering the goods," whatever they are, as quickly and efficiently as possible—fails to distinguish between different kinds of goods and different ways of receiving them, how quickness and efficiency may affect their quality, and how, in general, the modern approach fails to take into account the diverse needs and abilities of individuals and communities.

In this chapter, I'd like to make a pitch for "slow liturgy." I will explain why our basic mental framework should not be capturable in the question, "What do I get out of the 60-minute Sunday Mass?," but rather, "What will I get out of an entire lifetime of faithfully immersing myself in the mysteries of the Mass?" If liturgical reformers and church leaders make it their basic assumption that liturgy is to be assessed on the basis of what one can immediately understand in that 60-minute Sunday Mass, they are setting up the people of God for a catastrophic failure. They should be asking how a liturgy should be if it is to be capable of sustaining and rewarding an entire lifetime's participation, so that it will be experienced less as a repetitious and burdensome duty and more as an ever-deeper entry into something both familiar and strange.

Justifying the Revolution

In the heyday of liturgical reform, which was the decade from 1964 to 1974, and for many long decades thereafter, the avalanche of changes to Catholic worship was often justified by a few magical phrases that would be thrown about almost talismanically, with an air of infinite superiority to the meager mentalities of lowly laity. The leading contender was certainly the phrase "active participation," which turned out to be quite ironic considering how many millions of people simply stopped going to church altogether (and therefore ceased to participate in *any* way), but along with that phrase, you'd often hear about "the needs of Modern Man," "meeting people where they're at," "doing like the early Church," and, what is of most interest to me at present, "greater accessibility."

The revised liturgy was supposed to be, and was claimed and asserted to be, "more accessible," but this is a monumental smokescreen if ever there was one. After all, nothing is more or less accessible in the abstract or without further qualification. One must always ask: "Accessible *to whom*? And giving access *to what*? And for the purpose of . . . ?" To the liturgical reformers, accessibility was primarily or exclusively a verbal-conceptual phenomenon: if you can immediately grasp this bite-sized chunk of content, without further preparation, explanation, or remainder of bewilderment, then it's considered to be accessible to you. The object of such immediate and complete comprehension obviously cannot be God, whom every orthodox theologian declares right off the bat to be incomprehensible; nor can it be man, who, as made unto God's image, is a mystery to himself; nor can it be the world, which is far too complicated and vast to fit into man's mind, even if a thousand Einsteins were to chip away at it; nor can it be the mysteries revealed by God in history and delivered in Scripture, since each one of these is a combination of all of the above. Therefore, a perfectly accessible liturgy, in the sense given above, would have to be about nothing, address no one, and lead nowhere.

This, admittedly, is a limit case fortunately never reached: there is always a residue of unintelligibility in *anything* human beings do, even if they are trying to avoid it. To the extent that any elements of traditional Christian liturgy remained intact, the incomprehensibility of God, of man, of the cosmos, and of the mysteries of Christ remained as well. Still, the reform introduced a fundamental tension between allowing the liturgy to be mysterious, as it must be, and trying, in the name of liturgical science, to purge it of the very features that tended to make it darksome, intricate, wondrous, full of awe, and yet, paradoxically, also orderly and ordering, familiar and comforting, unassuming and free of invasive sources of irritation.

It seems to me that there is a mighty irony at work in the revival of the traditional Latin liturgy of the Roman church. In spite of all the handwringing of scholars and tinkerers about the horrible Middle Ages that led us into what Archbishop Bugnini called "lack of understanding, ignorance, and the 'dark night' of a worship that lacks a face and light, at least for those out in the nave,"[318] the irony is that new generations find the old rites in general quite sufficiently accessible, indeed *more* so than they do the new rites—provided one has a broader and deeper definition of "accessibility." The reason is not far to seek. The old liturgy appeals more consistently, more powerfully, to the *full range* of reality, natural and supernatural; of what it is to be human; of how we express ourselves, and what we are trying to express in words, gestures, songs, and quiet sighs. It appeals to all the senses, the various ages and temperaments and personalities, the different levels on which our interior life plays out and intersects with the external world.[319]

Non-Verbal Communication

The traditional Roman liturgy—and this is true of any of Christianity's organically-developed apostolic rites—recognizes a truth on which psychologists never tire of discoursing: human beings primarily communicate non-verbally. As a matter of fact, we are never *not* communicating something, even if we are not talking or have no intention of conveying a meaning. Orderliness and deferentiality speak volumes, just as carelessness and casualness do. A liturgy, like any human ceremony, is constantly communicating through every word, stance, gesture, position, action, and silence. The old liturgy, by harnessing and regulating these things in a harmonious way to bring out their full interactive meaning, is *more communicative*; in that sense, it proffers more to access, and in more ways. The reformed liturgy, by eliminating traditional non-verbal language and then leaving so much to chance and idiosyncrasy, thins the content and its delivery, while mingling it with extraneous and contradictory matter.

A video on body language by a former FBI agent, Joe Navarro, sharpened my awareness of the importance of small *and non-verbal* details in liturgy (and, therefore, the importance of being aware of them and being faithful to their proper execution). This expert looks at people from the point of view of an agent trying to assess potential threats or the trustworthiness of witnesses:

---

[318] Bugnini, *The Reform of the Liturgy,* 283; see also Ostrowski, "A 1969 Quote."

[319] For example, on the relationship of children with the TLM, see Kwasniewski, *Reclaiming Our Roman Catholic Birthright,* 235–80.

> How we dress, how we walk, have meaning, and we use that to interpret what's in the mind of the person. We are never in a state where we're not transmitting information. We're all transmitting at all times; we choose the clothes that we wear, how we groom ourselves, how we dress, but also how do we carry ourselves, are we coming to the office on this particular day with a lot of energy, or are we coming in with a different sort of pace . . . and what we look for are differences in behavior, down to the minutiae of: what is this individual's posture as they walk down the street, are they on the inside of the sidewalk, on the outside, can we see his blink rate, how often he is looking at his watch . . . You can have a poker face, but you can't have a poker body—somewhere it's going to be revealed. We talk about non-verbals because it matters, because it has gravitas, because it affects how we communicate with each other. When it comes to non-verbals, this is no small matter. We primarily communicate non-verbally and we always will.[320]

Phrases like: "we primarily communicate non-verbally" and "we're never not communicating something" are very relevant to the celebration of Mass. Every gesture—for example, the course and speed of movement around the altar; where, and when, the priest is standing or sitting; how he places his hands or bows his head; whether the priest's gaze is directed out to the people or modestly downcast; how the sacred vessels are treated, and how the Blessed Sacrament is approached and handled—every gesture like this confesses what the celebrant, and the people, believe they are doing.

Why is it that the liturgical reformers seemed so tone-deaf or clueless about the most obvious things in life? Did they not realize that changing the body language, the gestures, postures, orientation, signs of veneration, custody of the eyes, would effect a sea change in mentality and spirituality? Or . . . was it that they understood this *perfectly well*, and therefore abolished, piece by piece, a non-verbal language based in the Catholic Faith, substituting for it another with a contrary message? Consider the well-documented loss of faith in the Real Presence of Our Lord. This was not an unfortunate result of a "lack of catechesis." It was the result of a *renovated* catechesis. It was not an accidental byproduct of liturgical reform

[320] Navarro, "Former FBI Agent Explains How to Read Body Language."

gone awry; it was the outcome of a new ecclesiology that identified the worshiping community with "the Body of Christ" and sought to oppose the supposed "fetishism" or "magic" of the Eucharistic cultus that had developed in the Church for at least a thousand years. As Martin Mosebach points out:

> An entire bouquet of respectful gestures had surrounded the sacrament of the altar, and these gestures were the most effective homily, which continually showed priests and faithful quite clearly the mysterious presence of the Lord under the forms of bread and wine. We can be certain: no theological indoctrination of so-called enlightened theologians has so harmed the belief of Western Catholics in the presence of the Lord in the consecrated Host as the innovation of receiving communion in the hand, accompanied by the abandoning of all care in the handling of the particles of the Host.
>
> Yet can one really not receive communion reverently in the hand? Of course that is possible. Yet once the traditional forms of reverence were in place, exercising their blessed influence on the consciousness of the faithful, their discontinuation contained the message—and not just for the simple faithful—that so much reverence was not really necessary, and along with that there consequently grew the (initially unspoken) conviction that there was *nothing there* that demanded respect.[321]

Fr. Roberto Spataro makes a similar but broader point:

> Humility is more than a virtue. It is the condition for a virtuous life. Watch the bows and genuflections the humble man makes faithfully before God in a spirit of obedience, acknowledging His merciful sovereignty, His love without bounds, His creative wisdom. . . . It [the old rite] turns to Him through the means of a sacred language differing from ordinary speech, because in the harmonious order of creation that the liturgy represents in its rituals, there is never a monotonous repetition or tedious uniformity, but a symphony of diversity, sacred and profane, without opposition, respecting the alterity of each. Here reason also renounces an excessive use of words that unfortunately exists in the liturgical praxis inaugurated by the *Novus Ordo*, interpreted by

[321] Mosebach, *Subversive Catholicism,* 80–81.

> many priests as the opportunity for pure garrulousness. In the old rite, on the other hand, reason appeals to other dimensions of communication and, besides words pronounced or sung, also gives silence a place. This silence becomes the atmosphere, impregnated with the Holy Spirit, in which believing thought and prayerful word is born.[322]

What we do with our bodies is just as communicative as what we say with our lips. The liturgy should therefore govern the motions and dispositions of our limbs and senses, harnessing them as symbols of truth and instruments of sanctification. This will help us to pray, to enter more deeply into communion with the Lord, and to yield ourselves to truths that cannot be put into words or captured in concepts. As St. Paul says in the Epistle to the Romans, we should make our bodily members instruments of righteousness: "Neither yield ye your members as instruments of iniquity unto sin"—the sin of irreverence, of disrespect for holy things, of casual, haphazard, and inconsiderate behavior during our formal audience before the great King—"but present yourselves *to God*," in theocentric worship that governs our self-presentation, "as those that are alive from the dead"—the living death of modern anti-natural, anti-Christian culture—"and your members as instruments of justice unto God,"[323] the justice, namely, of the virtue of religion.

Incomprehension, Wonder, and the Search for Truth

After this discussion of non-verbal communication, I would like to circle back to my remarks about accessibility as a function of rational understanding, as this is an area in which many huge mistakes were made in the twentieth century—mistakes from which we are still reeling decades later. It was (and remains) a commonplace of liturgical reform that the people in the pews "must understand *all* the prayers and ceremonies": there must be no remainder, no residue of incomprehension. This drove the total vernacularization, the dumbed-down translations, the saying of nearly everything out loud, the visibility of the priest *versus populum*, and so forth. Nothing must be left inaccessible, implicit, hidden, or difficult to access.

---

[322] Spataro, *In Praise of the Tridentine Mass,* 54.

[323] Rom. 6:13, emphasis added.

What I find curious is that this is completely contrary to the normal way in which human beings learn and grow.

As babies and children, we are constantly up against what we cannot understand. Those who spend time with little ones see heart-wrenching (and sometimes amusing) exhibitions of frustration every day, as these eager souls struggle to grasp and navigate the giant world they must live in. Our intellectual growth occurs as a result of the inward drive to know ("all men by nature desire to know," Aristotle famously said at the opening of his *Metaphysics*). Wonder is the name of our reaction to what we cannot instantly grasp, what we can see but not see through. In a healthy soul, this wonder then moves us to seek to understand. When we lose the capacity for wonder, we lose the capacity for learning.

In the Gospels, we see several instances of incomprehension, where Our Lord does not say, "Okay, let's break down into synodal discussion groups and get to the bottom of this. Voting will follow, then a post-synodal dominical exhortation." He lets His companions stew in their lack of understanding because they still need to grow, and they need the challenge of not getting it. Mary and Joseph didn't understand the words He was saying; His Apostles didn't understand, either.[324] Jesus often did things without explaining why, as when He sent His Apostles across the lake without Him, knowing He would later walk across it and scare the living daylights out of them; or when He slept in the hull during the big storm; or when He escaped to go into remote places to pray, in spite of the crowds clamoring for more sermons.[325] Scripture tells us that many of the most important things Jesus said were understood by His disciples only after the Resurrection or after Pentecost. With his usual eloquence, Anthony Esolen explains why this is to be expected:

> The word of God is always beyond our comprehension and sometimes even beyond our apprehension. We never know all that it means; and sometimes we hardly know what it means at all, or that it means anything at all. It must be so. God is our Creator. We cannot have it out with Him in mere rational debate, as Job seems to want to have done.

---

[324] See Luke 2:50; Matt. 16:9; Luke 18:34.

[325] See Mark 6:45–51; Matt. 8:23–27; Luke 6:12.

> We must then wait upon him. We do not see so that we might obey. We obey that we might see: increase of vision and understanding is dependent upon obedience. It is not I who say so. The Lord says it. If we love Him, we will keep his commandments, and then he will dwell within us, making Himself manifest to us (see John 14:15–24). Many of those commandments will be hard for us to understand.[326]

St. Augustine's *De Doctrina Christiana*—a work justly deemed the most important and influential writing on scriptural exegesis in Church history—proposes that our Divine Teacher has made parts of Scripture difficult for us as a deliberate pedagogical strategy:

> Some of the expressions are so obscure as to shroud the meaning in the thickest darkness. And I do not doubt that all this was divinely arranged for the purpose of subduing pride by toil, and of preventing a feeling of satiety in the intellect, which generally holds in small esteem what is discovered without difficulty. . . . Nobody, however, has any doubt about the facts, both that it is pleasanter in some cases to have knowledge communicated through figures, and that what is attended with difficulty in the seeking gives greater pleasure in the finding. For those who seek but do not find suffer from hunger. Those, again, who do not seek at all because they have what they require just beside them often grow languid from satiety. Now weakness from either of these causes is to be avoided. Accordingly the Holy Spirit has, with admirable wisdom and care for our welfare, so arranged the Holy Scriptures as by the plainer passages to satisfy our hunger, and by the more obscure to stimulate our appetite.[327]

If all of Scripture were transparently obvious, we would quickly get bored and toss the book aside. In fact, we would not be able to believe it held the words of the eternal, infinite, and therefore incomprehensible God. Yes, these words are proportioned to us and our abilities, much as the Incarnation "proportions" God to our humanity; yet they also outstrip our abilities and will always do so. The most audacious sin of biblical scholarship consists not in any particular error but in the rationalism that aspires

---

326 Esolen, "Male and Female He Made Them."

327 Augustine, *On Christian Doctrine,* Bk. 2, ch. 6 (or in some editions, ch. 7).

either to arrive at a total explanation with no remainders or, failing that, to identify the text's supposed errors. Unpacking the insights of Augustine, Joseph Shaw writes:

> An opaque symbol may stick in the memory and stimulate the imagination more than a clear one, and it can more easily bear multiple and profound meanings. A symbol which conveys something too deep for words is not a symbol whose meaning can be explained in a couple of sentences.
>
> These realities were certainly not lost on the authors of Scripture. Here we find a collection of stories, sayings, and other texts which are complex and frequently opaque. If many confusing passages can be clarified with a little exegesis, other passages, which appear reasonably clear at first glance, can on closer inspection reveal unexpected complexity. This is not exactly a problem: it is simply a reflection of the richness of the text. Our participation in God's Word would not be improved by the substitution of a simplified, children's version of the text. Our Lord spoke in parables not to confuse people or limit the impact of his preaching, but to reach the sincere seeker after truth who was prepared to ponder his words. The most baffling of stories, like Jacob wrestling with God, can be the objects of the most powerful religious art, and make a home for themselves in readers' imaginative lives. Some things, again, can be understood by those who cannot articulate their understanding. Other things can rest in our memory before being activated, like an unexploded bomb, perhaps decades later, by some chance event or conversation. We should not expect, or even desire, to recover the full meaning of a passage of Scripture, without leaving anything behind, as we might squeeze a sponge dry. We can rather look forward to seeing another aspect of it when we return to meditate upon it years later.[328]

Traditional Liturgy: Before Us and Beyond Us

The Augustinian insight into Scripture can be applied analogously to the Church's traditional rites of divine worship. As visible, audible, tangible events that take place in our midst, such liturgies are proportioned to human abilities and needs, yet they also challenge us to go beyond where we happen

[328] Shaw, *Liturgy, Family, and Crisis,* 26–27.

to be at any point in our lives. The asceticism of penitential seasons and scattered days of fasting is an obvious way in which traditional rites challenge worshipers; but a more subtle challenge comes from the length, complexity, and density of their prayers and ceremonies, which confront us with content we cannot fully grasp all at once.[329] It will take a lifetime of patient experience and diligent pondering to get to the bottom of what the Church, with the inherited prayer of millennia, is doing and conveying to us. The liturgy sparks our wonder: Why is *this* being said or done? Reflection, or sometimes a flash of intuition, shows us that what may have initially appeared random, incidental, awkward, even downright useless, is a venerable relic, a sweet secret, a precious mnemonic, a lesson in piety. Our humility grows when we realize that we will never, as a matter of fact, "get to the bottom of it."

The most poisonous mentality we could possibly bring to the liturgy is that of rationalism: the assumption either that the liturgy is full of errors and in need of correction by specialists, or that it can be totally and adequately explained to the mental satisfaction of a person living in, say, 1945 or 1965 or 2025. Not surprisingly, a centuries-old liturgical rite baffles people and attracts people in different ways, for different reasons, at different times across history and even at different phases across the lifespan of one and the same person. This is as it *should* be; were we to succeed in creating a liturgy perfectly accessible, transparent, and comprehensible to the people of our day (or to a man at a particular age of life), it would no doubt cease to be of much help to people from a sufficiently different period (or to the same person at a different age). Not to mention the fact—too often ignored, it would seem, by modern liturgists—that at any given moment, a church building will be holding a large variety of people with quite varied backgrounds, abilities, learning styles, needs, and desires. The proportion of the congregation consisting of logical, analytical, word-oriented aural learners will always be rather small. What of the "infant, mewling and puking"[330]

---

[329] Thus, although the Byzantine Divine Liturgy is often celebrated in the language of the people, it is at the same time so diffuse, prolix, and repetitious, so saturated with imagery, and so complex in the number and variety of its components that it presents a *different* kind of difficulty of access than the shorter Roman Rite with its intervals of Latin and silence. Both, in very different ways, confront the worshiper with a wall that cannot be seen through but must be patiently scaled.

[330] Shakespeare, *As You Like It,* Act II, scene 7.

and the baby's harried parents; the daydreaming artist; the weary worker in search of a quiet pew; the old lady who basks in the warm light of the stained glass as she enjoys the touch of God without words? There is room for everyone in a Catholic church, but not in a rationalist rite.

Indeed, a good case can be made that it is the logical, analytical, word-oriented aural learner who most of all needs the traditional Roman Rite, in order to be liberated from excessive attachment to rational analysis and thrown into a wonder-bearing milieu that eludes immediate resolution. We shouldn't forget that St. Thomas Aquinas, who is a fair candidate for the most analytical human being who ever lived, was nourished by a daily fare of two Low Masses—one that he offered, and another that he served. In the monastic ambiance of the Dominican rite, he had the contemplative leisure to yield himself to (in Pope John Paul II's phrase) "Eucharistic amazement." The beloved poem *Adoro te devote* is handed down to us as a prayer that Friar Thomas would recite during the elevations.

The liturgy must be rather vast and complicated and full of symbolic words and gestures if it is to offer plenty for *anyone* to connect with or hold on to or become "hooked" by. In this way, it is like Scripture—a huge library of very diverse types of writing with "something for everyone," but more importantly, something that goes beyond everyone: the mystery of God who simultaneously reveals and conceals Himself, as if delighting to be chased and caught and chased again. The Italian poet and liturgical traditionalist Cristina Campo sees exactly this parallel:

> Rite is life, like the Scriptures—like the sun that every day rises, shines, and sets, yet remains inexhaustibly mysterious and different. The immutability of the true rite and all traditions was willed by God precisely so that in that cosmic, infallible return of figures we might proceed each day a little further into the unfathomable complexity of their meanings: that which will never allow itself to be expressed in rational concepts, but only to be indicated, alluded to in divinely ordained gestures, sounds, symbols.[331]

St. John Henry Newman describes this trait of Scripture in words that apply no less readily to ancient forms of worship:

---

[331] "Cristina Campo," translation mine.

> It is in point to notice also the structure and style of Scripture, a structure so unsystematic and various, and a style so figurative and indirect, that no one would presume at first sight to say what is in it and what is not. It cannot, as it were, be mapped, or its contents catalogued; but after all our diligence, to the end of our lives and to the end of the Church, it must be an unexplored and unsubdued land, with heights and valleys, forests and streams, on the right and left of our path and close about us, full of concealed wonders and choice treasures.[332]

"Concealed wonders and choice treasures": think of the veil in front of the tabernacle, the veil over the chalice, the veils on ladies' heads, the humeral veil around the paten held up by the subdeacon . . . all of these things reveal something by concealing it, but without a logical "plan" that governs them such as a committee might have drafted.

Summarizing much of what has been said so far, Urban Hannon draws out the parallels between Scripture and the liturgy:

> Like all the best things, the Mass is hard for us to understand. Its texts are hieratic and exotic and often inaudible, its movements hierarchical and ritualized and often invisible. In recent years, we have seen many liturgists try to solve for this difficulty, by calling for the Mass to be simplified, made transparent and plain, and translated into an everyday idiom. But if the mystical meaning of the Mass is something like the spiritual sense of sacred scripture, then on St. Thomas Aquinas's principles, this push for vulgarization is a terrible mistake. It would be like replacing the inspired word of God—which is often similarly difficult and obscure—with a children's picture Bible. Whereas for St. Thomas, the scriptures are difficult by design, not only because the richness of the form should fit the richness of the content, but also because an easier text would not hold our attention anyway. St. Thomas's *expositiones Missae* suggest that the same logic applies to the rites of the Mass. It is not a mistake that the liturgy is mysterious—it unveils precisely by veiling. After the example of St. Thomas, the right response to the difficulty of understanding the Mass is not to dispel the difficulty, to dispel the mystery, but to contemplate it.[333]

332 Newman, *Essay on the Development of Christian Doctrine,* I, 2, §1, no. 14, p. 71.

333 Hannon, *Thomistic Mystagogy,* 96–98.

Enemies of the "Sense of Mystery"

Now, someone might take offense at Augustine's claim that God intentionally made the path to Himself difficult. In his letter *Desiderio Desideravi*, Pope Francis complains about liturgy that employs what he calls a "sense of mystery," which can be defined as a "being overcome in the face of an obscure reality or a mysterious rite."[334] From the context, he seems to have in mind things like the priest "with his back to the people," prayers said *sotto voce* in a sacral tongue, clouds of incense blurring the line of vision, the ringing of little bells and big bells during the elevations of the Host and chalice, the making of many signs of the cross to which medievals attributed allegorical significance.[335] These sorts of things heighten the feeling of something special, different, strange, beyond reach, something that is in our midst but somehow off limits, beyond our control and demanding our utmost respect. The pope, in company with professional liturgists, has no patience for such things: "If the reform has eliminated that vague 'sense of mystery,'" he writes, "then more than a cause for accusations, it is to its credit." How can one not be reminded here of Alexis De Tocqueville's description of American frontiersmen—a description that equally befits the modern Europeans who drove the liturgical reform:

> As it is on their own testimony that they are accustomed to rely, they like to discern the object which engages their attention with extreme clearness; they therefore strip off as much as possible all that covers it, they rid themselves of whatever separates them from it, they remove whatever conceals it from sight, in order to view it more closely in the broad light of day. This disposition of mind soon leads them to condemn forms, which they regard as useless and inconvenient veils placed between them and the truth.[336]

Yet when we try to expose the nakedness of reality, we are stymied; just as we understand one thing, we stumble upon another gap we cannot cross. By the time we learn to cross it, another gap has opened. Can we truly deny that life, the soul, the universe, reality, above all God and the things of

[334] Francis, *Desiderio Desideravi,* no. 25.

[335] See Barthe, *A Forest of Symbols.*

[336] de Tocqueville, *Democracy in America,* Bk. II, sect. 1, ch. I.

God, are deeply mystifying and cannot be stripped bare "in the broad light of day"? To write off the "sense of mystery" would betray a Kantian belief that the human mind is capable of wrapping itself around God's revelation and digesting it for breakfast: "religion within the limits of reason alone." Mystery is truth that is luminous and yet inexhaustible, unconquerable. As in Rudolf Otto's definition of the sacred, mystery is both fascinating and overwhelming, even at times terrifying. Mystery is ineluctably mystifying.

Jesus mystified His parents and His Apostles. He remains for all time the prince of peace and provoker of paradox, the Truth that gives Himself to us not as a tidy possession but as a Life to live and a Way to follow. We are promised that at the end, when we pass through the final mysterious gate of death, we will see Him face to face, gaze upon His beauty, understand Him at last—but still not comprehend, for only God is fully transparent to Himself. There's not the remotest possibility of boredom in heaven; we are too busy resting in the Eternal Act, too enamored of Love to fall back on ourselves.

What Do We Mean by "Mystery" Anyway?

As a professor of theology, I often wondered what new college students were thinking when they heard the word "mystery" in class. In the wide world out there, I suspect that the term only comes up in connection with novels, where the mystery—that is, the initially unexplained crime, usually murder—has to be figured out, the clues deciphered, the inexplicable accounted for, by a brilliant detective who, as we say, solves the mystery. The term means nothing other than a set of circumstances that are temporarily obscure due to lack of data and intellectual acumen. It is something that can be *solved*: the mystery is something you intend to get rid of, if you can. Another place where you find the word in common use today is in the David Attenborough-type nature program, whose narrator might say: "The brown-crested billy-bong-bird's predilection for a diet of poisonous purple fungus is a mystery to ornithologists to this day"—implying that they just haven't figured out the answer yet, but stay tuned for next year's documentary.

To clear away these distracting reductionist meanings, I made a point of asking my students in theology class what we mean when we say that, for example, the Blessed Trinity or the Incarnation is a mystery. They usually said something like this: "A mystery is something you can't understand, something you don't see and can't explain, a secret or a puzzle or a paradox. But maybe it will all get cleared up in the next life: God's a mystery to us here below, but surely, He's plain as day in the world to come?" It was a moment of special joy to be able to say in response: "Actually, no—God is an infinite mystery that can never be fathomed or comprehended. He will be a mystery to us forever in heaven, *indeed more than he is now.*"

But this assertion demands unpacking if one doesn't wish to be a tease. Fortunately, the heavy lifting has been done by one of the most brilliant theologians of modern times, Matthias Scheeben, who writes in his masterpiece, *The Mysteries of Christianity*:

> Christianity entered the world as a religion replete with mysteries. It was proclaimed as the mystery of Christ (Rom 16:25–27; Col 1:25–27), as the "mystery of the kingdom of God" (Mk 4:11; Lk 8:10). Its ideas and doctrines were unknown, unprecedented; and they were to remain inscrutable and unfathomable. The mysterious character of Christianity, which was sufficiently intelligible in its simplest fundamentals, was foolishness to the Gentiles and a stumbling block to the Jews; and since Christianity in the course of time never relinquished and could never relinquish this character of mystery without belying its nature, it remained ever a foolishness, a stumbling block to all those who, like the Gentiles, looked upon it with unconsecrated eyes or, like the Jews, encountered it with uncircumcised heart. . . .
>
> The greater, the more sublime, and the more divine Christianity is, the more inexhaustible, inscrutable, unfathomable, and mysterious its subject matter must be. If its teaching is worthy of the only-begotten Son of God, if the Son of God had to descend from the bosom of His Father to initiate us into this teaching, could we expect anything else than the revelation of the deepest mysteries locked up in God's heart? Could we expect anything else than disclosures concerning a higher, invisible world, about divine and heavenly things, which "eye hath not seen, nor ear heard," and which could not enter into the heart of any man (cf. 1 Cor 2:9)? . . .

> Mysteries must in themselves be lucid, glorious truths. The darkness can be only on our side, so far as our eyes are turned away from the mysteries, or at any rate are not keen enough to confront them and see through them. There must be truths that baffle our scrutiny not because of their intrinsic darkness and confusion, but because of their excessive brilliance, sublimity, and beauty, which not even the sturdiest human eye can encounter without going blind. . . .
>
> Only God's cognition excludes all mysteries, because it springs from an infinite Light which with infinite power penetrates and illuminates the innermost depths of everything that exists. . . .
>
> Mysteries become luminous and appear in their true nature, their entire grandeur and beauty, only when we definitely recognize that they are mysteries, and clearly perceive how high they stand above our own orbit, how completely they are distinct from all objects within our natural ken. And when, supported by the all-powerful word of divine revelation, we soar upon the wings of faith over the chasm dividing us from them and mount up to them, they temper themselves to our eyes in the light of faith which is supernatural, as they themselves are; then they display themselves to us in their true form, in their heavenly, divine nature. The moment we perceive the depth of the darkness with which heaven veils its mysteries from our minds, they will shine over us in the light of faith like brilliant stars mutually illuminating, supporting, and emphasizing one another; like stars that form themselves into a marvelous system and that can be known in their full power and magnificence only in this system.[337]

Many of the points made by Scheeben have their analogy in the experience of the traditional Latin Mass. There, we encounter a world of mysteries, interlaced and overawing, in which God is at home and we are, so to speak, the outsiders who have dared to enter. Our intellect is never fully adequate to the sheer massiveness and volume of what we behold, in part because it is *presented* to us in a density of overlapping words and actions that go beyond the powers of any one finite agent to grasp. Not everything "makes sense," even after many visits. Thank God for that. My mind, and

[337] Scheeben, *Mysteries of Christianity*, 3, 4, 6, 8, 19. The introduction to this book (pages 3–21) counts as one of the most outstanding texts ever written in Catholic theology.

your mind, is too small to compass the elaborate language of encounter distilled over thousands of years of pagan, Jewish, and Christian worship. We are allowed to be there and to absorb what we can, when and as we can, because it is *good*: "Master, it is good for us to be here . . ."[338] There is always plenty going on "up there" in the sanctuary, but also a strange serenity all around, at times so palpable it feels as if time has stopped, space has condensed, eons have collapsed, individuals have coalesced around the sovereign Other who is "more within than the innermost in me and higher than the highest in me."[339]

"Lost in Wonder at the God Thou Art"[340]

The specific perfection I have tried to describe is one that authors on the subject frequently circle around as they seek words for something at once obvious and subtle. Fr. Spataro observes:

> Reason is not tempted to be puffed up, as happens in the revolutionary process, because in the old rite not everything can or ought to be explained by reason which, for its part, is content to adore God without comprehending Him.[341]

Joseph Ratzinger notes the supreme fittingness of the silence that descends on a church during the Roman Canon as whispered in the old rite:

> Anyone who has experienced a church united in the silent praying of the Canon will know what a really filled silence is. It is at once a loud and penetrating cry to God and a Spirit-filled act of prayer. Here everyone does pray the Canon together, albeit in a bond with the special task of the priestly ministry. Here everyone is united, laid hold of by Christ, and led by the Holy Spirit into that common prayer to the Father which is the true sacrifice—the love that reconciles and unites God and the world.[342]

---

338 Luke 9:33.

339 Augustine, *Confessions* III.6.11: "*interior intimo meo et superior summo meo.*"

340 The phrase is taken from Gerard Manley Hopkins's translation of St. Thomas's hymn *Adoro te devote.*

341 Spataro, *In Praise of the Tridentine Mass,* 54.

342 Ratzinger, *The Spirit of the Liturgy,* 215–16.

As the prophet Habakkuk says: "The Lord is in his holy temple; let all the earth keep silence before him!"[343] Some spiritual writers parallel the inaudible recitation of the Canon to the invisible miracle of transubstantiation: the incomprehensibility of a mystery that transcends the created mind is underlined in both ways. The Savior's presence is concealed to bodily senses, as an invitation to open the eye and ear of the heart.

Those of us who love the traditional Roman liturgy find one of its great and consistent attractions to be the way it does not attempt to hand itself to us on a platter, affirming our rationalistic tendencies and patting us on the back for participation ("'A' for Active!"). Instead, it keeps its focus inflexibly on God and seems almost indifferent to whoever is around—paradoxically, a fine pedagogy for stimulating interest in what is so real that it not only exceeds our poor powers but outweighs us entirely. As we said earlier, the copious rubrics make the priest, in St. Thomas's placid description, an "animate instrument": he, too, is nowhere near as important as the One whom he serves, in whom he sinks his distinctive personality.[344] We are allowed to be anonymous, quiet, focused, free—"lost, all lost in wonder at the God Thou art." A lady with whom I was corresponding wrote to me:

> I continue to be awestruck by the overwhelming sense of God's presence in the TLM. I'm still reeling from the contrast [with where I used to go] but in a good way. I finally understand all of the references to the Mass as a *cosmic reality*. I finally understand why preconciliar authors attained to such profundity and to such reverence for the Mass. I keep waiting for all of this to wear off as novelty recedes, but it isn't wearing off. Deep down, I don't expect it to.

As to that last sentence: I myself have been attending the old Latin Mass for over thirty years, and the sense of wonder, the regimented peace, the freedom of prayer, the desire awakened again and again for God, the joy (and frankly the relief) of never seeing any human being as the center of attention—all of this hasn't "worn off." The old rite is ever-new and ever-renewing. This "time outside of time," this immersion in God, has become the haven of my heart; it structures my day, my week, my life. I could not live well without it.

---

[343] Hab. 2:20.

[344] See chapter 4.

Wonder Is Meant to Lead to Wisdom

A final clarification is in order. My thesis is not that we should just float sleepily in a sea of confusion. *Not understanding* is beneficial to the extent that we *seek to understand*, just as wonder should provoke us to go "further up and further in."[345] For we are driven by grace to the *vision* of God, and likewise we are driven by grace to know the meanings of Scripture and to know the meanings of the liturgical rites. The lover wants to know the beloved and everything about the beloved. A laziness contented with passivity would have nothing admirable about it.[346]

In a remarkable 1978 speech, Pope John Paul II quoted Cicero: *Non enim tam praeclarum est scire Latine, quam turpe nescire*—"It is not . . . so great a distinction to know Latin as it is a disgrace not to know it."[347] In other words, we mustn't be lazy about educating ourselves. We should acquire some knowledge of the principal language of Western civilization and of the Roman Church. Assuredly, such knowledge does not reduce the mystery of the traditional liturgy; if anything, it intensifies one's astonishment at its spiritual subtleties and literary allusions.[348] Intellectual enrichment and cultural literacy are always that way: so far from narrowing one's life, they multiply occasions of wonder and open new possibilities for contemplation. Beauty itself seems to grow as one's capacity to see it or hear it grows.

Perhaps we could put it this way: the traditional Mass is good not *because* it baffles us or presents barriers, but because it humbles our pride and whets our appetite, with the barriers as so many provocations to intimacy. As the Lord says through the prophet Isaias: "I will give thee hidden treasures, and the concealed riches of secret places: that thou mayest know that I am the Lord Who calls thee by thy name, the God of Israel."[349] The mystic is the one who ardently follows the truth into the fiercest thickets and

---

[345] A phrase repeated often in C.S. Lewis's *The Last Battle* in *The Chronicles of Narnia.*

[346] Wonder is meant to lead to wisdom. My main point in this chapter is that, in this life, when one engages with the sacred mysteries in their traditional home, one will never reach a plateau at which he could say: "Okay, it's all clear now, there's nothing left to know, nothing left to puzzle, overwhelm, challenge, or humble me." In fact, the more we come to see, the more we will see what we do not see, and the more desire we will have for that embrace of God that will finally satisfy us and fill us beyond all imagining.

[347] Address of John Paul II to Participants in the *Certamen Vaticanum,* citing *Brutus* 37, 140.

[348] See Foley, *Lost in Translation,* and Martindale, *The Words of the Missal.*

[349] Is. 45:3.

fieriest trials. The Mass, as the mystical re-presentation of the sacrifice of Christ on the Cross, should be a place where everyday mystics are bred and fed—members of that Body we call Mystical. Against the rationalists of yesterday and today—the reformers at the Synod of Pistoia, the *periti* at the sacrosanct Council—let us thank God, in the aforementioned words of the Divine Liturgy of St. John Chrysostom, "for all things we know and do not know, for blessings manifest and hidden that have been bestowed on us."[350]

This chapter's title says it is better not to understand everything immediately. By now, it should be abundantly clear that, in point of fact, it is impossible for us to understand everything immediately—*that* is a prerogative of God alone; and to the extent that we are led to think we understand more than we actually do, we are being done a disservice, for knowledge and pride enjoy a subterranean link, and it is often for our good, for our humbling, that we are left in the dark. It is advantageous for us to come to know the two greatest mysteries with which our minds are in contact—namely, God and our own souls—*slowly*, lest we be blinded by the truth, overwhelmed and confused. Just as it befits the natural order that we are fed first mother's milk, then soft foods, then tougher foods, until we can eat nearly anything, so too it belongs to the divine pedagogy in the spiritual life that, as St. Paul says in 1 Corinthians, we start on milk and move eventually to meat. The traditional liturgy feeds us in just this way, by starting with the milk of outward splendor—the pomp of the ceremonies, the sweetness of the music, the "smells and bells" that capture our attention and keep it focused on the external symbols—and then moving us over time to the meat of the prayers in their dense content (think of the towering mysteries of the Roman Canon!) and the subtleties of the rite that one comes to see only after years of attending it, and for the understanding of which one must put in some effort of study and mental exercise. In short, traditionalists should challenge themselves and one another to live a life of prayer and study that fully accords with "slow liturgy," for in this way, they will absorb its wisdom, vindicate its perfections, and extend its earthly empire.

---

350 Quoted from www.goarch.org/-/the-divine-liturgy-of-saint-john-chrysostom.

9

Why We Kneel for Communion and Receive on the Tongue

"No posture is better or worse than another if your heart is in the right place."

Imagine eating the sun—and imagine you could do it without perishing. What would happen? You would receive into your body the source of light and warmth. You would have within you all the light and heat that you could possibly ever need or want.

When we receive Jesus in the Most Blessed Sacrament, we receive the source of all supernatural light and warmth, the light of truth, the warmth of love, for indeed He is the "Sun of Justice." We receive God Himself, the very Son of God, who is inseparable from the Father and the Holy Spirit. St. Ephrem the Syrian wrote: "He called the bread his living body and he filled it with himself and his Spirit. . . . He who eats it with faith, eats Fire and Spirit. . . . Take and eat this, all of you, and eat with it the Holy Spirit. For it is truly my body and whoever eats it will have eternal life."[351] That we are not killed instantly by this contact with eternal and infinite Fire is, in its own way, a greater miracle than would be eating the sun without perishing. Our Lord protects us, courteously hiding His blazing glory lest we be overwhelmed, and gently radiates His peace.

---

[351] *Sermo IV in Hebdomadam Sanctam:* CSCO 413/Syr. 182, 55, cited in John Paul II, *Ecclesia de Eucharistia,* no. 17.

It is because we receive divine fire—a fire far more potent in the range and reach of its possible spiritual effects than any physical fire—that the *worthy* reception of the Eucharist is purifying, illuminating, and unitive. The Holy Eucharist does within and upon the soul that which fire does within and upon combustible matter, burning away contrary dispositions and transforming the matter into itself. But since the spiritual soul is incorruptible, the soul can become fire without perishing, like the miraculous burning bush. The Eucharist does for the soul what the sun does for the earth, spreading light, warming bodies, causing growth.

As we learn from the Fathers, Doctors, and mystics of the Church, the Real Presence of Jesus has a proper effect on our soul *and* our body. Like the healing of the woman with the flow of blood,[352] the diseased blood of the old Adam cannot be healed by any human medicine, but only by the touch of the new Adam, the physician of souls. The Lord touches first the essence of the soul, increasing in it the grace that makes the soul pleasing to God, an adopted son of the Father, a spouse of the Word, a temple of the Holy Spirit.[353] He touches the powers of the soul, informing them with virtues, strengthening virtuous habits. Only in the life to come will we be given to know just how many times it was Jesus who, faced with the laziness of our fallen condition, animated our souls into action and prompted us to bear fruits pleasing to God and profitable to us.

Resurrection and Eternal Life

Holy Communion influences the body, too. This is very important to see, even if we cannot understand it completely. By means of the Holy Eucharist, our flesh is made more obedient and docile to the soul, rendered more receptive to the power of soul and virtue. The Lord is sown into the flesh as a seed of immortality: He radiates divine life, divine existence, upon what has merely earthly life and earthly existence. His presence is like a beneficial radiation. We know that ordinary radiation causes deformity of cells. But the radiation of the Son of God is exactly the opposite; it causes a hidden perfection in all the matter of the body, so that on the last day the flesh will be recognized in the

---

352 See Luke 8:43.

353 See St. Thomas Aquinas, *Summa Theologiæ* I–II, Q. 110.

sight of God as flesh marked by and belonging to Christ, as flesh worthy and able to be resurrected in the image of the glorified King. He wants to change the flesh, day by day, into flesh that He will resurrect as if it were His very own.

Those who have eaten the Eucharist have eaten the flesh and drunk the blood of Him who is the Resurrection and the Life. Their own flesh and blood are invisibly stamped with the signature, the seal, of the eternally living flesh and blood of Jesus. To the all-seeing eyes of God the Father, the man or woman fed on the Eucharist *looks different* from the one who has not been so fed. Not only in his soul but also in his flesh, he bears the marks of the Lord Jesus.[354] As St. Thomas says, we receive *Christus passus,* "the Christ who suffered," who is now glorified.[355] The body that is conformed to the suffering Christ is conformed to His glory, St. Paul tells us.[356] St. John Chrysostom cries out:

> Let us not, I beg you, slay ourselves by our irreverence, but with awe and purity draw near to it; and when you see it set before you, say to yourself: "Because of this Body am I no longer earth and ashes, no longer a prisoner, but free: because of this I hope for heaven, and [I hope] to receive the good things therein, immortal life, the portion of angels, to converse with Christ."[357]

The Real Presence

It is the faith of the Church—it has always been the faith of the Church, *pace* Protestants—that Jesus is really, truly, substantially, personally present in the Most Holy Sacrament of the Altar. Therefore, *how* we approach and receive Holy Communion is how we approach and receive Jesus Christ Himself. It is a personal act, an interpersonal union, a sign of the most intimate friendship—or the opposite, a sign of the most horrible betrayal. When Judas led the high priests and their guard to apprehend Christ in the Garden of Gethsemane, Jesus asked him: "Friend, why are you here? Would you betray the Son of man with a kiss?"[358]

---

354 See Gal. 6:17.

355 *Summa Theologiæ* III, Q. 66, art. 9.

356 See, *inter alia,* Rom. 8:17.

357 John Chrysostom, *In epistulam I ad Corinthos* 24.4 (PG 61:203); translated from the Latin given there.

358 Matt. 26:50; Luke 22:48 RSVCE.

Here, then, is the question we must ask ourselves: *Do* we believe that Jesus Christ is truly present in the Most Holy Eucharist? If so, we can do far more than just follow Him at a distance, like the timid Apostles during the Passion: we can *eat* the Way, the Truth, and the Life, we can become *one* with Him and allow His reality to shape our very selves. The Truth we are striving to know and to behold face to face in the beatific vision—that same Truth is our food, we can *consume* it and be one with it. The Life we long for, the blessed life, the life of heaven, free of suffering and death: this Life we can take into ourselves. That God should give us *Himself* is completely beyond our limited understanding, but not at all beyond His unlimited power. The Way we seek to follow, the Gospel way, is not a philosophy but a Person, the Word made Flesh, and this Person gives Himself to us. Do we believe He is Emmanuel, "God with us," God dwelling in our midst? Hidden, yes, but also real—indeed, *far more real than we are.* Let us go to Him, let us run to reality! God is the source of all reality, all goodness, all holiness, all happiness.

Holy Mass is the Sacrifice of Christ made real again in our midst; it is His self-offering and ours, too, united with His. It brings us the sacrament of His passion, death, and resurrection, and through communion with the Lord Himself, we suffer, die, and rise again. It may not always *feel* like the height of one's interior life or one's Christian life, but that is beside the point. Our religion does not consist in feelings or even in true thoughts, but in *communion with mysteries.* It is about massive realities too big for our comprehension: God thrusts them upon us, and we respond in the darkness of faith. We have to trust not our changing feelings or our uncertain thoughts but His everlasting Word, which is the only rock we can safely build on. All this takes place *in faith,* in the darkness of faith, but as long as we rely on the invincible and infallible promises of Jesus Christ, the Eucharist becomes for us the great reassurance that we are heading toward heaven as well as the great source of power to reach this goal.

Freedom from Mortal Sin

As I mentioned a moment ago, Judas betrayed Our Lord with a kiss, with a pretend sign of friendship that was actually a death warrant. We do not want to be like Judas, betraying Our Lord first by committing mortal sin, and then making our state infinitely worse by receiving Him in the midst of the guilt of unconfessed and unforgiven mortal sin. The Council of Trent expressed with incomparable brevity and clarity the reason why we must be concerned to present ourselves *worthily* for Holy Communion:

> If it is unbecoming for anyone to approach any of the sacred functions except in a spirit of piety, assuredly, the more the holiness and divinity of this heavenly sacrament are understood by a Christian, the more diligently ought he to give heed lest he receive it without great reverence and holiness, especially when we read those terrifying words of the Apostle: "He that eateth and drinketh unworthily, eateth and drinketh judgment to himself, not discerning the body of the Lord" (1 Cor 11:29). Wherefore, he who would communicate, must recall to mind his precept: "Let a man prove himself" (1 Cor 11:28).[359]

The collective and indiscriminate reception of Holy Communion by all or nearly all Catholics who attend Mass, even by those who are not properly disposed to receive the Lord to their benefit, is a major problem straightforwardly acknowledged by Popes John Paul II and Benedict XVI.[360] For example, John Paul II wrote:

> Sometimes, indeed quite frequently, everybody participating in the Eucharistic assembly goes to Communion; and on some such occasions, as experienced pastors confirm, there has not been due care to approach the sacrament of Penance so as to purify one's conscience.[361]

While this passage might win an award for understatement, its meaning is unambiguous. Purifying one's conscience through sacramental Confession on a regular basis—certainly whenever a grave or mortal sin has been committed—is the only way to guarantee that we are showing proper reverence to Our Lord, the Holy One of Israel, when we approach to receive Him.

---

359 Session 13, chapter 7. Note that the word "judgment" in 1 Cor. 11:29 could also be translated "damnation." It is clear that by "worthy" is not meant the absolute worthiness of one who is sinless and all-holy (for only God could be said to be worthy of Himself in that sense!), but rather, worthy in (at least) the minimum way demanded of us—namely, to be without the stain of mortal sin on our souls, with a moral certainty that we are dressed in the wedding garment of sanctifying grace.

360 As I noted in chapter 6, the total absence of 1 Cor. 11:27–29 in the Novus Ordo is partly to blame for this lamentable state of affairs.

361 John Paul II, *Dominicae Cenae,* no. 11.

As the Church teaches, the Eucharist is not a remedy for those whose souls are *dead,* but a food for those who, being alive, need to be strengthened for the life of charity.[362] You can put food all day long into a corpse and it will never do any good. In the spiritual life, it is worse: when a spiritually dead man takes the Bread of Life, he becomes *more* guilty; he dies again. And the giving of such food to unrepentant public sinners—as when priests or bishops give the Lord to politicians who vote in favor of abortion—calls down the wrath of God upon the heads of both the recipient and the minister.

Receiving the Lord Well

However, to be conscious of no unconfessed grave sin and to be morally certain that we are in a state of sanctifying grace is the *minimum* we can do for so awesome a gift as Jesus Himself. Catholic tradition shows us that we should do all in our power to prepare well and to act appropriately when the time comes for communing with the Lord.

As regards preparation, we should be fasting before Mass. One hour before Communion is the minimum required, but the older custom of three hours or even from midnight has much to commend it, if Mass is early enough in the day to make it realistic. We should "have a right and devout intention," which is defined by the Church as follows: "He who approaches the Holy Table should do so, not out of routine, or vainglory, or human respect, but that he wish to please God, to be more closely united with Him by charity, and to have recourse to this divine remedy for his weakness and defects."[363] In other words, the communicant should be conscious of what he is doing and whom he is approaching (hence, not from routine), and that he is doing it to please the Lord and sanctify his soul through a closer union with Him, not because of what others may be thinking (hence, not from vainglory or human respect). The Church also recommends that we should spend time *before* Mass getting into a recollected and prayerful frame of mind, to the best of our ability. The Mass itself should be such as to assist us in preparing for communion with

---

[362] See John Paul II, *Ecclesia de Eucharistia,* nos. 35–36.

[363] From the 1905 decree *Sacra Tridentina Synodus* of the Sacred Congregation of the Council.

the Lord; it does so traditionally by emphasizing the adoration of God, contrition for our sins, and the remembrance of what Christ has done and is doing for us, as well as by providing plenty of silence within which to make these interior acts. Spending time *after* Mass in thanksgiving greatly augments the effect that Communion will have in our lives.

Kneeling and Receiving on the Tongue

Traditional practices teach us proper behavior toward the Eucharist and habituate us in it. For the better part of Church history, Latin-rite Catholics have received Communion on the tongue and in a kneeling posture. Let's look at kneeling first. In his *Commentary on Ephesians,* St. Thomas Aquinas underlines the intimate connection between kneeling and humility:

> Humility makes a prayer worthy of being heard . . . [And kneeling] is a symbol of humility for two reasons. First, a man belittles himself, in a certain way, when he bends the knee, and he subjects himself to the one he kneels before. In such a way he recognizes his own weakness and insignificance. Secondly, physical strength is present in the knees; in bending them a man confesses openly to his lack of strength. Thus external, physical symbols are shown to God for the purpose of renewing and spiritually training the inner soul . . .[364]

Traditional Christian liturgies of East and West dramatically emphasize God's transcendence over us, His benevolent reign, His rightful demand of our whole heart, soul, mind, and strength, and our corresponding duty to worship Him by offering sacrifice with contrite and humble hearts. In spite of the illusions fostered by modern democracy, we are *not* equals before Jesus Christ; He is Our Lord and Master, and we are His disciples, servants, and adorers. Yes, He lovingly calls us His friends; but He is not just *any* friend, He is the Lord of heaven and earth who has called us "out of darkness into His marvelous light,"[365] and who deserves (and rewards) our absolute self-surrender, which no creature can rightly demand or receive. This is why kneeling, within a tradition that has long expressed and cultivated the attitude of humility by means of it, is no mere incidental external feature

[364] Thomas Aquinas, *Commentary on Ephesians,* ch. 3, lect. 4, n. 166, 248.

[365] 1 Pet. 2:9.

that we can take or leave. It is part of our fundamental spiritual discipline. Kneeling is a vivid and heartfelt expression of worship, of the adoration that is due to Our Lord and God. The devil knows this, too:

> According to Abba Apollo, a desert father who lived about 1,700 years ago, the devil has no knees; he cannot kneel; he cannot adore; he cannot pray; he can only look down his nose in contempt. Being unwilling to bend the knee at the name of Jesus is the essence of evil (cf. Is 45:23, Rom 14:11).[366]

Note how well everything fits together in the Roman liturgy as it developed over the millennia. As long as Communion is given on the tongue, there is good reason to kneel—not only for its symbolic and formative value, but also because kneeling makes it easier for the priest to place the Host on the tongue. And once this custom is firmly established, a Communion rail is obviously helpful, not only to affirm the symbolic distinction between the sanctuary and the nave, but also to offer bodily support to those who are kneeling. Moreover, the priest is always accompanied by a server holding a paten, out of respect for the Blessed Sacrament and lest it or any fragment of it fall to the ground. All of these customs grew up in support of each other, once the fundamental principle was allowed to breathe freely, namely, that Our Lord Jesus Christ is really present in the Most Holy Sacrament of the Altar. If "at the *Name* of Jesus, every knee should bow . . .,"[367] all the more should our knees bend when it is *Jesus Himself* before whom we come, as we see throughout the New Testament whenever people approach Him to profess their faith and ask His help. Pope Benedict XVI once said: "Kneeling in adoration before the Lord . . . is the most valid and radical remedy against the idolatries of yesterday and today."[368]

That is also why, if I may slightly digress, the practice of Adoration of the Blessed Sacrament outside of Mass is so crucial a part of any authentic

---

[366] Olmsted, "Knees to Love Christ." As Joseph Ratzinger relates the story: "The devil was compelled by God to show himself to a certain Abba Apollo. He looked black and ugly, with frighteningly thin limbs, but, most strikingly, *he had no knees.* The inability to kneel is seen as the very essence of the diabolical" (*Theology of the Liturgy,* 121).

[367] Phil 2:10 RSVCE, emphasis added.

[368] Benedict XVI, Homily for Corpus Christi, May 22, 2008; translated from the Italian.

Eucharistic revival. As the same pope liked to remind us, we grow in faith and love for the Lord when we spend time in His Presence—and we are given an opportunity to make reparation for the sins of those who do not believe in His Real Presence or who treat the Lord, truly present, with contempt or indifference. We do not hear the word "reparation" nearly enough; it is thought to be too old-fashioned, or perhaps the concept is simply unknown. And yet, the entire work of Our Lord Jesus Christ was a work of reparation, the work of repairing fallen human nature and repairing the broken relationship between God and man. He is the Reparator par excellence, and when we fast, abstain, keep vigil, make Holy Hours, or do other penances, we enter more deeply into His work of redemption, for the liberation of souls and the glorification of the Father. On the basis of what we learn from Church history and the revelations of countless mystics, we can be quite certain there will never be any Eucharistic revival without earnest and widespread reparation for sins committed against the Most Blessed Sacrament.

The Priest's Anointed Hands

Resuming our main topic, a second point to focus on is that the priest's hands are specially anointed with holy oil in his ordination so that he may fittingly handle the Blessed Sacrament and administer to others the holy gifts of the altar. In the words of Pope John Paul II:

> One must not forget the primary office of priests, who have been consecrated by their ordination to represent Christ the Priest: for this reason their hands, like their words and their will, have become the direct instruments of Christ. Through this fact, that is, as ministers of the Holy Eucharist, they have a primary responsibility for the sacred species, because it is a total responsibility: they offer the bread and wine, they consecrate it, and then distribute the sacred species to the participants in the assembly who wish to receive them. . . . How eloquent therefore . . . is the rite of the anointing of the hands in our Latin ordination, as though precisely for these hands a special grace and power of the Holy Spirit is necessary! To touch the sacred species and to distribute them with their own hands is a privilege of the ordained . . .[369]

[369] John Paul II, *Dominicae Cenae,* no. 11. Unfortunately, the pope goes on to say that the

A layman's hands, in contrast, are not anointed in this way, because no simple layman represents Christ the Priest in the Mass and serves as His direct instrument.[370]

A third point is receiving on the tongue. It is absolutely fitting that Christ's faithful should go before the ordained minister who represents Him, and *receive* on bended knee and with open mouth the nourishment of body and soul, like a baby bird fed in the nest by its parent, or like a child too young to feed itself. From this symbolic vantage, it is wholly inappropriate for the priest to put the Host into our *hands*, so that we may then *administer Communion to ourselves.* This gesture means: "I'm grown up and can feed myself, thank you very much." But this is false. We cannot feed ourselves supernaturally. In the prophet Ezekiel, we read: "Open thy mouth, and eat what *I* give thee."[371] In the Psalms, we read, "Open thy mouth wide, and *I* will fill it."[372] Who is the "I" in these statements? It is the Lord. The Lord alone may feed us, His children. Only Christ the High Priest can give us the Bread of Life, and His ordained minister acts in His place, set apart by Holy Orders, and with hands likewise set apart for the task of divine bestowal.

In fact, so pervasive and profound was the Church's reverence toward Christ our God in His Holy Sacrament that she even forbade the laity to touch the *vessels* that touched Christ. The *Catechism of the Council of Trent*—the Magisterium's first universal catechism, published in 1566 and obviously still authoritative as a witness to the Faith—explained this point with unanswerable logic:

> To safeguard in every possible way the dignity of so august a Sacrament, not only is the power of its administration entrusted exclusively to priests, but the Church has also prohibited by law any but

faculty of handling and distributing the Blessed Sacrament can be extended beyond its ordinary ministers "to meet a just need," which compromises the theological point he is making, and introduces incoherence between office, sign, and praxis. For an explanation of why this incoherence is unavoidable and undesirable, see Kwasniewski, *Ministers of Christ.*

370 The involvement of deacons in distributing Holy Communion to the faithful—a practice that started in the eighteenth century and was confirmed by the 1917 Code of Canon Law (albeit as "extraordinary")—can be defended from the vantage of their being ordained with the lowest grade of Holy Orders; but it is less fitting than when priests or bishops distribute Communion, for the reasons given by John Paul II.

371 Ezech. 2:8, emphasis added.

372 Ps. 80:11, emphasis added.

consecrated persons, unless some case of great necessity intervene, to dare handle or touch the sacred vessels, the linen, or other instruments necessary to its completion. Priests themselves and the rest of the faithful may hence understand how great should be the piety and holiness of those who approach to consecrate, administer or receive the Eucharist.[373]

The Magisterium Supports Tradition

The Magisterium of the Church, in the 1969 Instruction *Memoriale Domini* of the Congregation for Divine Worship, approved by Pope Paul VI, defends Communion on the tongue—a practice that the vast majority of the world's bishops, when polled at that time by Paul VI, agreed should continue:

> In view of the state of the Church as a whole today, this manner of distributing Holy Communion must be retained, not only because it rests upon a tradition of many centuries, but especially because it is a sign of the reverence of the faithful toward the Eucharist. The practice in no way detracts from the personal dignity of those who approach this great Sacrament,[374] and it is a part of the preparation needed for the most fruitful reception of the Lord's body.
>
> This reverence is a sign of Holy Communion not in "common bread and drink" but in the Body and Blood of the Lord. . . .
>
> In addition, this manner of communicating, which is now to be considered as prescribed by custom, gives more effective assurance that Holy Communion will be distributed with the appropriate reverence, decorum, and dignity; that any danger of profaning the Eucharistic species, in which "the whole and entire Christ, God and man, is substantially contained and permanently present in a unique way," will be avoided; and finally that the diligent care which the Church has always commended for the very fragments of the consecrated bread will be maintained: "If you have allowed anything to be lost, consider this a lessening of your own members."[375]

---

[373] *Catechism of the Council of Trent,* 270.

[374] As I've mentioned a couple of times already in this book, some agitators in the 1960s were saying it was undignified for adults to kneel and be fed by another. Behold, the arrogant inanities into which progressivism devolves in its revolt against divine authority!

[375] For text and commentary, see Shaw, *The Case for Liturgical Restoration,* 59–63.

This last point is very important. Studies done with black gloves have shown that hosts, even when designed to be compact and firm, still shed particles. Some brands of hosts are crumblier than others, and sometimes particular hosts can be damaged so that they fragment more easily. Anyone with extensive experience handling or watching the handling of hosts knows that this is true. Over the centuries, the Church was careful to develop practices and rubrics that guaranteed that fragments would always be caught on linen or metal, and then consumed. In the modern way of distributing hosts directly into people's hands, the scattering of particles cannot be avoided—not to mention other horror stories about evil people who take away hosts, or confused individuals who don't know what to do with the host and put it in a hymnal or in a purse.

Even if it is possible to imagine a tightly controlled situation in which reception in the hand might not run the risk of sacrilege, it is impossible to avoid sacrilege when this practice is carried out on a large scale over long periods of time. To this day—although one would hardly know it from the aggressive policies framed by most bishops' conferences, and the iron grip of bad custom—the Church's *universal norm* is still Communion on the tongue; Communion in the hand requires an indult, or special permission, from the Holy See. To those who still believe in the Real Presence, it is blindingly obvious that such permission should never have been given and it must someday be rescinded when the Church on earth is better governed than at present. We must do everything in our power—with patience, yes, but also with a perseverance that never quits—to overturn the practice of Communion in the hand and to restore the practice of Communion on the tongue, administered to the kneeling faithful by the clergy alone. Even if the latter customs cannot prevent unworthy Communions from ever happening, they limit or eliminate many evils, and greatly foster the goods of supernatural faith, interior devotion, and external reverence.

You might be asking yourself what you personally can do to bring about this goal. The one course of action open to all the laity is to make a firm commitment to kneel before the Eucharistic Lord and receive Him *only* on the tongue, no matter what Mass you attend or where.[376]

---

[376] If you happen to attend a Byzantine liturgy, however, please note that it is their tradition for

But Didn't the Ancient Church Do It?

So far, so good. But bringing up this topic with other Catholics is guaranteed to elicit, sooner or later, the following objection: "Didn't the ancient church practice Communion in the hand, standing? If they did, why shouldn't we?" The answer is: "Yes, it once happened . . . and no, their practice wasn't the same as ours." Let's take a closer look at this crucial matter.

Proponents of the modern Communion practice always quote a passage from the *Mystagogical Catecheses* of St. Cyril of Jerusalem, a Church Father who lived in the fourth century:

> Coming up to receive, therefore, do not approach with your wrists extended or your fingers splayed, but making your left hand a throne for the right (for it is about to receive a King) and cupping your palm, so receive the Body of Christ; and answer: "Amen." Carefully hallow your eyes by the touch of the sacred Body, and then partake, taking care to lose no part of It. Such a loss would be like a mutilation of your own body. Why, if you had been given gold-dust, would you not take the utmost care to hold it fast, not letting a grain slip through your fingers, lest you be by so much the poorer? How much more carefully, then, will you guard against losing so much as a crumb of that which is more precious than gold and precious stones![377]

We should take note of several things about this passage: First, there are some very odd aspects to Cyril's description: no one in our times, as far as I know, has ever suggested that the Host should be touched to one's eyes! And the reason for quietly passing over *that* part of the text is obvious: whatever might have been the custom in fourth-century Jerusalem, no one thinks this would be a good idea today, if only because it stands in tension with Cyril's own insistence on not risking the loss of even the slightest crumb of the heavenly gift. But if the praxis described here was already deserving of criticism in this detail, why couldn't it be flawed in other respects too? That is the whole point of ritual development: better ideas and practices come along and church leaders adopt them because they are better.

---

the communicant to stand, tilt his head back, open his mouth, and receive the Body and Blood of the Lord by means of a metal spoon handled by the priest.

[377] Cyril of Jerusalem, *Mystagogical Catecheses* 5.21, p. 203.

In any case, notice the extreme carefulness that St. Cyril demands of the one about to receive the Lord Himself, the King: not a speck of the consecrated Bread should be lost—that would be like a mutilation of one's body, a loss of something more precious than any created thing! It was, in fact, this very emphasis on the immense care to be taken toward the Eucharist, together with an ever-deepening appreciation of the sheer magnitude of so divine a gift, that led the Church over time to *abandon* Communion in the hand and to prefer Communion directly into the mouth. This is a primary example of organic development in the liturgy, which pursues the implications of a belief or attitude until the external expression most perfectly reflects that belief and inculcates that attitude. Conversely, the artificial return to a much earlier but long since discontinued practice—and one that *now*, reappearing in a very different socio-cultural context, carries with it overtones of casualness and lack of faith in the Real Presence—is a primary example of the error of antiquarianism condemned in 1947 by Pope Pius XII in *Mediator Dei*.[378]

Second, if we look more carefully at what Cyril describes, and combine this passage with other hints from antiquity, we can see that even when Communion in the hand *was* practiced, it involved marks of reverence that (curiously?) never accompanied its re-invention in the late 1960s.

> It is significant that the Eucharist, laid on the right hand, is not then received by means of the less-valued left hand, but rather directly by the mouth. What appears at first glance to be Communion in the hand reveals itself on closer examination to be Communion in the mouth, with the right hand serving as a sort of paten. Bishop Cyril's description shows that "the attitude of the communicant is, then, not one of taking and capturing, but rather of reverent and humble reception, accompanied by a sign of adoration."[379]

Bishop Athanasius Schneider, an expert in patristics, writes:

> The practice had a different form in ancient times than it does today: the Holy Eucharist was received on the palm of the right hand and

---

[378] See Pius XII, *Mediator Dei,* nos. 62–64; for extended commentary, see my books *Once and Future Roman Rite,* chapters 2 and 7, and *Reclaiming Our Roman Catholic Birthright,* chapter 10.

[379] Fiedrowicz, *The Traditional Mass,* 115–16, quoting M. Lugmayr.

> the faithful were not allowed to touch the Holy Host with their fingers, but they had to bow down their head to the palm of the hand and take the Sacrament directly with their mouth, thus, in a position of a profound bow and not standing upright. The common practice today is to receive the Eucharist standing upright, taking it with the left hand. This is something which, symbolically, the Church Fathers would find horrific—how can the Holy of Holies be taken with the left hand? What is more, today the faithful take and touch the Host directly with their [right-hand] fingers and then put the Host in the mouth: this gesture has never been known in the entire history of the Catholic Church but was invented by Calvin—not even by Martin Luther. . . . The Calvinists . . . who do not believe at all in the Real Presence of Christ in the Eucharist, invented a rite which is void of almost all gestures of sacredness and of exterior adoration, i.e., receiving "Communion" standing upright, and touching the bread with their fingers and putting it in their mouth in the way people treat ordinary bread. . . . For them, this was just a symbol, so their exterior behavior towards Communion was similar to behavior towards a symbol. During the Second Vatican Council, Catholic Modernists—especially in the Netherlands—took this Calvinist Communion rite and wrongly attributed it to the Early Church, in order to spread it more easily throughout the Church. We have to dismantle this myth and these insidious tactics . . .[380]

Third, in the early Church, a Communion cloth was, at least in some places and times, laid over the hands of recipients so that they would not directly touch the Holy Sacrament and any fragments could be easily gathered. The Byzantine rite still utilizes such a cloth, held under the chins of those who are receiving in their mouths from a spoon handled by the priest. Some traditional Latin-rite parishes retain the use of a "houseling cloth" that covers the Communion rail. While the invention of the so-called chin paten renders the houseling cloth no longer necessary, traditional Catholic churches and chapels often retain it as an additional reminder of the sacredness of the Eucharistic banquet and a symbolic link between the people's reception of the Lord and the linen-covered altar of sacrifice on which the

---

[380] Schneider, *Christus Vincit,* 223–24.

divine Victim has been offered. It underlines that they, like the priest, are partaking of a mystical sacrifice.[381]

In short: the ancient record bears witness to beliefs and attitudes that would, over time, develop into the longstanding Communion customs of *both* the Latin West and the Byzantine East. In the West, Communion on the tongue, kneeling, is the natural and suitable result of St. Cyril's Eucharistic piety. The attempt to turn back the clock to antiquity—an antiquity, moreover, deceptively misrepresented and fictitiously reconstructed—is, in the end, nothing but a Trojan horse for Calvinistic sacramental theology.

What is at stake, therefore, is no minor issue of personal preference or private devotion, but precisely those distinctively Catholic dogmas at the center of our Faith that surveys show are being rapidly abandoned by Catholics, even among those who still attend Mass regularly.[382] Undoubtedly, poor catechesis outside of Mass is part of the explanation, but the single greatest catechizer in the Church is *the liturgy itself*, as it forms the minds and hearts of worshipers week in and week out. The only path to a true Eucharistic revival is to abandon harmful, heresy-induced practices from the 1960s and 1970s and to restore our traditional customs of utmost reverence toward the Bread of Angels.

The Tongue Is Special

Sometimes one will also hear a silly objection that goes like this: "Why do you think the tongue is holier than the hand? If you are in a state of grace, your hands are as holy as your tongue." Or the related objection: "What matters is what's inside our hearts, not what we do with our bodies. As long as you believe in and love Jesus, it doesn't matter whether you stand or kneel, etc."

Anyone who has read the preceding chapters of this book can see right away that these objections totally miss the point. What we do with our bodies during worship both expresses the belief in our souls—what we believe we are doing—*and* helps to shape our attitude. Everyone recognizes this fact. A man would not propose marriage to a woman in the same way

---

381 See Kwasniewski, *Reclaiming Our Roman Catholic Birthright*, 321.

382 See Smith, "Just one-third of U.S. Catholics agree with their church."

as he stands in line at the post office to buy stamps. A mother would not handle her baby roughly or negligently and make the excuse that "it's only the love in my heart that matters, not what I do outwardly." A president would not go before Congress wearing swim trunks and speak slang. We all instinctively know that our bodily disposition, clothing, and behavior tell others, and even tell ourselves, what we are doing and why it's important (or not important) to us.

It is simply *obvious* that kneeling is a sign of reverence. Even the Novus Ordo requires that the faithful kneel for the duration of the Eucharistic Prayer of the Mass. How bizarre is it that we would kneel for the time when Our Lord comes into our midst on the altar at the hands of the priest, but we would not kneel for Our Lord when we come right before Him to receive Him! That's what I call backwards and upside-down. And how bizarre that we would think it beautiful for newlyweds to feed each other cake or for a mother to feed a child milk and yet we would not recognize that Christ our Bridegroom is here to feed us with Himself and that the Church, our Mother, is offering us this heavenly nourishment from her abundance.

But there is more! The tongue, as a matter of fact, *was* specially blessed by the Church in the traditional rite of baptism, and wherever this traditional rite continues to be used, we will see it happen. A pinch of exorcised and blessed salt is placed on the infant's tongue, with a command that looks ahead to the reception of Communion: *Accipe sal sapientiae: propitiatio sit tibi in vitam aeternam* ("Receive the salt of wisdom: may it be propitious to you unto eternal life"), followed by a prayer:

> O God of our fathers, O God the Author of all truth, vouchsafe, we humbly beseech Thee, to look graciously down upon this Thy servant, *N.*, and as he tastes this first nutriment of salt, suffer him no longer to hunger for want of heavenly food, to the end that he may be always fervent in spirit, rejoicing in hope, always serving Thy name. Lead him, O Lord, we beseech Thee, to the laver of the new regeneration, that, together with Thy faithful, he may deserve to attain the everlasting rewards of Thy promises.[383]

---

383 The texts of the traditional rite of baptism in Latin and English may be found at www.fisheaters.com/baptism2.html.

No other part of the body is set aside in this manner for blessed food. The salt serves as a symbolic "substitute" for Communion, an anticipation of and preparation for the Eucharist for the one who cannot yet receive it. It is no wonder that the removal of this precious ceremony from the modern rite of baptism (1970) more or less coincided with the toleration of Communion on the hand.

Ways in Which the Latin Mass Helps Us

All that we have covered in this chapter points to a single resounding conclusion: the Catholic Church knew what it was doing for the past thousand years (and more), in regard to how the clergy and the faithful should treat the Most Holy Eucharist. Let's briefly review how the traditional Latin Mass practices, and thereby inculcates, utmost reverence for the Most Holy Eucharist, and in this way serves as the "gold standard."

In order to prevent the scattering of any particles and to remind himself of the awesomeness of what he is doing, the priest holds his thumb and forefinger together after the consecration of the Host and keeps them thus until the careful ablutions after Communion. He bows and genuflects many times toward the Blessed Sacrament, never passing before It without doing so. His anointed hands are the only ones that touch the sacred species and distribute them to the faithful, who receive on their tongue, kneeling, in a posture of humble submission.[384] This millennium-old practice of kneeling before the Holy One of Israel, and of receiving Him on the tongue from the hand of an ordained minister, literally *embodies* our dependency on God, our lowliness and unworthiness, our need to fall in adoration before the Lord, and our desire for healing and elevation. In the supernatural domain, we are all children who must be fed by the Father, fed with the Bread that is His Son.

Accurate catechesis is very good; accurate homilies are good; diocesan or national programs can be good. But none of these alone is enough, or even of lasting value. What is needed, above all, is a permanent form of liturgy that cries out Real Presence and humbles itself to the dust in adoration. What is needed, in short, is reverential fear. As the Psalmist says: *Servite*

384 As mentioned before, a deacon, as a minister in Holy Orders, is allowed to distribute as well.

Domino in timore, et exsultate ei cum tremore, "Serve ye the Lord with fear: and rejoice unto Him with trembling."[385] God's merciful closeness gives us no cause for abandoning reverential fear and expressions of our smallness, dependency, and need for purification. Quite the contrary: since in modern times man exalts himself too highly for false reasons, he must be reminded of his true place before the Divine Majesty.

Another way the revival of the traditional Mass helps us today is by presenting to us a ritual that is manifestly ordered to the worship of God Himself, rather than seeming to be directed to the people. One of the widespread errors of our age is the belief that Mass is more or less a fancied-up Communion service for the sake of getting the Eucharist—so much so that it is thought strange to attend Mass *without* going up for Communion. Undoubtedly, the sacramental union of the members of the Mystical Body with Christ their Head is *included* in the purpose of the Mass. But we can receive Communion also *outside of* Mass, as when it is brought to the sick in hospital, or to soldiers on a battlefield. The primary purpose of the Mass *as such* is to adore, praise, placate, and supplicate the Most Holy Trinity. It is the perfect act of divine worship, by which the Father is well-pleased with the Son; through it, the Church Militant receives an outpouring of grace, the Church Triumphant an increase of joy, the Church Suffering an alleviation of pains. The truth of the inherent value of the Mass was better understood in olden times, when people spoke of "*assisting* at Mass." We *assist* in this outpouring, this increase, this alleviation, by our presence and our personal prayer united to the Holy Sacrifice. We are already mightily blessed simply to *be* there for the august Mystery, the all-worthy Offering. Even if there were nothing else "in it for us," so to speak, the Holy Sacrifice of the Mass, all by itself, would give us matter for a lifetime of thanksgiving, or more truly, an eternity. In heaven, so perfect is the communion we enjoy with God that there is no need any more for sacraments, yet the worship of the Mystical Body still continues—the Son still offers His divine humanity and His holy wounds to the Father, and we offer ourselves with Him.

---

[385] Ps. 2:11.

The Right Diagnosis and the Right Cure

When a community is lacking at the center, in its core identity, it begins to crumble around the edges, like a garment that unravels when the seam is torn. This is exactly what has happened in the Catholic Church in the past several decades. Far too many Catholics have lost their core identity as sons in the Son, soldiers of Christ, citizens of the City of God, heirs of immortality, priests of divine worship, prophets of truth, kings over their bodies and lesser goods. The fundamental reason for this confusion or amnesia about who we are and what we are supposed to be doing is the devastation wrought on the central act of the Catholic religion, the Holy Sacrifice of the Mass, and on all that happens during it.

As John Senior says, the whole of Christian civilization was built around the Mass and the Holy Eucharist, the world ministering to the altar and the tabernacle.[386] If we get this wrong, it's as if the soul has departed from the body; the body starts decomposing, and nothing we do can make it come alive again, unless the Lord breathes the soul back into it, as He did for His friend Lazarus. As He once said "Lazarus, come forth!,"[387] Jesus says to His Church today: "My people, come forth from the tomb in which you have buried yourselves by compromises with the world, by surrendering to the flesh, by collaborating with the devil in the destruction of Christian civilization, Catholic culture, and the sacred liturgy. Come forth and live again the life you once knew. I will make you whole again."

A good physician does not rest content with the palliating of symptoms—in our case, liberally applying "smells and bells" to a Mass already gutted, trivialized, secularized. He goes straight to the root cause of the disease, namely, the unconscionable rupture from a bimillennial tradition of continuous divine worship, and heals it through the restoration of its rich tradition of prayers and music, ceremonies and customs, together with the exaltation of the beauty, mystery, and holiness of the Mass.

When the Mass shines forth once again as the glorious pinnacle of our life together; when the clergy approach it as the holy mountain and the burning bush, in awe, with head bowed and vanity slain; when the laity

386 Senior, *Restoration of Christian Culture,* 16–17.

387 John 11:43.

enter into it as into a spiritual Garden of Eden where they may taste the sweetest fruit of the Tree of Life—then, and *only* then, will the Church flourish in a new springtime.

The Church's greatest theologian, St. Thomas Aquinas, teaches that the common good of the entire universe is contained in the Holy Eucharist. If we care about our own souls and, beyond that, our families and the parish of which we are members, and the universal Church and indeed all mankind, we will orient our lives around the worthy celebration of this awesome sacrifice and will do our utmost to partake worthily of it.

10

The Mass Is the Faith and the Faith Is the Mass

"Why are you people always going on about 'the TLM this' and 'the TLM that'?"

Hilaire Belloc is famous for many sayings, but perhaps the most famous—and among the most heavily criticized—is his claim: "Europe is the Faith, and the Faith is Europe."

It is in the nature of hyperbole to be . . . exaggerated. The very *modus operandi* of the mythical beast George Bernard Shaw called the "Chesterbelloc" was to say extreme, provocative things that stood precariously balanced on one leg of truth. We all know that the Faith has taken root in many places other than Europe. We know that Asia Minor, that is, modern-day Turkey, hardly "counts" as Europe, yet this is where so much of apostolic Christianity flourished.

Nevertheless, Belloc's statement is more true than false, as Joseph Ratzinger himself recognized (not with explicit reference to Belloc, but with reference to the debate about "hellenization" and "dehellenization"). The Catholic Faith flourished above all in the lands that were once embraced by the Roman Empire, and Europe is the fairest fruit of this Roman miracle. As Pope Benedict XVI put it in his Regensburg Address:

> This inner rapprochement between Biblical faith and Greek philosophical inquiry was an event of decisive importance not only from the standpoint of the history of religions, but also from that of world history—it is an event which concerns us even today. Given this convergence, it is not surprising that Christianity, despite its origins and

> some significant developments in the East, finally took on its historically decisive character in Europe. We can also express this the other way around: this convergence, with the subsequent addition of the Roman heritage, created Europe and remains the foundation of what can rightly be called Europe.

I shall make a similarly bold assertion: "The Mass is the Faith, and the Faith is the Mass."

A flood of objections will rise against this claim. Surely, the Faith is much more than the Mass! It is orthodox dogma; it is the life shaped by the Decalogue and the Beatitudes, lived in many vocations and friendships, spilling over into works of mercy; it is devotion, meditation, wordless prayer. Indeed, even in the realm of liturgy, there is far more than the Mass: there is the Divine Office, the Word of God offered in worship; there are other sacramental rites; blessings, processions, penances, pilgrimages.

However, no one can really dispute the point that the Mass is the burning heart of the Faith, the axis, the pith, the focal point, the *fons et culmen*. Once we know that Jesus is *there*—that He reigns as King in our midst from the altar and in the Holy Eucharist—we know that all things in this world of pilgrimage culminate and are meant to culminate in the Holy Sacrifice of the Mass. The Mass, in itself, expresses the dogmatic content and doxological purpose of our religion. It is the summation, the synopsis, the synaxis.

St. Leonard of Port Maurice wrote in his popular treatise *The Hidden Treasure*:

> The thrice-holy Sacrifice of the Mass . . . is the sun of Christianity, the soul of Faith, the center of the Catholic religion, the grand object of all her rites, ceremonies, and Sacraments; in a word, it is the condensation of all that is good and beautiful in the Church of God.[388]

In history, it functioned in just this way, as Fr. William Slattery observes, quoting Christopher Dawson:

> The Ancient Rite's impact is due not only to the fact that it is the Mass but to the fact that it is this concrete rite, this "Ancient Rite," a clearly defined complex ceremonial embodying "everything that the

[388] Leonard of Port Maurice, *The Hidden Treasure,* 1.

> [Western] Christian world possessed of doctrine and poetry, music and art . . . poured into the liturgy, moulded into an organic whole which centered round the Divine Mysteries."[389]

Traditional Catholics[390] are sometimes criticized for "making too much of the Mass." "Why are you people always going on about 'the TLM this' and 'the TLM that'? It's as if you think of only one thing!"

Of course we don't think about just one thing. If someone is married, he has a wife and children to think about and take care of. If he has a job, he has to pay attention to it and carry it out well. If he is studying, he bends to his studies; if teaching, he prepares for his classes; if welding, he fires up the blow-torch; if building, he swings the hammer. And so on and so forth. But the traditionalist intuitively perceives, intellectually grasps, and passionately feels that the Mass is the concrete symbol and mediation of the *unum necessarium*, the one thing necessary. He knows that, if the Mass *is* as it *should* be, all other things will find a way to fall into place around it, like iron filings drawn to a magnet, or bodies drawn to a center of gravity. He knows with no less certainty that if it is *not* as it should be, all other things will fall apart around it, fly away from it, crash into chaos.

Catholicism fully believed and fully lived is centripetal toward the Mass in its full "thickness," its full-fledged form; Catholicism in a state of decline is centrifugal from the Mass, falling apart and breaking down. This, tragically, can happen even *within* the Mass, when certain actions, practices, customs, adaptations, inculturations,[391] cause it to disintegrate into the ambient worldview, the horizontal environs, the religious titillation of the moment, the project of a department, the ideological tool of a dicastery.

Indeed, the Mass is the microcosm in which we see reflected the macrocosm of the Church. As goes the Mass, so goes the Church. The Mass is the center of all the concentric circles that define Catholicism as a religion[392]—as the true religion offering the true sacrifice of Jesus Christ, in continuity with the Chosen People who looked in faith for Him, with His Apostles ordained

---

389 Slattery, *Heroism and Genius,* 140, citing Dawson's *The Formation of Christendom.*

390 For a defense of the phrase "traditional Catholics" or "traditionalists," see Kwasniewski, "Can We Call Ourselves 'Traditional Catholics'?"

391 See Hickson, "Official draft of new Mayan rite of Mass."

392 See Kwasniewski, "Processing through the Courts of the Great King."

by Him, and with the Church that His Spirit has guided over the course of 2,000 years of divine worship.

Dom Pius de Hemptinne, a disciple of Dom Columba Marmion, well expresses the Catholic vision of a world caught up in the supreme sacrifice of love that unites man to God, earth to heaven, time to eternity, death to life, and our poor souls to infinite riches:

> Although Jesus Christ the divine High Priest appeared only once on earth, to offer up His great sacrifice on Calvary; yet, every day He appears in the person of each one of His ministers, to renew His sacrifice on the altar. In every altar, then, Calvary is seen: every altar becomes an august place, the Holy of holies, the source of all holiness. Thither all must go to seek Life, and thither all must continually return, as to the source of God's mercies.
>
> Those who are the Master's privileged ones never leave this holy place, but there they "find a dwelling," near to the altar, so that they never need go far from it; such are monks, whose first care it is to raise temples worthy to contain altars. Making their home by the Sanctuary, they consecrate their life to the divine worship, and every day sees them grouped around the altar for the holy sacrifice.
>
> This is the event of the day, the centre to which the Hours, like the centuries, all converge: some as Hours of preparation and awaiting in the recollection of the divine praise—these begin with Lauds and Prime continued by Terce, the third Hour of the day; the others, Sext, None, Vespers, and Compline, flow on in the joys of thanksgiving until sunset when the monks chant the closing in of night.
>
> Thus the days of life pass, at the foot of the altar; thus the life of man finds its greatness and its holiness in flowing out, so to say, upon the altar, there to mingle with that Precious Blood which is daily shed in that hallowed place: for, if the life of man is as a valueless drop of water, when lost in the Blood of Christ it acquires an infinite value and can merit the divine mercy for us. He who knows what the altar is, from it learns to live; to live by the altar is to be holy, pleasing to God,—and to go up to the altar to perform the sacred Mysteries is to be clothed upon with the most sublime of all dignities after that of the Son of God and His holy Mother.[393]

[393] de Hemptinne, *A Benedictine Soul,* 145–47.

So far from being the province of dreamy monks, such a grand vision of the Holy Mass, the priesthood, the liturgy, and the calling of Christians to participate in the mysteries of Christ could—prior to the last Council—be found everywhere in the Catholic world, expressed in luxurious variety. Yes, we can thank the Liturgical Movement in its original phase for reviving awareness of the treasures of tradition; and, lamentably, we can blame the Liturgical Movement in its radical phase for smashing them to bits in the vain pursuit of fabled antiquity and modern relevance.

It's no secret to Catholics today that liturgy has become a battlefield of conflicting opinions, practices, experiments, improvisations, and abuses. It hardly seems that a day passes when we don't hear about how the Mass somewhere or other has been harnessed into the service of the latest fad or trend, reducing divine worship to a means to some further end—usually a practical end, like motivating teens to help immigrants or to save Mother Earth.

This is fundamentally the wrong way of looking at our highest act, in which we approach our Maker, Lord, and Judge. As bequeathed to us along the path of apostolic tradition, the sacred liturgy is the gateway to the mystery of Christ, the best and most perfect way He has left us for drawing near to Him in our pilgrimage. The liturgy is the pinnacle, the exemplar, of all human activity, and at the same time, the home where men open their souls to God's divinizing action.

Since all grace is given through Christ, and Christ gives Himself to us in the Eucharist, the Eucharist must be at the center of our lives. The entire supernatural life of the Christian can be accurately described as *Eucharistic*: the giving of thanks and worship to the Father. Removing the liturgy, one would remove the action and passion of Christ from our midst. This would strip the Christian life of its fundamental purpose: to make us knowers and lovers of God.

The good of anything is its perfection. The perfection of a thing whose end is outside of itself consists in the attainment of that end. The end of man is God, and the activity by which we are united to God is both loving (on the part of the will) and knowing (on the part of the intellect). On earth as in heaven, the expression of our relationship to God is the act of worship, which perfects both the will and the intellect. For this reason, holy contemplation—understood as union with and adoration of God—is the good activity that corresponds to our attainment of the ultimate good.

Everything in human life is to be judged by the contribution it makes to the activity of adoring God and reaching union with Him. Since liturgy is the privileged way in which this activity is carried out and perfected—so much so that many of the Fathers of the Church, the Eastern ones in particular, describe heaven as an eternal liturgy—it follows that all human perfections are ordered to our liturgical participation in divine mysteries. If Christian life culminates in the enrapturing vision of the Blessed Trinity and the Incarnate Word, and if to us pilgrims these realities are manifested and made present most of all in the sacred liturgy, then the ultimate end of everything that man *is* and *does* on earth is the adoration of God through the Holy Sacrifice of the Mass. Everything God gives to us is for the sake of adoring the one true God, the all-holy Trinity, through, with, and in Jesus Christ, true God and true man. "He who knows what the altar is, from it learns to live; to live by the altar is to be holy, pleasing to God."

It must be remembered that theology and spirituality are about *one thing* and have only *one purpose*: God. This means they also comprise the gradual ascent to God, the hearing of His revealed word, the sharing in His divine life through the sacraments. The liturgy, again, is the privileged setting of Scripture not just by giving the readings their original and abiding home, but, infinitely more, by containing the essence of the entire revelation of Christ—the highest wisdom, the greatest power, the all-conquering love—in the mystical, sacrificial banquet.

The Fathers of the Church concur that if you want to understand Scripture, you must live a holy life in imitation of Christ, the Word whom the words of Scripture teach about and point to. The Bible was given for those striving to be holy, and that is why its pages can be so obscure—as St. Augustine says, they discourage all but the unwearying laborer, the tireless seeker of God. Without Scripture, you can have no theology, which is the highest wisdom attainable by the human mind; but without participation in the living Christ, you cannot understand Scripture or interiorize its meaning; and without the liturgy, there is no participation in the mystery, since the liturgy contains the *mysterium fidei* in its living, breathing reality, as the center from which all the radii of the Church's mission in the world project outwards, like the rays of a dazzling sun.

Like the monastic life, the liturgy too has been called "the school of sanctity." Liturgy educates by presenting the mysterious Truths of Faith to each faculty of the human person and demanding some response from us. The very language of the liturgy in all its dimensions is a continual exegesis of Scripture, a living and penetrating presentation of the mysteries of faith to the eyes of the soul. The many-layered symbolism in the ceremonies, gestures, vestments, and sacred objects leads the soul into the realm of divine truth, guiding our senses and our intellect to what lies beyond them. The meaning of these symbols is easily discerned (though never exhausted) by a soul *fully awake*, and this helps us to see that a successful "reform" of liturgy would have had the effect of helping people to wake up and stay awake, rather than dumbing things down so that they might remain asleep in their worldly or conventional ideas. But what am I saying? There is no need to reform tradition; there is only the need to understand it, to teach it, and to live it better.

The liturgy must be a spacious home to the divine symbols and the realities they convey, letting them shine through words and chants, gestures and ceremonies, indeed the entire language of appearances. If there is going to be singing and speaking during Mass, all of it ought to be focused entirely *on the mystery*—as it is in the Eastern liturgies, with their escalating waves of sung prayers, or in the Solemn Latin Mass, when Gregorian chant, dignified rituals, and moments of saturated silence combine to place the soul outside of time, outside of place, into the very Heart of Christ, the Teacher, Shepherd, and Savior.

Epilogue

A global objection to this entire book might be on the minds of some of its readers, an objection often voiced by conservatives critical of traditionalists. "The aspects or features you call *distinctive* of the traditional Latin Mass are actually, to a greater or lesser extent, still available in the Novus Ordo. It is only due to the unfortunate cultural climate at the time of its introduction in 1970, followed by decades of bad ecclesiastical habits and lackluster episcopal leadership, that we have not seen the new rite done in a manner more continuous with tradition, such as facing eastwards, in Latin, with chant, only males serving in ministerial roles, Communion on the tongue and kneeling, and so forth. Today's younger clergy are more inclined to do it that way, and we should constructively emphasize the common ground between old and new, rather than pitting the old against the new."

I respect that point of view, which used to be mine as well.[394] I do not hold it anymore, for reasons I have gone into elsewhere.[395] The most basic reason is that the old rite is integrally and necessarily *determined* by its texts and rubrics: it *must* include *all* of the features we have discussed in this book, and in context they all make sense, mutually reinforced and reinforcing. This was the main point of chapter 4, although I have touched on it in many places. To use a favorite metaphor of our times, you see there, in the TLM, the harmonious working-together of the flora and fauna of the liturgical ecosystem: the *ad orientem* position is required, as is the use of Latin;

[394] See Kwasniewski, "Imbuing the Ordinary Form with Extraordinary Form Spirituality" and "Two Attitudes toward Ordinary Form Rubrics." The *ne plus ultra* in this regard is Cipolla's "A Primer for a Tradition-Minded Celebration of the OF Mass."

[395] See Kwasniewski, *Once and Future Roman Rite.* For further thoughts on the improbabilities and impossibilities of both the "hermeneutic of continuity" and the Reform of the Reform, see, in addition, the following articles of mine: "Why the 'Reform of the Reform' Is Doomed"; "Can a Case Still Be Made for Reforming the Reform?"; "The 'Latin Novus Ordo' Is Not the Solution"; "Restoration, Not Reform, Is the Only Way Forward."

the clergy's roles are tightly defined, and if laity (male only) are to assist in the capacity of acolytes, they do so dressed in cassock and surplice—there are no "extraordinary ministers of Holy Communion"; the atmosphere of the prayers and ceremonies is simply what it is and must be: kingly, courtly, hierarchical, ordered to the service of Christ the King, who is received by His subjects on bended knee, in a posture of submissive humility. There is, indeed, no room for spontaneity or adaptation, and that is on purpose; there are no options within the rite, no choices to be made by the celebrant that might advertise either his piety and good taste or the lack thereof. In short, what you see in the missal and its rubrics is what you get, *every time*.[396] It is meant to be utterly consistent, stable, and predictable, because that is the only way it can really be *prayed*, with our ego safely out of the way. A foundation of rock is meant to be immovable so that a building can be placed on top of it. The same holds for the liturgy: if it is to serve as the foundation of our spiritual life, it needs to be immovable. As Marcel De Corte perfectly expressed it:

> Because the soul of each member of the faithful is oriented towards God, the unchanging [traditional] Mass realizes the union in God of all those who take part. Each goes according to his or her personal disposition, and according to the grace of God that sustains them. Some unite themselves to God in this or that part of the Mass, this or that phrase, this or that formula; others do so in others. Even those who are present only in body take part in the Mass to a degree that is not nil. The Tridentine Mass is the only one that is truly "personal and communal."
>
> For the Mass to be attended and participated in with such analogical degrees, it must always remain the same in its meaning and signs. Any change introduced disrupts the accustomed momentum of the soul as it rises to God above the vicissitudes of this world. Any change breaks the cohesion of the faithful. The mere fact of having allowed different Eucharistic Prayers [in the modern rite of Paul VI] can only disperse attention, diminish it, extinguish it. Because it's always the same,

[396] Provided, of course, that the clergy involved are well-trained in the rite; my argument takes that for granted, and my extensive travels visiting TLM communities in the United States and across the world have persuaded me that it is usually the case.

> the Tridentine Mass creates habits (in Latin, *habitus*)—stable qualities that perfect the faithful's faculties, their being and their actions. Regularly repeated physical exercise strengthens the limbs. Regularly repeated religious practice brings the action of the supernatural ever more deeply into the soul. God does not despise this psychological law, which He Himself created, and which the most rudimentary experience of human life reveals to the most untrained eye. In order to live, and above all to access the spiritual life, man urgently needs all those earthly substitutes for eternity: identity, permanence, repetition, refrains, accumulation of synonymous expressions, etc.[397]

If a liturgy is successfully to nourish a healthy and balanced Catholic interior life and all the good works that should flow therefrom, that liturgy also *needs* all the other aspects this book has explained—and it needs them as intrinsic properties, not as extrinsic accidents.

The Novus Ordo *can* be done *ad orientem*, but as we have seen for years, and continue to see, priests are rebuked, bullied, even canceled, when they try to return to this tradition. Worries, woes, and wrath have descended upon the heads of priests for other "crimes" too, such as reintroducing Latin and traditional sacred music. If not even Pope Paul VI expected these things to be part of the Novus Ordo, which was designed for immediate comprehension and the most active involvement possible for everyone,[398] it is not clear how the reintroduction of a hieratic language and an utterly non-contemporary and talent-based style of singing corresponds to the stated goals of the new rite's architects and current ecclesiastical patrons. Because the new rite is emptied of much of the tradition's textual and ceremonial content, it does not function nearly as well at forming and guiding the priest in the action *and spirit* of the high-priestly sacrifice, and thereby also cheats the faithful of the vicarious formation they can receive from a more sacerdotally elaborate and manifestly sacrificial act (as I argued in chapter 2). The superficial understanding of "active participation" has so melded with the new rite that, apart from the rarest exotic species at an Oratory, one will be hard-pressed to find a Mass that does not conscript

---

[397] De Corte, "Sur les variations du clergé catholique."

[398] See Kwasniewski, *Once and Future Roman Rite,* 117–43.

various unvested laity into service—usually women, out of an egalitarian notion of "giving them what they can do" to "balance out" the male clergy.

Thanks to this activism and populism, accompanied by the unavoidable verbosity of a rite in which almost everything is required to be said aloud and at short intervals, comes an atmosphere lethal to meditation and inimical to higher acts of prayer. As we saw in chapters 4, 5, and 6, the textual and rubrical deficiencies of the Novus Ordo are hard-wired into its books, which have been in use now for more than half a century, and there is nothing that can be done to improve them—at least, nothing that can be done by anyone who is unwilling to ignore or contradict canon law and liturgical law on his own initiative.[399] And so the rite of Paul VI will remain as dull and denuded as it is, until and unless a future pope decides to reanimate Joseph Ratzinger's well-intended but papally unsupported (and, at the moment, totally eclipsed) project of a "reform of the reform," a program that has as many interpretations and possible instantiations as there are liturgically awake individuals.

Moreover, let's be honest with ourselves: if this reform were thoroughly executed, leaving no stone unturned, would it not amount to a herculean effort to rebuild an intact system that *already exists* in the Tridentine liturgical books? After all that laborious tinkeritis, the final result will *still* not possess the internal coherence and continuity of the authentic Roman Rite, stretching back into the mists of the third century,[400] with its roots in the first origins of the Church of Rome, hallowed by the blood of Sts. Peter and Paul. The perfections we are after—the perfections we so urgently need for the good of souls and for the health of the Church—*are already in our God-given patrimony of liturgical rites*. All we need to do is take them up again in their preexisting integrity, restoring them to the place of honor they once enjoyed and ought to enjoy until the end of time.[401]

---

[399] See Kwasniewski, "Two 'Disobediences' Compared."

[400] As shown by Uwe Michael Lang in his magnificent book *The Roman Mass*.

[401] The "defects" of the TLM frequently criticized in the "old days" had to do mostly with *how* it was celebrated (too fast, too muttered, poor music, etc.) and with how the faithful related to it. These things can obviously be addressed without turning the liturgy upside-down and inside-out. At the end of the day, it is simply not possible to rid the world of every liturgical abuse, less-than-ideal execution of ceremonies, or uninvolved, indifferent laity. The better question to ask is the one asked by the Council of Trent: How do we improve the formation of clergy and the ongoing formation of the people? Without this commitment to real formation-in-tradition,

Many clergy and laity are suffering now from the unmerciful "accompaniment" and unjust restrictions unleashed by the despisers of tradition and the saboteurs of liturgical peace. I know that many in conscience believe that they can do nothing other, or nothing better, than a patchwork "traditionalized" Novus Ordo. Though I disagree, I understand their plight—the situation in many places is extremely bitter and difficult.[402] I would only counsel everyone to develop an ever-greater appreciation of what is at stake in the preservation of our integral and authentic Roman liturgical tradition, and then urge them to be ready to take whatever steps they can to recover it once and for all, after the open hunting season on it has passed with the inevitable passing of generations. Today's traducers of tradition, though powerful, are past their prime and curmudgeonly, while the Roman Rite, though besieged, is immortally youthful and attractive. The time will come when men will be surprised that it was ever under attack rather than being held aloft as the crown jewel of the Latin Church.

---

no amount of external reform can avoid dwindling results and mounting frustrations.

402 For close analysis of the post-*Traditionis Custodes* situation as well as concrete suggestions for clergy and laity who rightly refuse to give up the immense good of Catholic tradition, see my companion books *True Obedience in the Church* and *Bound by Truth.*

What Next?

The first thing I always recommend is this: if you haven't already done so, pick up a good daily missal and get to be familiar with it. There's no need to feel *glued* to the missal; there will be plenty of times when you'll simply want to pray quietly at the traditional Mass, and, thanks be to God, the TLM gives you that wonderful liberty of the sons of God. At the same time, the riches in the Roman missal are nothing short of astonishing, and they should become a staple food for our interior life.[403] I like to say that I was "converted by my missal," because following along with it not only taught me the differences between the old and new rites but also served as an incomparable school of spirituality. After using it a lot for many years, nowadays I don't need to consult it nearly so much, because I am already familiar with the Order of Mass as well as many of the Commons and Propers of saints. My favorite daily missal is the St. Andrew's from 1948 (available as a reprint), which is useful especially for its commentaries and its pre-55 content. For the 1962 missal, the Baronius Press and Angelus Press missals are praiseworthy candidates. If you would like an even easier way of access, take out a subscription to the *Benedictus* monthly missal mailed out from Sophia Institute Press, which gives you not only the full Ordinary and Propers for each Sunday and Holy Day of obligation, but also the daily Propers together with seasonal or festal meditations and devotions (in other words, it's the "*Magnificat* for the old rite"). Be sure to check out Sophia's full-color poster-sized Illustrated Liturgical Calendar as well.

The next step is to delve into the meaning of the prayers and ceremonies themselves. For that, I recommend Lisa Bergman's *Treasure and Tradition* (St. Augustine Academy Press, 2014), a colorful, illustration-packed

[403] For superabundant proof, consult Foley, *Lost in Translation.*

guide to the TLM, appropriate for all ages, and, what's more, suitable as a homeschooling text. Pick up Joseph Shaw's non-polemical and insightful pamphlet *Sacred and Great: A Brief Introduction to the Traditional Latin Mass* (Os Justi Press, 2023). This unthreatening pocket-sized pamphlet is an ideal giveaway for relatives, friends, or people you bump into who are open-minded, curious, or even skeptical about the TLM. It also has well-curated lists of recommended resources at the end, including books, websites, videos, and smartphone apps. My book *Reclaiming Our Roman Catholic Birthright* (Angelico Press, 2020) is a one-stop shop for apologetics in favor of liturgical tradition and in refutation of arguments brought against it, but with broader social commentary and more pointed ecclesiastical commentary than one finds in the present book. Like Shaw's pamphlet, *Reclaiming Our Roman Catholic Birthright* ends with a select bibliography of recommended reading divided into categories, including books specifically for younger readers. In a related vein, the anthology *Illusions of Reform: Responses to Cavadini, Healy, and Weinandy in Defense of the Traditional Mass and the Faithful Who Attend It* (Os Justi Press, 2023) offers a complete synopsis of all the typical arguments given against the old rite and thoroughly refutes them, with humor as well as scholarship.

When you are ready for a "deep dive," the single best and most accessible book on the Roman Rite is Michael Fiedrowicz's *The Traditional Mass: History, Form, and Theology of the Classical Roman Rite* (Angelico Press, 2020). The definitive scholarly history of the Roman Rite from antiquity to 1570 is Uwe Michael Lang's *The Roman Mass: From Early Christian Origins to Tridentine Reform* (Cambridge University Press, 2022). My book *The Once and Future Roman Rite: Returning to the Traditional Latin Liturgy after Seventy Years of Exile* (TAN Books, 2022) presents a thorough investigation of the "unique Roman Rite," that is, the Tridentine rite, comparing it with the Eastern rites and the modern rite of Paul VI, and providing an extended treatment of the concept of "organic development," a wide-ranging meditation on the Roman Canon, and a synopsis of the superiority of the pre-55 (i.e., Tridentine) missal in contrast to the 1962 edition. If you are particularly interested in the music that belongs, by right, to the Mass, check out my book *Good Music, Sacred Music, and Silence: Three Gifts of God for Liturgy and for Life* (TAN Books, 2023).

If you're interested in how our forefathers engaged with the traditional liturgy, rejoicing in its complex symbolism, take a look at Fr. Claude Barthe's *A Forest of Symbols: The Traditional Mass and Its Meaning* (Angelico Press, 2023). The more adventuresome may check out Honorius Augustodunensis's *Jewel of the Soul* (Harvard University Press, 2023), Pope Innocent III's *The Mysteries of the Mass & The Four Kinds of Marriage* (Angelus Press, 2023), and Urban Hannon's *Thomistic Mystagogy: St. Thomas Aquinas's Commentaries on the Mass* (Os Justi Press, 2024). Two other accessible classics are Martin von Cochem's 1704 work *Explanation of the Holy Sacrifice of the Mass* (retitled *The Incredible Catholic Mass* when reprinted by TAN Books, 2012) and St. Leonard of Port Maurice's eighteenth-century *The Hidden Treasure* (TAN Books, 2012). Books such as these benefit the reader with profuse and profound insights; but they also serve to demonstrate the substantive continuity of Catholic spiritual and theological writing on the Holy Mass—a body of commentary stretching from the Church Fathers through the medieval mystics and scholastics down into the Counter-Reformation and right up to the eve of the Second Vatican Council. In spite of differences in emphasis and style, it is a single body of literature looking to a stable body of traditional rites. In this way, it bears witness to the magnitude of the rupture that occurred after Vatican II and the urgency of repairing it, or rather, of responding to it with the wholesale restoration of traditional rites.

Lastly, given the hostile attitude of certain members of the hierarchy toward liturgical tradition, you may find benefit in reading—or may bring insight and comfort to your friends and acquaintances among the clergy by distributing copies of—my little book *True Obedience in the Church: A Guide to Discernment in Challenging Times* (Sophia Institute Press, 2022) and, for more ambitious readers, my follow-up, *Bound by Truth: Authority, Obedience, Tradition, and the Common Good* (Angelico Press, 2023). The anthology *From Benedict's Peace to Francis's War: Catholics Respond to the Motu Proprio* Traditionis Custodes *on the Latin Mass* (Angelico Press, 2021) includes dozens of essays and articles by a "who's who" of cardinals, bishops, priests, religious, and laity, defending traditional Catholics from their critics and persecutors.

The movement to preserve, propagate, and pass on tradition is alive and well, *Deo gratias*! What a privilege it is to be a part of this reawakening of the Church at prayer.

Acknowledgments

Several of these chapters began as lectures I was invited to give at various places, and many have seen multiple revisions over time. I thank all the kind people who facilitated the trips here, there, and everywhere—you know who you are, and more importantly, the Lord knows who you are. May He reward you for your invitations and hospitality.

Two substantial portions of Chapter 1 were published at *New Liturgical Movement* as "How Contrary Orientations Signify Contradictory Theologies" on November 5, 2018 and "Mass 'Facing the People' as Counter-Catechesis and Irreligion" on August 20, 2018. Chapter 2 incorporates "How the Clergy's 'Distance' from the People Facilitates the Laity's Offering," *OnePeterFive*, September 1, 2021, and "The Priest Praying for Himself at Mass," *OnePeterFive*, September 8, 2021, as well as improvements from the lecture version "The Relationship between Priest and People in the Latin Mass: Space and Time for Divine Intimacy" published at *Rorate Caeli*, August 23, 2022. Chapter 3 was first published at *New Liturgical Movement* on May 2, 2022 as "Enter His Courts With Praise: Liturgical Reverence for Christ the King." Chapter 4 was published as "Liturgical Obedience, the Imitation of Christ, and the Seductions of Autonomy" at my Substack *Tradition & Sanity* on November 13, 2023. Chapter 5 originally appeared at *Rorate Caeli* on February 19, 2019, under the title "Poets, Lovers, Children, Madmen—and Worshipers: Why We Repeat Ourselves in the Liturgy." Chapter 6 incorporates the lecture "Mythbusting: Why the TLM's Lectionary Is Superior to the New Lectionary," published at *Rorate Caeli* on March 30, 2022, and based, in turn, on my "The Reform of the Lectionary," in Alcuin Reid, ed., *Liturgy in the Twenty-First Century: Contemporary Issues and Perspectives* (London/New York: Bloomsbury T&T Clark, 2016), 287–320, while Chapter 7 incorporates the lecture "Why Latin Is the Right Language for Roman Catholic Worship," published at

Rorate Caeli on June 8, 2022. Chapter 8 was published in three parts at *Tradition & Sanity*, on May 9, 13, and 16, 2024. Chapter 9 has been developed out of so many different articles and lectures that it would be impossible to list all of them; there are some parallel passages in my book *The Holy Bread of Eternal Life*. Chapter 10 incorporates an article under the same title at *New Liturgical Movement*, as well as my article "The sacred liturgy is the best and most perfect way to draw near to God" at *LifeSiteNews* on July 19, 2018. A number of the preceding pieces also appeared in the pages of *Latin Mass* magazine. All of the foregoing essays and articles have been revised for inclusion in this book, with many notes added.

Bibliography

In order to avoid clutter, hyperlinks for articles at several popular websites—*New Liturgical Movement*, *OnePeterFive*, *Crisis Magazine*, *Rorate Caeli*, etc.—are not included, as all these articles come up instantly with a title search. Hyperlinks are given for more obscure items.

Augustine. *On Christian Doctrine*. Translated by James Shaw. *Nicene and Post-Nicene Fathers, First Series*, vol. 2. Translated by James Shaw and Edited by Philip Schaff. Buffalo, NY: Christian Literature Publishing Co., 1887. Revised and edited for New Advent by Kevin Knight, http://www.newadvent.org/fathers/12022.htm.

——. *Expositions of the Psalms 1–32*. Translated by Maria Boulding. Hyde Park, NY: New City Press, 2000.

Augustinus. "The 50th Anniversary of Paul VI's First Italian Mass: Some hard truths about the '1965 Missal' and the Liturgical Reform." *Rorate Caeli*, March 7, 2015.

Bagshawe, J.B. *The Treasure of the Church*. New York: Burns & Oates, 1902.

Baresel, James. "Archbishop Roche: 'The Traditional Mass Must Go,'" *Inside the Vatican*, March–April 2022, https://issuu.com/insidethevaticanmagazine/docs/inside_the_vatican_magazine_march-april_2022/s/15214344.

Barthe, Claude. *A Forest of Symbols: The Traditional Mass and Its Meaning*. Translated by David J. Critchley. Brooklyn, NY: Angelico Press, 2023.

——. "A Sacrificial and Royal Liturgy." Homily for the Feast of Christ the King, October 31, 2021. *Rorate Caeli*, December 17, 2023.

Basil of Caesarea. *On the Holy Spirit*. Translated by Blomfield Jackson. Edited by Philip Schaff and Henry Wace. Nicene and Post-Nicene Fathers, Second Series, vol. 8. Buffalo, NY: Christian Literature Publishing Co., 1895. Revised and edited for New Advent by Kevin Knight, www.newadvent.org/fathers/3203.htm.

The Beauties of St. Francis de Sales. Selected and translated from the writings of John Peter Camus. London: Longman, Rees, Orme, Brown, and Green, 1829.

Bell, Luke. *The Mystery of Identity*. Brooklyn, NY: Angelico Press, 2022.

Benedict of Nursia. *The Rule of Saint Benedict in English and Latin*. Translated by Justin McCann. Fort Collins, CO: Roman Catholic Books, n.d.

Benedict XVI. Homily for Corpus Christi. May 22, 2008.

——. Lecture of the Holy Father at the Aula Magna of the University of Regensburg. September 12, 2006.

——. Post-Synodal Apostolic Exhortation *Verbum Domini*. September 30, 2010.

Benson, Robert Hugh. *By What Authority?* Stamullen: Cenacle Press, 2022.

——. *Papers of a Pariah*. Stamullen: Cenacle Press, 2022.

Bergman, Lisa. *Treasure and Tradition*. Homer Glen, IL: St. Augustine Academy Press, 2014.

Berquist, Marcus R. *Learning and Discipleship*. Edited by Anne S. Forsyth. Santa Paula, CA: Thomas Aquinas College, 2019.

Bougaud, Émile. *Revelations of the Sacred Heart to Blessed Margaret Mary and the History of Her Life*. Translated by a Visitandine of Baltimore. New York: Benziger Brothers, 1890.

Bouyer, Louis. *The Invisible Father: Approaches to the Mystery of the Divinity*. Translated by Hugh Gilbert. Edinburgh: T&T Clark. Petersham, MA: St. Bede's Publications, 1999.

——. *Liturgy and Architecture*. Notre Dame, IN: University of Notre Dame Press, 1967.

——. *Rite and Man: Natural Sacredness and Christian Liturgy*. Translated by M. Joseph Costelloe. Notre Dame, IN: University of Notre Dame Press, 1963.

Buck, Roger. *Cor Jesu Sacratissimum: From Secularism and the New Age to Christendom Renewed*. Kettering, OH: Angelico Press, 2016.

Bugnini, Annibale. *The Reform of the Liturgy, 1948–1975*. Translated by Matthew J. O'Connell. Collegeville, MN: The Liturgical Press, 1990.

Cantalamessa, Raniero. "Mysterium Fidei! On the Liturgy—Fourth Lenten Sermon 2023." March 24, 2023. http://www.cantalamessa.org/?p=4080&lang=en.

Catechism of the Council of Trent for Parish Priests. Translated by John A. McHugh and Charles J. Callan. Rockford, IL: TAN Books and Publishers, 1982.

Chautard, Jean-Baptiste. *The Soul of the Apostolate*. Translated by a Monk of Our Lady of Gethsemani. Trappist, KY: The Abbey of Gethsemani, Inc., 1946; republished Rockfold, IL: TAN Books, 2012.

Chesterton, G.K. *Orthodoxy*. London: The Bodley Head, 1908.

Chiron, Yves. *Annibale Bugnini: Reformer of the Liturgy*. Translated by John Pepino. Brooklyn, NY: Angelico Press, 2018.

——. *Paul VI: The Divided Pope*. Translated by James Walther. Brooklyn, NY: Angelico Press, 2022.

Cipolla, Richard. "A Primer for a Tradition-Minded Celebration of the OF Mass." *New Liturgical Movement*, September 14, 2017.

Clarke, Veronica. "Why I Went to a Catholic College." First Things, December 2022. https://www.firstthings.com/article/2022/12/why-i-went-to-a-catholic-college.

Claudel, Paul. "La Messe à l'envers." *Le Figaro*, January 23, 1955. Translation published at *Rorate Caeli*, July 28, 2017.

Clayton, David. "Connecting *Ad Orientem*, Sacred Art, an Ordered Environmentalism, Social Graces, and a Hierarchical Society." *New Liturgical Movement*, April 10, 2018.

——. "The Smoke of Satan Enters From the West . . . at Our Invitation." *New Liturgical Movement*, October 31, 2018.

——. *The Way of Beauty: Liturgy, Education, and Inspiration for Family, School, and College*. Kettering, OH: Angelico Press, 2015.

Congregation for Divine Worship and the Discipline of the Sacraments. Instruction *Liturgiam Authenticam*. March 28, 2001.

Consilium. *Comme le Prévoit*. January 25, 1969.

Crean, Thomas. *"Letters from that City…": A Guide to Holy Scripture for Students of Theology*. Lincoln, NE: Os Justi Press, 2023.

"Cristina Campo." *L'Astero Rosso,* April 25, 2023. https://www.asterorosso.com/2023/04/25/cristina-campo/.

Cyril of Jerusalem. *Mystagogical Catecheses.* Translated by Leo P. McCauley. *Fathers of the Church,* vol. 64. Washington, DC: Catholic University of America Press, 1970.

Davies, Michael. *Pope Paul's New Mass.* Kansas City, MO: Angelus Press, 2009.

de Corte, Marcel. "Sur les variations du clergé catholique." *Itinéraires* 210 (February 1977).

de Hemptinne, Pius. *A Benedictine Soul: Biography, Letters, and Spiritual Writings of Dom Pius De Hemptinne.* Stamullen: Cenacle Press, 2022.

de Tocqueville, Alexis. *Democracy in America,* vol. 2. Translated by Henry Reeve. www.gutenberg.org/files/816/816-h/816-h.htm.

DeVille, Adam A.J. "When it comes to liturgy, we're all mutually-enriching mongrels." *The Catholic World Report,* February 10, 2017.

DiPippo, Gregory. "Liturgical Improvisation Must End." *New Liturgical Movement,* August 26, 2020.

——. "Other Readings for the Octave of Corpus Christi." *New Liturgical Movement,* June 4, 2021.

——. "Reforming the Canon of the Mass: Some Considerations from Fr Hunwicke." *New Liturgical Movement,* April 25, 2015.

——. "The Theology of the Offertory—Series to Resume." *New Liturgical Movement,* February 27, 2015.

——. "The Unfunded Mandate." *New Liturgical Movement,* March 6, 2022.

The Divine Liturgy of Our Father Among the Saints John Chrysostom. Ruthenian Recension—A Study Text. October 2015. www.byzcath.org/forums/ubbthreads.php/ubb/download/Number/1617/filename/Study-Liturgicon-Chrysostom.pdf.

Dix, Gregory. *The Shape of the Liturgy.* London: Continuum, 2005 (first published 1945).

Dubay, Thomas. *Fire Within: Teresa of Avila, John of the Cross and the Gospel on Prayer.* San Francisco: Ignatius Press, 1989.

Esolen, Anthony. "A Bumping Boxcar Language." *First Things,* June 2011. https://www.firstthings.com/article/2011/06/a-bumping-boxcar-language.

——. "Male and Female He Made Them." *Crisis Magazine,* October 17, 2023.

Everitt, Gabriel. "Let them learn some of the Psalter." Ampleforth Abbey, accessed October 24, 2017 but apparently no longer on the website www.abbey.ampleforth.org.uk.

Fiedrowicz, Michael. *The Traditional Mass: History, Form, and Theology of the Classical Roman Rite.* Translated by Rose Pfeifer. Brooklyn, NY: Angelico Press, 2020.

Foley, Michael P. "The Feasts of Saint Monica and a New Conjecture about Her Dies Obitus." *New Liturgical Movement,* May 3, 2024.

——. *Lost in Translation: Meditating on the Orations of the Traditional Roman Rite.* Brooklyn, NY: Angelico Press, 2023.

——. "The Reform of the Calendar and the Reduction of Liturgical Recapitulation." In Alcuin Reid, ed., *Liturgy in the Twenty-first Century: Contemporary Issues and Perspectives,* 321–41. London/New York: Bloomsbury T&T Clark, 2016.

Francis, Pope. Apostolic Letter *Desiderio Desideravi.* June 29, 2022.

Grillo, Andrea. "Rito tridentino e nullità matrimoniale: le inattese analogie." *Munera: Rivista Europea di Cultura,* November 8, 2022. www.cittadellaeditrice.com /munera/rito-tridentino-e-nullita-matrimoniale-le-inattese-analogie/.

Guardini, Romano. *The Spirit of the Liturgy*. Translated by Ada Lane. New York: Crossroad, n.d.

Hahn, Scott. *The Lamb's Supper: The Mass as Heaven on Earth*. New York: Doubleday, 1999.

——. *Letter and Spirit: From Written Text to Living Word in the Liturgy*. New York: Doubleday, 2005.

Hannon, Urban. "The Politics of Hell." In P. Edmund Waldstein, O.Cist., ed., *Integralism and the Common Good*, vol. 2: *The Two Powers*, 209–29. Brooklyn, NY: Angelico Press, 2022.

——. *Thomistic Mystagogy: St. Thomas Aquinas's Commentaries on the Mass*. Lincoln, NE: Os Justi Press, 2024.

Harrison, Brian W. "The Biblical Dimension of Paul VI's Liturgical Vision." *Living Tradition*, no. 154 (September 2011): 1–6.

Hauke, Manfred. *Women in the Priesthood? A Systematic Analysis in the Light of the Order of Creation and Redemption*. San Francisco: Ignatius Press, 1988.

Hausherr, Irénée. *The Name of Jesus*. Translated by Charles Cummings. Cistercian Studies 44. Collegeville, MN: Liturgical Press, 1978.

Hayden, Evagrius. "*Convertere, Israël, ad Dominum Deum Tuum!*: A Benedictine Monk Defends Worshiping Eastwards." *New Liturgical Movement*, November 16, 2015.

Heid, Stefan. *Altar and Church: Principles of Liturgy from Early Christianity*. Washington, DC: Catholic University of America Press, 2023.

Hickson, Maike. "Official draft of new Mayan rite of Mass confirms elements of ancient pagan worship, lay 'principals.'" *LifeSiteNews*, March 22, 2023.

Hillier, Paul, and Tõnu Tormis. *On Pärt*. Copenhagen: Edition Samfundet, 2005.

Honorius Augustodunensis. *Jewel of the Soul*. Translated by Zachary Thomas and Gerhard Eger. Cambridge, MA: Harvard University Press, 2023.

Hopkins, Gerard Manley. Translation of the hymn *Adoro te devote*. https://spicathedral.org/blog/adoro-te-devote-a-eucharistic-hymn/.

Howard, Thomas. *The Secret of New York Revealed: Being the Autobiographical Fragments of the Then Recently Married Thomas Howard Chronicling His Numerous Discoveries in the City of That Name*. San Francisco: Ignatius Press, 2002.

Hunwicke, John. "Facing the Mystery; or Catholic Crustaceans." *Fr Hunwicke's Mutual Enrichment*, February 4, 2020.

Innocent III, Pope. *The Mysteries of the Mass & The Four Kinds of Marriage*. St. Marys, KS: Angelus Press, 2023.

John XXIII, Pope. Apostolic Constitution *Veterum Sapientia*. February 22, 1962. The English translation is from papalencyclicals.net.

John Damascene. *De fide orthodoxa*. In St. John of Damascus, *Writings*. Translated by F.H. Chase. *The Fathers of the Church*, vol. 37. Washington, DC: Catholic University of America Press, 1958.

John Paul II, Pope. Apostolic Letter *Dominicae Cenae*. February 24, 1980.

——. Encyclical Letter *Ecclesia de Eucharistia*. April 17, 2003.

——. Encyclical Letter *Orientale Lumen*. May 2, 1995.

——. General Audience. November 3, 2004.

——. Post-Synodal Apostolic Exhortation *Christifideles Laici*. December 30, 1988.
——. Speech to Participants in the "Certamen Vaticanum." November 27, 1978.
Julian of Norwich. *Revelations of Divine Love*. Translated by Elizabeth Spearing. London: Penguin Books, 1998.
Jungmann, Joseph. *The Early Liturgy to the Time of Gregory the Great*. Translated by Francis A. Brunner. Notre Dame, IN: University of Notre Dame Press, 1959.
Knox, Ronald A. *The Pastoral Sermons*. Edited by Philip Caraman. New York: Sheed & Ward, 1960.
Kwasniewski, Peter. "Between Christ the King and 'We Have No King But Caesar.'" *OnePeterFive*, October 25, 2020.
——. *Bound by Truth: Authority, Obedience, Tradition, and the Common Good*. Brooklyn, NY: Angelico Press, 2023.
——. "Can a Case Still Be Made for Reforming the Reform?" *OnePeterFive*, May 3, 2023.
——. "Can We Call Ourselves 'Traditional Catholics'?" *OnePeterFive*, April 12, 2023.
——. "The Chop-Chop Reform and the Mass of the Ages." *New Liturgical Movement*, July 25, 2022.
——. "Christian Militancy in the Prayer of the Church." *OnePeterFive*, March 16, 2022.
——. "Clothed in the Vesture of Royalty: Sharing the Beauty of Our Mass." *OnePeterFive*, January 8, 2021.
——. "The Council Fathers in Support of Latin: Correcting a Narrative Bias." *New Liturgical Movement*, September 13, 2017.
——. *The Ecstasy of Love in the Thought of St. Thomas Aquinas*. Steubenville, OH: Emmaus Academic, 2021.
——. "Escaping the Closed Circle: Why in the TLM the Epistle Is Read Eastwards and the Gospel Northwards." www.youtube.com/watch?v=xUfBFRJNUQE.
——. "'For I Will Not Give You a Kiss as Did Judas': On Sacred and Profane Kissing." *New Liturgical Movement*, April 6, 2020.
——. "Formation and Malformation: Why Catechesis Isn't Enough if the Liturgy is Countercatechetical." *New Liturgical Movement*, June 21, 2021.
——, ed. *From Benedict's Peace to Francis's War: Catholics Respond to the Motu Proprio* Traditionis Custodes *on the Latin Mass* Brooklyn, NY: Angelico Press, 2021.
——. "From Extemporaneity to Fixity of Form: The Grace of Liturgical Stability." *New Liturgical Movement*, October 11, 2021.
——. *Good Music, Sacred Music, and Silence: Three Gifts of God for Liturgy and for Life*. Gastonia, NC: TAN Books, 2023.
——. *The Holy Bread of Eternal Life: Restoring Eucharistic Reverence in an Age of Impiety*. Manchester, NH: Sophia Institute Press, 2020.
——. "The Homily Is Not Part of the Liturgy." *The Remnant*, January 15, 2021.
——, ed. *Illusions of Reform: Responses to Cavadini, Healy, and Weinandy in Defense of the Traditional Mass and the Faithful Who Attend It*. Lincoln, NE: Os Justi Press, 2023.
——. "Imbuing the Ordinary Form with Extraordinary Form Spirituality." *New Liturgical Movement*, April 13, 2015.
——. "The 'Latin Novus Ordo' Is Not the Solution." *OnePeterFive*, August 24, 2022.
——. "The Lie That Was Told to Over 2,000 Council Fathers at Vatican II." *New Liturgical Movement*, May 27, 2024.

——. "Men Must Be Changed by Sacred Things, and Not Sacred Things by Men." *OnePeterFive*, September 15, 2021.

——. *Ministers of Christ: Recovering the Roles of Clergy and Laity in an Age of Confusion.* Manchester, NH: Sophia Institute Press, 2021.

——. "'Moments of Liturgical Action': Recovering the Sacramentality of Biblical Lections." *New Liturgical Movement*, January 24, 2022.

——. *Noble Beauty, Transcendent Holiness: Why the Modern Age Needs the Mass of Ages.* Kettering, OH: Angelico Press, 2017.

——. "The Normativity of *Ad Orientem* Worship According to the Ordinary Form's Rubrics." *New Liturgical Movement*, November 23, 2015.

——. "Not Abandoning the Flock—Not Abandoning the Truth." *OnePeterFive*, July 13, 2022.

——. "The Omission of 'Difficult' Psalms and the Spreading-Thin of the Psalter." *Rorate Caeli*, November 15, 2016.

——. *The Once and Future Roman Rite: Returning to the Traditional Latin Liturgy after Seventy Years of Exile.* Gastonia, NC: TAN Books, 2022.

——. "Praying in the Same Words with which the Saints Prayed." *New Liturgical Movement*, August 1, 2022.

——. "Processing through the Courts of the Great King." *New Liturgical Movement*, February 13, 2023.

——. *Reclaiming Our Roman Catholic Birthright: The Genius and Timeliness of the Traditional Latin Mass.* Brooklyn, NY: Angelico Press, 2020.

——. "Refuting the Commonplace that 'Liturgy' Means 'Work of the People.'" *New Liturgical Movement*, May 9, 2022.

——. "Restoration, Not Reform, Is the Only Way Forward." *New Liturgical Movement*, June 6, 2022.

——. *Resurgent in the Midst of Crisis: Sacred Liturgy, the Traditional Latin Mass, and Renewal in the Church.* Kettering, OH: Angelico Press, 2014.

——. "The Sacrifice of Praise and the Ecstatic Orientation of Man." *Rorate Caeli*, July 28, 2016.

——. "The Sanctoral Killing Fields: On the Removal of Saints from the General Roman Calendar." *New Liturgical Movement*, November 16, 2020.

——. *Treasuring the Goods of Marriage in a Throwaway Society.* Manchester, NH: Sophia Institute Press, 2023.

——. *True Obedience in the Church: A Guide to Discernment in Challenging Times.* Manchester, NH: Sophia Institute Press, 2022.

——. "Two Attitudes toward Ordinary Form Rubrics: Kantian Duty and Aristotelian *Epikeia*." *New Liturgical Movement*, January 8, 2018

——. "Two 'Disobediences' Compared." *OnePeterFive*, January 18, 2023.

——. "Two Modest Proposals for Improving the Prayerfulness of Low Mass." *New Liturgical Movement*, November 12, 2018.

——, ed. *Ultramontanism and Tradition: The Role of Papal Authority in the Catholic Faith.* Lincoln, NE: Os Justi Press, 2024.

——, ed. *Unresolved Tensions in Papal-Episcopal Relations: Essays Occasioned by the Deposition of Bishop Joseph Strickland.* Lincoln, NE: Os Justi Press, 2024.

——. "What They Requested, What They Expected, and What Happened: Council Fathers on the Latin Roman Canon." *New Liturgical Movement*, August 8, 2022.

——. "Who Was Captain of the Ship in the Liturgical Reform? The 50th Anniversary of an Embarrassing Letter." *New Liturgical Movement*, June 24, 2019.

——. "Why 1962 Must Eventually Perish: The Case of St. John." *New Liturgical Movement*, December 26, 2022.

——. "Why the 'Reform of the Reform' Is Doomed." *OnePeterFive*, April 22, 2020.

Lamont, John. "Dominican Theologian Attacks Catholic Tradition: Defending Kwasniewski against Donneaud's Positivist Reductionism." Published in four parts at *Rorate Caeli,* September 2023; available as a single PDF via https://rorate-caeli.blogspot.com/2023/09/dominican-theologian-attacks-catholic_20.html.

Lang, Uwe Michael. *The Roman Mass: From Early Christian Origins to Tridentine Reform*. Cambridge: Cambridge University Press, 2022.

Lanzetta, Serafina M. *Super Hanc Petram: The Pope and the Church at a Dramatic Moment in History*. Lincoln, NE: Os Justi Press, 2023.

Leclercq, Jean. *The Love of Learning and the Desire for God: A Study of Monastic Culture*. Translated by Catharine Misrahi. New York: Fordham University Press, 1982.

Lemna, Keith. *The Apocalypse of Wisdom: Louis Bouyer's Theological Recovery of the Cosmos*. Brooklyn, NY: Angelico Press, 2019.

Leonard of Port Maurice. *The Hidden Treasure: or The Immense Excellence of the Holy Sacrifice of the Mass; Together with a Practical and Devout Method of Assisting at It with Fruit*. Dublin: James Duffy, 1861.

Lewis, C.S. *A Preface to Paradise Lost*. Oxford: Oxford University Press, 1942.

——. *Screwtape Letters*. New York: The Macmillan Company, 1946.

Longenecker, Dwight. "From a Priest at the Altar." May 29, 2014. www.patheos.com/blogs/standingonmyhead/2014/05/from-a-priest-at-the-altar.html.

Magister, Francis. "What Attracts Homosexuals to the Priesthood?" *Crisis Magazine*, December 12, 2023.

Marini, Guido. "Clergy Conference in Rome: Address of Msgr. Guido Marini, Papal Master of Ceremonies." *New Liturgical Movement*, January 6, 2010.

Maritain, Jacques. *Existence and the Existent*. Translated by Lewis Galantiere and Gerald B. Phelan. Garden City, NY: Image Books, 1956.

——. *God and the Permission of Evil*. Translated by Joseph W. Evans. Milwaukee: Bruce, 1966.

Martindale, C.C. *The Words of the Missal*. Lincoln, NE: Os Justi Press, 2023.

McCabe, Herbert. *God, Christ, and Us*. Edited by Brian Davies. New York: Continuum, 2003.

Mectilde of the Blessed Sacrament. *The "Breviary of Fire": Letters by Mother Mectilde of the Blessed Sacrament, Chosen and Arranged by the Countess of Châteauvieux*. Translated by an Oblate of Silverstream Priory. Brooklyn, NY: Angelico Press, 2021.

——. *The True Spirit of the Perpetual Adorers of the Most Holy Sacrament of the Altar*. Translated by a Benedictine Oblate. Brooklyn, NY: Angelico Press, forthcoming.

Miller, Peter. "Bible by the Pound: Would the Holy Spirit Agree that More Bible Is Better at Mass?" In Kwasniewski, *Illusions of Reform*, 180–97.

Moore, Jeffrey. "Liturgical Participation." *Fr. Moore* (blog), February 2, 2020, https://frmoore.com/2020/02/01/february-02-2020-liturgical-participation/.

Morrill, Bruce T. "Tradition and the Roman Rite: The Ongoing Struggle." *Doxology* 32.3 (2021): 28–36.

Mosebach, Martin. *The Heresy of Formlessness: The Roman Liturgy and Its Enemy.* Revised and expanded edition. Brooklyn, NY: Angelico Press, 2018.

——. "Holy Routine: The Mystery of Repetition." *First Things,* September 14, 2017. www.firstthings.com/web-exclusives/2017/09/holy-routine.

——. *Subversive Catholicism: Papacy, Liturgy, Church.* Translated by Sebastian Condon and Graham Harrison. Brooklyn, NY: Angelico Press, 2019.

Navarro, Joe. "Former FBI Agent Explains How to Read Body Language." WIRED, May 21, 2019. https://youtu.be/4jwUXV4QaTw.

Newman, John Henry. *Certain Difficulties Felt by Anglicans in Catholic Teaching,* vol. 1. London: Longmans, Green, and Co., 1901.

——. *An Essay on the Development of Christian Doctrine.* London: Longmans, Green, and Co., 1909.

——. *The Idea of a University.* London: Longmans, Green, and Co., 1907.

——. *Loss and Gain: The Story of a Convert.* London and New York: Longmans, Green, and Co., 1906.

——. "Reverence in Worship." In *Parochial and Plain Sermons,* vol. 8. London: Longmans, Green, and Co., 1908.

Nichols, Aidan. *Looking at the Liturgy: A Critical View of Its Contemporary Form.* San Francisco: Ignatius Press, 1996.

Olmsted, Thomas J. "Knees to Love Christ." *The Catholic Sun* (Phoenix), February 17, 2005. Reprinted at www.catholicculture.org/culture/library/view.cfm?recnum=6378.

O'Loughlin, Thomas. "Liturgy is not a visit to a museum." *La Croix,* August 13, 2022.

Oppenheimer, Daniel Augustine. "Towards the Second Coming: Facing the Liturgical East." *OnePeterFive,* May 20, 2015.

Ostrowski, Jeff. "A 1969 Quote Bugnini Wishes He Could Retract." *Views from the Choir Loft* of Corpus Christi Watershed, July 8, 2014.

Otto, Rudolf. *The Idea of the Holy.* Translated by John W. Harvey. London: Oxford University Press, 1958.

Pickstock, Catherine. *After Writing: On the Liturgical Consummation of Philosophy.* Oxford: Blackwell Publishers, 1998.

Pieper, Josef. *Divine Madness: Plato's Case Against Secular Humanism.* Translated by Lothar Krauth. San Francisco: Ignatius Press, 1995.

——. *The Silence of St. Thomas.* Translated by John Murray and Daniel O'Connor. South Bend, IN: St. Augustine's Press, 1999.

Pius XI, Pope. Encyclical Letter *Officiorum Omnium.* August 1, 1922.

Pius XII, Pope. Encyclical Letter *Ad Caeli Reginam.* October 11, 1954.

——. Encyclical Letter *Mediator Dei.* November 20, 1947.

——. Encyclical Letter *Mystici Corporis Christi.* June 29, 1943.

Pluth, Kathleen. "The First Step in Ecclesiastical Reform: Turn the Altars Around." *The Chant Café,* July 30, 2018.

Poe, Edgar Allen. "The Raven." www.poetryfoundation.org/poems/48860/the-raven.

Pristas, Lauren. *The Collects of the Roman Missals: A Comparative Study of the Sundays in Proper Seasons Before and After the Second Vatican Council.* London/New York: Bloomsbury T&T Clark, 2013.

Ratzinger, Joseph. "The Ecclesiology of the Constitution on the Church *Lumen Gentium.*" *L'Osservatore Romano,* English ed., September 19, 2001.

——. "The Image of the World and of Human Beings in the Liturgy and Its Expression in Church Music." In *A New Song for the Lord: Faith in Christ and Liturgy Today*, 111–27. Translated by Martha M. Matesich. New York: Crossroad, 1997.

——. *Milestones: Memoirs 1927–1977*. Translated by Erasmo Leiva-Merikakis. San Francisco: Ignatius Press, 1988.

——. *Pilgrim Fellowship of Faith: The Church as Communion*. Edited by Stephan Otto Horn and Vinzenz Pfnür. San Francisco: Ignatius Press, 2005.

——. *The Spirit of the Liturgy*. Translated by John Saward. San Francisco: Ignatius Press, 2000.

——. *Theology of the Liturgy: The Sacramental Foundation of Christian Existence*. Translated by John Saward, et al. Edited by Michael J. Miller, et al. *Collected Works*, vol. 11. San Francisco: Ignatius Press, 2014.

——. *Truth and Tolerance: Christian Belief and World Religions*. Translated by Henry Taylor. San Francisco: Ignatius Press, 2004.

Reid, Alcuin. "Elements of the New Liturgical Movement." Lecture given at St. Mary's, Norwalk, CT, in June 2014. www.academia.edu/9282429/Elements_of_the_New_Liturgical_Movement.

Roche, Arthur. "'In the earthly liturgy we take part in a foretaste of that heavenly liturgy' (*Sacrosanctum Concilium* n. 8): The study of the liturgy as an ecclesial service for a renewed spirituality." Inaugural Address at the Athenaeum Sant'Anselmo, 2021–22, October 4, 2021. https://praytellblog.com/index.php/2021/10/07/the-study-of-the-liturgy-as-an-ecclesial-service-for-a-renewed-spirituality/.

——. "The Roman Missal of Saint Paul VI: A witness to unchanging faith and uninterrupted tradition." *Notitiae* 597 (2020): 248–58.

Ruff, Anthony. "Cardinal Sarah on Mass Not Facing the People." *PrayTell*, May 26, 2016.

——. "The Worst Reasons for *Ad Orientem*." *PrayTell*, August 18, 2016.

Sacred Congregation of the Council. Decree *Sacra Tridentina Synodus*. December 20, 1905.

Saint-Exupéry, Antoine de. *Le Petit Prince*. Paris: Gallimard, 1999.

Salmerón, Alfonso. *De Passione et Morte D.N.I.C.* (1604). In *Comentarii in Evangelicam Historiam, et in Acta Apostolorum*, 16 vols. Cologne, 1602–1605.

Saward, John. *World Invisible: The Catholic Doctrine of the Angels*. Brooklyn, NY: Angelico Press, 2023.

Scheeben, Matthias Joseph. *The Mysteries of Christianity*. Translated by Cyril Vollert. St. Louis: B. Herder Book Co., 1946.

Schneider, Athanasius, with Diane Montagna. *Christus Vincit: Christ's Triumph over the Darkness of the Age*. Brooklyn, NY: Angelico Press, 2019.

——. "Exclusive: Bishop Athanasius Schneider Interview." *Rorate Caeli*, February 2, 2016.

Schrader, Dylan. "'Altared' States: Easterly Orientation in the Celebration of the Eucharist." *Adoremus* Bulletin, July 15, 2021.

Senior, John. *The Restoration of Christian Culture*. Norfolk, VA: IHS Press, 2008.

Shakespeare, William. *As You Like It*. In *The Globe Illustrated Shakespeare: The Complete Works, Annotated*. Edited by Howard Staunton. New York: Greenwich House, 1983.

Shaw, Joseph. "Cardinal Roche on the Vatican II Rupture." *OnePeterFive*, March 24, 2023.

——. *The Case for Liturgical Restoration: Una Voce Studies on the Traditional Latin Mass*. Brooklyn, NY: Angelico Press, 2019.

——, ed. *A Defence of Monarchy: Catholics under a Protestant King*. Brooklyn, NY: Angelico Press, 2023.

——, ed. *The Latin Mass and the Intellectuals: Petitions to Save the Ancient Mass from 1966 to 2007*. Waterloo, ON: Arouca Press, 2023.

——. *The Liturgy, the Family, and the Crisis of Modernity: Essays of a Traditional Catholic*. Lincoln, NE: Os Justi Press, 2023.

——. "The Novus Ordo at 50: Loss or Gain? A Reply to Prof. Mary Healy." *Homiletic & Pastoral Review*, February 10, 2020.

——. *Sacred and Great: A Brief Introduction to the Traditional Latin Mass*. Lincoln, NE: Os Justi Press, 2023.

Skojec, Steve. "A Priest Just Doing His Job." *OnePeterFive*, July 23, 2020.

Slattery, William J. *Heroism and Genius: How Catholic Priests Helped Build—and Can Help Rebuild—Western Civilization*. San Francisco: Ignatius Press, 2017.

Smith, Gregory A. "Just one-third of U.S. Catholics agree with their church that Eucharist is body, blood of Christ." *Pew Research Center*, August 5, 2019. www.pewresearch.org/fact-tank/2019/08/05/transubstantiation-eucharist-u-s-catholics.

Smith, Janet. "Jesus Christ Is Our True King and Priest." *National Catholic Register*, March 31, 2022.

Spataro, Roberto. *In Praise of the Tridentine Mass and of Latin, Language of the Church*. Translated by Zachary Thomas. Brooklyn, NY: Angelico Press, 2019.

Sweeney, Terence. "Pope Francis: Guardian of Tradition." *Where Peter Is*, August 18, 2021.

Taft, Robert. "Robert Taft Acceptance Speech: Berakah Award." *PrayTell*, November 2, 2018.

——. "Recovering Western Liturgical Traditions." *America*, May 26, 2008. www.americamagazine.org/faith/2008/05/26/recovering-western-liturgical-traditions.

Teague, Matthew. "These devout young Catholics are embracing the old ways." *National Geographic* online, October 26, 2023.

Thomas Aquinas. *Commentary on the Letters of Saint Paul to the Galatians and Ephesians*. Translated by Fabian R. Larcher, OP, and Matthew Lamb. Green Bay, WI: Aquinas Institute, 2018.

——. *Commentary on the Sentences*. Book IV, Distinctions 1–13. Translated by Beth Mortensen. Latin/English Edition of the Works of St. Thomas Aquinas, vol. 7. Green Bay, WI: Aquinas Institute, 2018.

——. *The Summa Theologiæ of St. Thomas Aquinas*. Second and revised edition, 1920. Literally translated by Fathers of the English Dominican Province. Online edition by Kevin Knight, 2017. https://www.newadvent.org/summa/.

Thurian, Max. "La Liturgie, contemplation du mystère." *Notitiae* 32 (1996): 690–97. Reprinted in English in *L'Osservatore Romano*, June 24, 1996.

Turner, Paul. *In These or Similar Words: Praying and Crafting the Language of the Liturgy*. Franklin Park, IL: World Library Publications, 2014. A synopsis may be found at http://paulturner.org/wp-content/uploads/2015/01/ml-in-these-or-similar-words.pdf.

Vatican II. Dogmatic Constitution on the Church *Lumen Gentium*. November 21, 1964.

——. Constitution on the Sacred Liturgy *Sacrosanctum Concilium*. December 4, 1963.

Vico, Giambattista. *On the Study Methods of Our Time*. Translated by Elio Gianturco. Indianapolis: Bobbs-Merrill, 1965.

von Cochem, Martin. *The Incredible Catholic Mass*. (Originally: *Explanation of the Holy Sacrifice of the Mass*.) Charlotte, NC: TAN Books, 2012.

Wasserman-Soler, Daniel. *Truth in Many Tongues: Religious Conversion and the Languages of the Early Spanish Empire*. University Park, PA: Penn State University Press, 2020.

Wellborn, Amy. "It's not the reverence; It's the ego." *Charlotte was Both*, August 9, 2021.

——. "…wishful thinking and liturgical pretense." *Charlotte was Both*, September 23, 2023.

Zuhlsdorf, John. "More on liberal liturgists' attacks on 'ad orientem' worship, bishops and priests who support it." *Fr. Z's Blog*, August 24, 2019.

Index

abbreviation, 42, 48, 123; *see* simplification
abortion, politicians who vote for, 218
abuse, xiv, 172, 189, 238, 244
accessibility, 101, 172, 183, 193–212
acolytes, 4, 17, 30–31, 37, 41, 43, 52, 123, 126, 186, 220, 242
active participation, 30–32, 38, 42, 96, 110, 134, 158, 183, 193, 210, 243
activism, 42, 244
Ad Caeli Reginam (Pius XII), 62
ad orientem, xi, 1–28, 46, 63, 139–40, 168, 241, 243
adaptations, liturgical, 79, 156, 180, 187, 236, 242
adoration, xii, 6, 8, 11, 22, 28, 40–41, 59, 64, 68–78, 106, 126, 138, 142, 209, 219–21, 226–27, 230–31, 239
Adoro te devote, 203, 209
aggiornamento (updating), 72; *see* modernization
Agnus Dei, 106, 124, 165
Alcuin of York, 186
Alexandria, 9, 184
alleluia, 59, 82, 176
Alleluia (Proper), 59, 150, 155, 157, 163
altar, xi, 1–2, 4, 7, 17, 23–27, 31, 37, 41, 43–44, 48, 50–52, 59–61, 64, 73, 75, 82, 88, 92, 97, 106, 119–20, 122–23, 126, 129, 140, 149, 153, 155–57, 173, 186, 196–97, 221, 227, 229, 232, 235, 237; side-altar, 116
altar rail, *see* Communion rail
Ambrose of Milan, 140
Ambrosian rite, 5, 91, 130
anaphora, 33, 142, 229, 242; *see* Roman Canon
ancient practice, 5, 10, 19–20, 24, 26, 28, 68, 91, 135, 148, 158, 173–75, 181, 225–28; *see also* antiquarianism
angels, 41, 48, 54, 57, 61–62, 64, 66, 70, 80, 84–85, 115, 125–26, 164, 171, 187, 215
Anglican Ordinariates, 74, 172
Anglicans, Anglicanism, 19, 39, 74–75, 90, 172, 175
anointing of hands, 221–22, 230
anonymity, 14, 30, 210
Anselm of Canterbury, 186
anthropocentrism, 3–5, 19, 23, 26–28, 210
Antichrist, 80
antinomianism, 25
Antioch, 184
antiphons, 82, 106, 148, 150–52, 155, 164–65, 190; *see* Propers
antiquarianism, 42, 130, 226
Apocalypse of John, *see* Revelation
Apollo, Abba, 80, 220
Apostles, 8–9, 24, 43, 45, 55, 90, 124, 146, 170, 173, 187, 199, 206, 216, 236
Arabic, Quranic or classical, 175, 177, 190
Aramaic, 173, 175–76
architecture, 2, 4–6, 10, 22, 24, 57, 61, 73–77, 105, 116, 169, 188
Arius, Arianism, 20–21, 127
aristocracy, 65, 67, 69
Aristotle, 88, 199
Armenian, 5, 175, 181
Arminteros, Carolina, 171
ars celebrandi, 83, 107, 137, 154–56
artistry, need for finest of, 73–74, 77
Ascension, 7, 9, 145, 184, 186
asceticism, 84, 95, 126, 153–54, 202
Asperges, 127, 164
"assisting at Mass," 35, 38, 41, 56, 151, 190, 231
atheism, 83
Attenborough, David, 206
attention, attentiveness, 2–4, 13, 19–20, 26, 39, 50, 53, 56, 94–98, 131–32, 167, 204–5, 210, 212, 242
audibility, 33, 39–40, 50, 85, 125–26, 134, 142, 169, 183, 185, 201, 204, 210, 244

Augustine of Hippo, 118, 149, 200–201, 205, 209, 239
Austen, Jane, 118
autonomy, 99, 174
awakeness, 145, 210, 240, 244
awe, 171, 183, 194, 210, 215, 218, 230, 232–33

Babel, 80, 83, 184, 186–89
Babylon, 58, 83, 171
Bagshawe, Canon, 64
baldachin, 26
baptism, 5–6, 16, 25–26, 30, 36, 50, 58, 160, 186–87, 229–30
Baroque, xi, 31, 63, 65, 111, 131
barriers in church, 26, 33, 52, 56, 168–69, 176, 182, 211
Barthe, Claude, 68, 205, 248
Basil the Great, 7–8, 24
beatific vision, 58, 149, 125, 206–7, 211, 216
beating of the breast, 43, 45, 48
Beatitudes, 235
beauty as requisite to liturgy, 1, 4, 53, 71–77, 107, 114, 120–21, 154–55, 157–58, 188–89, 208, 232
Bell, Luke, 92
Belloc, Hilaire, 234
bells, 33, 205
Benedict XVI, 25, 134, 161, 217, 220, 234; *see also* Ratzinger
Benedict of Nursia, 91, 102, 127
Benedictines, 62, 119, 120, 128, 237
Benediction, 156
Benson, Robert Hugh, 39–41, 89
Bergman, Lisa, 246
Bible study, 141, 160
bishops, 14, 62, 68, 72, 83, 90, 124, 146, 170, 181–82, 218, 222–24, 249
blessings, xiv, 47–48, 90, 127, 165, 235
body language, *see* language
Book of Common Prayer, 175
boredom, 105, 200, 206
Borromeo, Charles, 123
Bouyer, Louis, 10, 65, 156, 184
bowing of the head, 4, 7, 41, 44, 46, 48, 62, 69, 96–97, 117, 126, 140, 196–97, 220, 227, 230, 232
breviary, *see* Divine Office
Buddhists, 175
Bugnini, Annibale, 113, 154, 182, 194
Byzantine rite, 5, 16, 26, 37, 62, 65, 69–72, 111–12, 118, 140, 188, 192, 202, 224, 227, 228; *see also* Eastern rites

calendar, liturgical, 111, 126, 135, 137, 149, 246
Calvary, 18, 25, 40, 50, 71, 116, 149, 159, 237; *see also* Christ, Passion of
Calvin, Calvinism, 39, 227–28
Campion, Edmund, 40, 186
Campo, Cristina, 203
Canaan, 83
canceled priests, 243
candles, 3, 25–27, 41, 58–59, 64, 69, 139, 154, 156, 172
Cantalamessa, Raniero, 33–34
Carolingians, 62–63, 68–69
Casini, Tito, 185
casual behavior, 25, 54, 74, 90, 96, 176, 195, 198, 226
catafalque, 172
catechesis, 4, 21, 27, 53, 55, 83, 100, 112, 134–35, 141, 147, 160, 170, 196, 228, 230
Catechism of the Catholic Church, 57, 140, 143
Catechism of the Council of Trent, 123, 222
Catherine of Siena, 49
celibacy, 81, 180–81
ceremonial, xii, 24, 52, 61, 64, 69, 73, 89, 111, 122, 140, 154, 159, 168, 235
chant, Gregorian, xiii, 3, 16, 37, 52, 54, 70, 75, 80, 90, 105–6, 112–13, 124, 137–40, 145, 154–56, 159, 173, 181, 183, 190, 237, 240–41
chanting of Scripture, 138–41, 154–56, 159
character, sacramental, 36, 48, 88
charity, works of, 77, 80, 92, 96, 218
Charlemagne, 63, 186
Charles de Foucauld, 186
Charles I, king, 171
Chautard, Jean-Baptiste, 51
Cherubic hymn, 7, 70
Chesterton, G.K., 119, 234
child, children, xii–xiii, 6, 14, 32, 41, 54, 82, 104, 110, 117–21, 131, 135, 142, 162–63, 167, 190, 195, 199, 201, 204, 222, 229–30, 236
Chiron, Yves, 72, 182
choir, 31, 37, 39, 80, 106, 128, 190
choir loft, 14, 106

Christ, as East or Orient, 7–9, 10, 16, 24, 27–28; Body and Blood of, 21, 40, 45–46, 54, 58, 75, 96, 98, 102, 125, 152, 158, 215, 223, 225, 237; imitation of, 84, 87, 91, 93, 239; kingship of, 56–78, 85, 215, 225–26, 235, 242; Passion of, 66, 71, 92, 125, 145, 153, 166, 186, 216; priesthood of, 34, 36–40, 48–49, 60, 66, 80, 88, 93, 104, 116, 125, 155, 222, 237, 243; wounds of, 91, 231
Christendom, xii, 68, 127, 130, 185–86, 189, 236
Christifideles Laici (John Paul II), 63
Christmas, 148
Christocentrism, 10, 19, 33, 66, 156
Christology, 73
Church Fathers, *see* Fathers of the Church
Church, militant, 84, 150, 231; suffering, 88, 93, 172, 231; triumphant, 66–67, 85, 89, 130, 150, 231
Church Slavonic, 70, 173–75, 177, 181
Cicero, 211
Cipolla, Richard, 241
Clarke, Veronica, 185
Claudel, Paul, 27
Clayton, David, 1–4, 16
clericalism, clericalization, xi, 26, 33, 50–51, 63, 83, 89
clericocentrism, 13, 30, 49
codification of liturgy, 98, 136
Comme le Prévoit, 113
common good, 233
communication, 2, 4, 16, 30, 73, 86, 113, 118, 125, 167–68, 177–78, 191, 195–98, 200; non-verbal, 171–72, 195–98
Communion cloth, *see* houseling cloth
communion of saints, 149
communion rail, 17, 26, 71, 220, 227
Communion, 9, 25, 68, 125–26, 159, 165, 214–16, 231; distribution of, 38, 63, 221–23, 230–31, 242; fast before, 84, 126, 130, 154, 218; manner of receiving, 16–17, 54, 104, 126, 197, 219–30, 241; priest's, 46–48, 123–25; under one kind, 125; unworthy vs. worthy, 125, 143, 152, 217, 224, 228
complexity, 31, 37, 80, 111, 114, 118, 201–3, 235, 248
Compline, 123, 127, 237
comprehension, 30, 59, 110–11, 116, 141, 168–69, 171–72, 174–75, 183, 189, 191–212, 216, 243
compunction, 108, 132
Confession, 51, 143, 217–18
Confirmation, 30, 232
Confiteor, 37, 43, 48, 109, 123–27, 129
conservative critics, 241
Consilium, 113, 126, 137, 153, 159
Constantine the Great, 65, 68, 188
Constantinople, 5, 69
contemplation, 11, 57, 110, 112–15, 118, 123, 128, 160, 203–4, 211, 239
conversion, xi, 1, 25, 35, 50, 140, 148, 171
Copts, Coptic, 5, 130, 173–75
Corpus Christi, 111, 152, 220
cosmos, 24, 65, 70, 194
countercultural, TLM as, xii, 191
courtliness, 56–78, 168, 242
Covenants, continuity between Old and New, 34, 37, 57, 61, 86–87, 89, 138–39, 173–76, 209, 236
creativity, liturgical, 100, 171; *see also* extemporization; spontaneity
Creed (at Mass), 5, 127, 140–41, 143, 190
crucifix on or above altar, 25–27, 50
cultural literacy, 211
cursing or imprecatory psalms, 153
custom, 5, 8, 20, 24, 54, 69, 76, 84, 98, 123, 126, 131–32, 146, 159, 170, 173, 178, 187, 189, 218, 220, 223–25, 228, 232, 236, 242
Cyril of Alexandria, 9
Cyril of Jerusalem, 225–28

daily missal, 40, 43, 51, 53, 135, 145, 151, 160, 169, 188, 190, 246
dance, liturgy as, xii, 85, 87, 89, 106
David, king, 9, 66, 71, 87, 90, 108
Davies, Michael, 29
Dawson, Christopher, 235
De Corte, Marcel, 242
de Hemptinne, Pius, 237
de Lubac, Henri, 35
de Maistre, Joseph, 171
De Tocqueville, Alexis, 205
deacon, 54, 80, 119, 124, 126, 155, 170, 181, 222, 230
dead, prayer for the, 41, 55, 88, 172, 231
defects, in celebration of Mass, 98, 244

dehellenization, 234
democracy, 16, 18, 36, 56, 62, 65–67, 69, 72, 80, 84, 123, 174, 205, 219
density, 42, 54, 98, 113, 132, 188, 202, 208, 212
Desert Fathers, 80, 127–28, 220
Desiderio Desideravi (Francis), 205
determinateness in worship, 89, 100, 102, 140, 174, 241
devil, the, *see* Satan
DeVille, Adam, 118–19
devotion, 39, 50, 68, 77, 85, 110, 119, 132, 169, 171, 218, 224, 228, 235
devotions, popular, 31, 49, 111, 114–15, 190, 246
dialogue, Mass as, 11, 15, 26, 42, 50, 101, 123–24
didacticism, 52, 146, 158
difficulties as deliberate pedagogy, 111, 154, 157, 200–205
"difficult" passages in the Bible, 126, 137, 152–54, 158, 200, 204
Dionysius (or Pseudo-Dionysius), 15
DiPippo, Gregory, 37, 44, 99, 111, 146
discipline, 83–84, 95, 102, 171, 220
distance between priest and people, 29–55
Divine Liturgy, 7, 37, 61, 69–70, 112, 192, 202, 212; *see also* Byzantine rite; Eastern rites
Divine Office, xiv, 6, 76, 82, 127, 129, 153, 159–60, 170, 182, 235
divinization, 9, 87, 238
Dix, Gregory, 6
Domine, non sum dignus, 46, 109, 116, 126–27, 131–32, 165
Dominicae Cenae (John Paul II), 217, 221
Dominican rite, 203
doxology, 18, 127, 235
drama, liturgy as, 31, 62–63, 67, 89
Dubay, Thomas, 147
Dupré, Stéphane, 87

east, symbolism of, see *ad orientem*
Easter, 6, 58, 136, 145–46, 148, 153, 155, 159
Eastern Orthodox, 22, 84, 145, 174–75, 181
Eastern rites, 5, 33, 71, 97, 100, 115, 130, 141, 144, 156, 173–77, 181, 219, 228, 247; *see also* Byzantine rite
eastward orientation, see *ad orientem*
Ecclesia de Eucharistia (John Paul II), 76–77, 180, 213, 218
ecclesiology, 67, 197
ecstasy, 12, 18, 80–81, 84, 121
effeminacy, 14
efficiency, 114, 124, 193; *see also* utilitarianism
egalitarianism, 42, 65, 66, 123, 244
elevations at Mass, 3–4, 33, 40, 68, 203, 205
Elizabeth I, 39
Elizabethan English, 175
embolism, 45, 48
emotions, 85, 87, 106, 118, 124, 167–68, 171, 205, 216
emotionalism, 92
environmentalism, 2, 238
Ephrem the Syrian, 213
epiclesis, 37
Epiphany, 141
Epistle of the Mass, 48, 87, 135, 139, 145–46, 148–50, 152, 155, 157, 162, 164, 185
eros, 121
eschatology, 6–7, 11, 17, 27–28, 60, 62, 92, 238; *see also* heaven; hell; purgatory
Esolen, Anthony, 113, 199
eternal life, 55, 66, 123–24, 213–15, 229
Ethiopian Orthodox, 5, 174
ethnic identity, 184–85, 189
etiquette, 63, 89
Eucharistic revival, 221, 228, 230
Europe, 17, 75, 177, 205, 234–35
evangelization, 77, 170–71
experimentation, 27, 108, 137, 188, 238
"experts," 10, 18, 29, 68, 122, 181
extemporization, 99–102; *see also* improvisation
extraordinary ministers of Holy Communion, 38, 63, 85, 222, 242
eyes, custody of, 2, 50, 96–97, 196

fasting, 84, 126, 130, 154, 166, 202, 218, 221
Fathers of the Church, 7, 34, 137, 180, 227, 239, 248
fear of the Lord, 4, 68, 70–71, 74, 92, 126, 230–31
feelings, role of, *see* emotions
ferias, 87, 135–36, 159–60
Fides et Ratio (John Paul II), 180
Fiedrowicz, Michael, 167–68, 172, 174–76, 226, 247
fingers, 54, 97, 117, 225–27, 230

fittingness, 11, 46, 50, 75, 84, 89, 98, 123, 144–47, 154, 169, 171, 176, 179, 190, 209, 221–22, 228
Florensky, Pavel, 141
Foley, Michael, 60–61, 66, 111, 149, 188, 211, 246
food and/or drink, 20, 25, 46, 54, 66, 70, 78, 84, 115, 152, 192, 212, 216, 218, 223, 229–30, 246
formality in liturgy, 12, 39, 73, 74, 84, 92, 100, 106, 109, 121, 127, 139, 148, 151, 167, 175–76, 190, 198
Fra Angelico, 85
fragments of the Eucharist, care for, 197, 220, 223–25, 227, 230
Francis de Sales, 132
Francis of Assisi, 75
Francis, pope, 30, 32, 35, 113, 179–80, 182, 205
Franciscans, 75, 136
friends of God, 19, 21, 66, 68, 126, 215–16, 219, 232

Gallican rite, 5, 31, 63
Gamber, Klaus, 1
Garden of Eden, 8–9, 17, 82, 184, 233
Ge'ez, 174
Gehenna, 83; *see also* hell
genuflections, 48, 54, 62, 88, 96–97, 109, 117, 140–41, 197, 230; *see also* kneeling
Gertrude the Great, 186
gestures, 7, 15–16, 37, 42, 48, 50, 52, 62, 69, 89, 92–93, 98, 105, 109, 113, 119, 125, 132, 195–97, 203, 222, 227, 240
Gethsemane, 112, 128, 215
Glagolitic rite, 173–74
globalism, 53, 185
Gloria, 18, 59, 106, 116, 126, 165, 190
Gospel of the Mass, 44, 63, 87, 130, 135, 139, 141–50, 155–57, 163–64, 185–86
grace, sanctifying, 72, 125, 150, 214, 217–18, 228
Gradual (Proper), 150, 155, 157, 162, 164, 166
Greek, 5, 57, 60, 97, 130, 169, 173–77, 181
Gregorian reform (11th cent.), 68
Gregory the Great, 10, 31, 108
Grillo, Andrea, 32–34
Guardini, Romano, 114–15
Guéranger, Prosper, 112
habits, in prayer, 24, 49, 51, 83, 96, 116, 122, 146, 171, 214, 219, 241, 243
Hahn, Scott, 57, 59, 61, 133
Hanc igitur, 37
hand missal, *see* daily missal
hands, xii, 7, 17, 37–38, 40–41, 44, 47, 50, 54, 64, 67, 69, 74, 86–88, 98, 104–5, 117, 125–26, 139, 196–97, 221–30
Hannon, Urban, 80, 204, 248
Harrison, Brian, 133
haste in prayer, 131–32
Hauke, Manfred, 14
Hausherr, Irénée, 128
head, movement of the, xii, 37–38, 41, 46, 48, 97, 117, 140, 196, 204, 225, 227, 232
heaven, ix, 7, 9, 12, 38, 46–47, 52, 55–70, 73, 78, 80, 84–87, 89, 121, 125, 130, 149, 157, 159, 184–85, 188, 192, 206–8, 215–16, 231, 237–39
Hebrew, 169, 173–77, 190
Hebrews, Epistle to the, 60, 164–65,
Heenan, John Carmel, 14
Heid, Stefan, 5
hell, 6, 66, 79–83, 85, 93, 107, 152, 217
hermeneutic of continuity, 241
hiddenness, v, 27, 30, 72, 92, 192, 198, 211–12, 216
hierarchy, 2, 15, 27, 35–36, 62, 67, 73, 80, 84, 90, 123, 154, 204, 242, 248
Hindus, 175
Hippolytus, 33
Holy Ghost, 8, 10–11, 43, 45–46, 60, 78, 82, 86, 90, 105, 116, 127, 140, 187, 192, 198, 200, 209, 213–14, 221
Holy of Holies, 15, 34, 43, 61, 127, 164, 171, 227, 237
Holy Orders, xii, 36, 38, 54, 67, 85, 88, 116, 125, 155, 221–22, 230
holy water, 53
Holy Week, 114–15, 130, 166
homily, homiletics, 4, 92, 142–43, 147, 156, 160, 197, 220, 230
homosexuality, 14
Honorius of Autun, 131, 248
Hopkins, Gerard Manley, 209
horizontal(ization), 15–16, 30, 236
Houghton, Bryan, 32
houseling cloth, 227
Howard, Thomas, 105–7
Howell, Clifford, 180

humanism, 19, 25, 27, 53; *see also* anthropocentrism
humility, xii, 13, 25, 45, 64, 79, 80–81, 87–91, 122–24, 126, 132, 138, 157, 163–64, 166, 168, 197, 202, 211–12, 219, 226, 230, 242
Hunwicke, John, 19

iconoclasm, 119
iconostasis, 26, 71; "sonic iconostatis," 52–54
icons or holy images, 8, 12, 16, 55, 57, 61, 64, 69, 75, 87, 99, 121, 138–40, 147, 181, 202
idolatry, 52, 58, 83, 220
Ignatius of Loyola, 186
illuminated manuscripts, 154
imagination, 41, 87, 116, 201
immanence, 14; divine, 22–24
improvisation, 87, 90, 92, 99, 104, 238
inaudibility, xi, 169, 204, 210
Incarnation, 3, 28, 85, 145, 186, 200, 207
incense, 3, 16, 34, 37, 52, 58–59, 64, 69, 82, 105, 139, 154, 156, 171, 205
incomprehensibility, 59, 169, 175, 184, 189, 194, 198–201, 208, 210
inculturation, 236
ineffability, 120, 167
infidelity, 58, 83, 96–97, 105
informality in liturgy, 12, 74, 84; *see also* casual behavior
Innocent III, 131, 248
integrity, ritual, 130, 151, 241, 244–45
intercession of saints, 45, 124, 126, 163
interior life, 25, 113, 195, 216, 243, 246
interlectional chants, 155
Introit, 126, 150, 153, 157, 162, 164, 166
Israel, v, 7, 28, 66, 83, 87, 211, 217, 230; modern state of, 190

Jesus Prayer, 120
Jewel of the Soul (Honorius), 131, 248
Jews, Judaism, 20, 58, 61, 128, 173–75, 190, 207, 209
Job, 199
John Chrysostom, 215; *see also* Divine Liturgy
John Damascene, 8–9, 62, 137
John Paul II, 57, 61, 63, 76, 111, 203, 211, 213, 217–18, 221–22
John the Baptist, 43, 124, 138
John Vianney, 51, 75
John XXIII, 72, 178–81, 185
Jones, David, 18–19
Joseph, St., 87, 199
Judas, 50, 70, 215–16
Julian of Norwich, 72
Jungmann, Joseph, 10
Just, Felix, 144
justice, 21, 43, 47, 71, 96, 198, 245; "sun of," 7, 9, 28, 213
Justin Martyr, 33

Kant, Immanuel, 206, 257
Keim, Robert W., 189
kingship of Christ, *see* Christ, kingship of
kisses, 70, 96, 215–16; to altar, 41, 44, 48, 50, 88, 97, 119–20; to hand, 69; to missal or lectionary, 139, 156
kneeling, xii, 3–4, 16, 50, 54, 80, 104, 117, 126, 154, 219–24, 228–30, 241; *see also* genuflections
Knox, Ronald, 88, 94
Kyrie, 106, 109, 112, 116, 126–27, 157, 164

laity, 29–30, 32, 35–36, 38, 42, 55, 63, 68, 80, 84, 158, 193, 222, 224, 232, 242, 244–45, 249
Lamb of God, 46, 54, 59, 138; see also *Agnus Dei*
Lamont, John, 188
Lang, Uwe Michael, 244, 247
language, xii, 16, 29, 31, 52–53, 56, 68, 79–80, 82, 90, 101, 113, 120, 151, 167–90, 192, 197, 202, 209, 211, 240, 243; body, 4, 26, 195–96; colloquial, 15, 172–77, 186–87, 204; levels of, 176–78; sacral (or sacred), xii, 16, 167–76, 187, 189, 197, 204, 243; vernacular, 13, 16, 83, 101, 112–13, 169–88, 198
Last Gospel, 47–48, 127, 130, 141, 151, 165
Last Supper, 18, 20, 58, 60, 125, 143, 175
Latin, in the liturgy, xii, 16, 31, 33, 39, 52–54, 68, 90, 97, 124, 132, 167–90, 202, 211, 229, 241, 243; learning of, 51, 53, 82, 117, 128, 189–90, 211–12; reaffirmation of at Vatican II, 181–82; *see* sacral language
Laud, William, 73–74
Lauds, 7, 91, 127, 237
Lavabo, 44, 164
Lawrence, St., 148

Lazarus, 232
laziness, 127, 211, 214
Leclercq, Jean, 117
lectio (semi-)continua, 137, 148–50
lectio divina, 128, 147, 160–61, 240
lectionary, xii, 119, 133–66
lectors, 38, 63, 156, 158
leisure, 111, 114, 118, 203
leitourgia, meaning of, 33, 60, 66
Lemna, Keith, 65
Lenten fast, 84
Leo the Great, 108
Leonard of Port Maurice, 235, 248
Lewis, C.S., 75, 85, 122, 211
lex orandi, lex credendi, 108
liberal arts, 185
Liberalism, 21, 25
lies, lying, 67, 81, 83, 105
litanies, 39, 78, 111–12, 128
Liturgiam Authenticam, 113
Liturgical Movement, 32–33, 112, 115, 238
Liturgy, of the Eucharist, 143, 158; of the Hours, *see* Divine Office; of the Word, 143, 151, 156, 158–60
Longenecker, Dwight, 2–3
Lord's Prayer, the, 45, 90, 114, 165
love of neighbor, 59
Lucifer, *see* Satan
Lumen Gentium (Vatican II), 36, 67
Luther, Martin, 227

madness, 121
magic, 172, 193, 197
Marcionism, 34, 61
Margaret Mary Alacoque, 78
Marini, Guido, 11–12
Maritain, Jacques, 35, 104
Marmion, Columba, 237
marriage, 58, 81, 105–6, 181, 228, 236
Martindale, C.C., 211
Martyrology, 87
Marxism, 67
Mary Magdalene, 64, 77
Mass, as communal gathering, 11–12, 17–18, 21, 24, 42, 63–64, 67, 89, 97, 99, 101, 171, 197, 231–32, 242; as meal or banquet, 5, 18–21, 23, 58–60, 64, 68, 138, 143, 175, 227, 239; as true and proper sacrifice, 5, 17–19, 21, 36–37, 41, 46–47, 70–71, 75, 116, 122, 125, 143, 149, 209, 216, 227–28, 236–37; biblical permeation in the, 150–51, 164–65; "dialogue," 124; low or private, 25, 116, 124, 155, 185, 203; of the Catechumens, 138, 157; of the Faithful, 138; pontifical, 63, 127; social nature of, 16, 21, 180, 184; solemn, xii, 71, 124, 154, 164, 240; sung or high, 37, 71, 106, 154, 156; votive, 87, 135–36, 139, 152
Mayan rite, 236
McCabe, Herbert, 82
Mectilde of Hackeborn, 188
Mectilde of the Blessed Sacrament, 93–96, 103
mediator, mediation, 10, 12–13, 35, 42, 51, 65, 123, 168, 236
Mediator Dei (Pius XII), 36, 112, 178, 226
Memoriale Domini, 223
memorization, 116–17, 147
memory, 116–17, 128, 140, 145, 157, 189, 201
Michael the Archangel, 43, 124
Michelangelo, 122
microphones, 183
Middle Ages, 23, 44, 49, 63, 65, 72, 101, 117, 126, 130–31, 136, 147, 154, 194, 205, 248
Miller, Peter, 141, 158
ministers, male-only, xiii, 14, 181, 241–42, 244
missal, altar, 2, 90, 98, 102, 135–36; *see also* daily missal
Missale Romanum (1570), 98, 135–36, 153, 247
Missale Romanum (pre-1955), 130, 246–47,
Missale Romanum (1962), 123, 130, 149, 246–47
modernism, modernists, 85, 108, 179, 181, 227
modernity, 27, 62, 65, 69, 79, 130
modernization, 130, 189
"Modern Man," 69, 101, 193
monarchy, xii, 36, 62, 65–67, 69, 174
Monica, St., 149–50
monks, monasticism, 62, 68, 91, 117, 119–20, 127–28, 160, 203, 237–38, 240
Montini, Giovanni Battista, 72; *see also* Paul VI
Moore, Jeffrey, 31–32, 34
Morello, Sebastian, 171, 185

Morrill, Bruce T., 32, 34
Mosaic Law, 89, 151
Mosebach, Martin, 17, 69, 91–92, 113, 122–24, 197
motherhood, 82, 149, 186–87, 212, 229
Mozarabic rite, 5, 130
Murray, Gregory, 29
muscle memory, 117
music, sacred, xiii, 4, 61, 73–76, 89, 105–6, 108, 115, 143, 154, 169, 171, 181, 185, 188, 212, 232, 236, 243, 248; *see also* chant; polyphony
Muslims, 175
mysteriousness, 2–4, 20, 38, 129, 194, 197, 203–8, 240
mystery, xii, 2, 4, 6, 8, 10, 24–25, 34–36, 40–41, 53, 57, 61, 77, 82, 89, 98, 110–11, 116, 119, 134, 145, 163, 167, 169, 171–72, 176, 183, 194, 203, 204–8, 210–11, 231–32, 238–40, meaning of, 207–8
Mystici Corporis Christi (Pius XII), 125

"Nabbish," 113, 180
Navarro, Joe, 195–96
nave, 6, 23–24, 71, 195, 220
Nero, 128
Nestorius, 9
New American Bible, 113, 180
Newman, John Henry, 5, 39, 90, 98, 203–4
Nichols, Aidan, 110–11
Nivakoff, Benedict, 120
noise, 85, 184–85
novelty, 5, 10, 99, 120, 136, 153, 159–60, 189, 197
numerology, 116

O'Connell, J.B., 32
O'Loughlin, Thomas, 62
obedience, 36, 88, 91, 95, 98, 103, 106, 158, 197, 200, 214, 244–45, 248
objective nature of liturgy, 12, 100, 115, 168, 171
obscurantism, 97
obscurity, xi–xii, 13, 40, 111, 114, 200–201, 204–6, 239
octaves, 110–11, 114, 130, 146, 170
Offertory of the Mass, 13, 37, 44, 48, 54, 68, 150, 164
Officiorum Omnium (Pius XI), 178
Olmsted, Thomas J., 220
options, xii, 28, 48, 83, 87, 96, 99–100, 137, 150–51, 153, 242
Oratory, Brompton, 2–3; cf. 243
Order of Mass, 43, 45, 48–49, 126–27, 150–51, 160, 164–65, 182, 246
order, orderliness, xii, 18, 27, 36, 58, 61, 74, 77, 80, 82, 86, 88–89, 91, 94–95, 101, 104, 106, 114, 138, 186–87, 194–95, 197, 210, 212, 231, 239, 242
ordination, 49–50, 221; *see also* Holy Orders
organic development, 17, 68, 86, 97, 99, 116, 130, 136, 170, 174–75, 184, 187–88, 195, 197, 220, 224–28, 235–36, 247
Orientale Lumen (John Paul II), 111
originality, 86, 89
"otherness" of God, 23, 172, 176
Otto, Rudolf, 169, 206

Padre Pio, 51, 91, 186
paganization of liturgy, 97
pagan religion, 69, 97, 128, 170, 174, 209
Palestrina, Giovanni Pierluigi da, 38
Palm Sunday, 142–43
papal authority, 108, 137, 189, 248
parables of Jesus, 138, 201
parallel liturgy, 37
Pärt, Arvo, 73
participatio actuosa, see active participation
particles of the Host, *see* fragments
Paschaltide, *see* Easter
passivity, xii, 122, 211; *see also* receptivity
Passover, 20, 34, 58, 60, 175
paten, 17, 204, 220, 226–27
Paul VI, xi, 17, 26, 29, 48–49, 66, 72, 83–84, 133–34, 137, 151, 153, 157, 182, 223, 242–44, 247
Pelagianism, 20–21
penance, 84, 124, 126, 217, 221, 235; *see also* Confession
Pentateuch, 86
Pentecost, 60, 80, 82, 145–46, 170, 184, 199
"People of God," 17, 25, 32, 67
Pickstock, Catherine, 130
Pieper, Josef, 81, 121
piety, 16, 25, 49, 91, 97–98, 112, 161, 172, 187, 202, 217, 223, 228, 242
pilgrimage, 12, 78, 235, 238
Pistoia, Synod of, 212
Pius V, ix, 31, 33, 98, 123
Pius XI, 66, 178–79, 181

Pius XII, 36, 62, 112, 115, 125, 136, 154, 178–81, 226
Plato, 121
pluralism, 83
Pluth, Kathleen, 14–15
Poe, Edgar Allen, 111
poetry, 18, 27, 53, 71, 111, 118, 120, 167, 169, 176, 178, 184, 203, 236
polyphony, xiii, 3, 38; *see also* chant; music
populism, 26, 62, 244
postmodernism, 86, 189
prayer of the faithful, 143
prayers at the foot of the altar, 43, 48, 123, 127, 151, 153, 157, 164, 237; *see also* Confiteor
pre-'55 Roman Rite, 114–15, 130, 246–47
preaching, 4, 19, 21, 40, 92, 105, 134, 142–43, 147, 156, 158, 160, 170–71, 187, 197, 201, 230; *see also* homily
Preface of the Mass, 7, 150
pride, 14, 17, 69, 118, 200, 211–12
priesthood, 37, 40, 83, 88–89, 181, 237–38, *et passim*; difference between ministerial and universal, 36–38, 124; *see also* Holy Orders; ordination
priest, as *alter Christus*, 10, 12, 41; as acting *in persona Christi*, 10, 41; as instrument, 13, 88–89, 93–94, 99, 104, 210, 221–22; personality of, 13, 89–91, 101, 210; as minister of Holy Communion, 38, 63, 221–23, 230–31, 242
Pristas, Lauren, 153
processions, 69, 74, 89, 105, 235
Prologue of John, *see* Last Gospel
Propers of the Mass, 150–51, 160, 162–63, 246; *see* Introit; Gradual; etc.
Protestants, Protestantism, xi, 9, 18–21, 39–40, 59, 85, 89, 105, 125, 147, 170, 215, 227–28
Psalms, praying of, 5–6, 43, 82, 87, 90–91, 102–3, 117–18, 127–28, 151–57, 164–66, 173
public nature of liturgy, 24–25, 28, 40, 49, 52, 60, 72–75, 97, 100, 102, 127, 154, 160, 167, 174, 184, 190
purgatory, 41, 88, 93, 172, 231

rationalism, 37, 118, 120, 129, 149, 167, 171, 181, 193, 200, 202–3, 210, 212
Ratzinger, Joseph, 11, 16, 24–25, 56–57, 61, 67, 97, 100, 129, 186, 209, 220, 234, 244; *see also* Benedict XVI
readings at Mass, purpose of, 116, 119, 128, 133–66, 239
Real Presence, ix, 9, 23, 78, 125, 140, 196, 214–15, 221, 224, 226–27, 230; *see also* transubstantiation
receptivity, 54, 79, 91–92, 113, 130–31, 155, 183, 214
redemption, xiv, 40–41, 67, 157, 188, 221; distinction between objective and subjective, 125
"Reform of the Reform," 241, 244
Regensburg Address (Benedict XVI), 234
Reid, Alcuin, 119
relics, 5, 44
religion, virtue of, 4, 11, 22, 59, 85, 96–97, 198, 236
religious life, 83, 192; *see also* vocations
Renaissance, 65
reparation, 49, 221
repentance, 85, 108, 218; *see also* penance
repetition, xii, 100, 109–32, 145, 168–69, 197, 243
Requiem aeternam, 172
responsorial psalm, 143, 155
resurrection, 5–6, 16, 58, 70–71, 125, 145, 186–87, 199, 214–16
Revelation, book of, 56–62, 70, 73, 164–65
revolution, 30, 69, 107, 182, 193, 209
ritual, rituality, 24, 32, 50, 69, 75–76, 79–108, 110, 119, 121–22, 149, 155, 168–69, 197, 204, 225, 231, 240
Roche, Arthur, 34, 36, 153, 179
Roman Canon, 18, 33, 37, 45, 48, 54, 68, 109, 137, 142, 150–51, 165, 183, 209–10, 212, 247
Roman Catechism, 123, 222–23
Roman emperor, 69, 188; empire, 69, 188, 234
Rome, Church of, 91, 184, 244
rood screen, 26
Rosary, 111–15, 120, 128
royalism, 64, 73; *see also* Christ, kingship of; courtliness
rubricism, 98
rubrics, xii, 50, 55, 67, 79–108, 149, 210, 224, 241–42

Ruff, Anthony, 62–63
Rule of St. Benedict, 91, 102, 127
rupture, 28, 34, 158, 232, 248

sacerdotalism, 33, 35, 66, 89
Sacra Tridentina Synodus, 218
Sacred Heart of Jesus, 78, 87
sacred language, *see* language
sacrilege, 224
Sacrosanctum Concilium (Vatican II), 109–15, 118, 134, 136, 144, 156–58, 160, 181–82; *see also* Vatican II
Saint-Exupery, Antoine de, 3
saints, communion of, 5, 8, 39, 52, 62, 66–67, 78, 83, 87, 90, 94, 102, 107, 123–24, 145, 150, 159, 186–87; intercession of, 43, 45, 112, 123–24, 136; as proof and manifestation of Scripture, 138, 148–49; relics of, 5, 44
Salmerón, Alfonso, 128
salvation history, 34, 134–35, 144, 147, 157, 173
sanctoral cycle, 126, 135, 148–51, 157, 159
sanctuary, xii–xiii, 23–24, 26–27, 30, 38, 42, 52, 61, 71, 74–75, 85, 87, 89, 108, 119, 121, 126, 189, 209, 220, 237
Sanctus, 59, 106, 121, 164
Sanskrit, 175, 177
Sarah, Robert, 63
Satan, xiv, 15–16, 58, 80–85, 102, 105, 108, 220, 232; smoke of, 16
Saward, John, 108
Scheeben, Matthias, 207–8
Schneider, Athanasius, 83, 93–94, 124, 226–27
Scripture, 7–10, 24, 54, 59–60, 62–64, 79, 90, 95, 103, 106, 108, 111, 121, 128, 133–61, 173, 194; as inspired and inerrant word of God, 60, 90, 135, 139, 146, 204; as ordered to worship, 59, 64, 90, 103, 121, 138–42, 147–49, 239; benefit of memorizing, 128, 145–47; chanting of, 106, 138–41, 154–56, 159; difficulty of understanding, 199–204, 211; veneration of, 138–42, 154–56
secularism, secularization, ix, 52, 63–64, 79, 84, 130, 232
Senior, John, 232
sentimentality, 74, 189
Septuagesima, 84, 155
Septuagint, 173
Sequence, 150
sequential liturgy, 37
seriousness, 3, 16, 30, 47, 49, 55, 107, 171
Shakespeare, 100, 122, 202
Shaw, George Bernard, 234
Shaw, Joseph, 14, 19, 32, 34, 65, 72, 113, 145, 154, 168–69, 171, 173–74, 182, 185, 201, 223, 247
signs of the cross, 43, 48, 59, 97, 109, 120, 139–40, 205
silence, 11, 39–40, 70, 85, 88, 90, 113, 117, 142, 151, 166, 183, 186, 195; criticism of, 31–32, 85; during Roman Canon, 142, 183, 209–10; value of, 48, 52–54, 121, 155, 171, 198, 202, 219, 240
simplicity, 64, 110–11, 114, 119
simplification, 109–10, 113, 129, 134, 143, 183, 201, 204, 244
sin, 6, 18, 37, 44–46, 49, 77, 85, 104, 123–26, 138, 143, 149, 198, 200, 216–19, 221
singing, 9, 31, 37, 39, 53, 71, 74, 85, 117, 121, 127, 129, 139, 167–68, 173, 182, 190, 192, 240, 243; *see also* music
Slattery, William, 235
slave, slavery, 87–88, 92–93, 95–96, 126
"smells and bells," 192, 212, 232
Smith, Janet, 68
Socrates, 128
solemnity, xii, 3, 57, 61, 71–73, 77, 90, 100, 106, 123, 127, 139, 145, 154, 156, 169, 171, 183, 188, 190
Solomon, king, 7
Spanish empire, 170–71
Spataro, Robert, 149, 157–58, 197–98, 209
splendor, 47, 61, 67, 77, 212
spontaneity, 90, 97, 105–6, 242
stability, ritual, 73, 84, 91, 97, 150–51, 158–59, 171, 180, 186, 242–43, 248
standing, posture of, 4, 6, 17, 26, 87, 104, 117, 126, 196, 225–29
Stephen, St., 45, 148
subdeacon, 80, 124, 155, 204
subjectivism, 92, 115
Summorum Pontificum (Benedict XVI), 179–80
Sunday as the Lord's Day, 5–6, 59, 120, 145, 149
Swain, Joseph, 181

Sweeney, Terence, 30, 34
symbolism, 10, 14–16, 23–24, 37, 52–53, 62, 69, 72–73, 92, 113–14, 116, 174, 178, 183–84, 187, 203, 220, 222, 227, 230, 240, 248
synagogue, 34, 144, 170, 175
Synod of Bishops (1967), 14
Synod of Pistoia, 212
Syriac, 177, 181

tabernacle, 26–27, 43, 66, 78, 204, 232
Taft, Robert, 100
Teague, Matthew, 192
technology, 24, 191
temple, soul as, 24, 72, 78, 214
Temple worship, 7, 33–34, 37, 64, 170, 173; *see also* Covenants
temporal cycle, 135
thanksgiving, 25, 47, 76, 139, 190, 192, 219, 231, 237
theocentricity of worship, 18, 21, 33, 48, 79, 168, 198
theology, purpose of, 239–40
Thérèse of Lisieux, 94, 96, 162–63, 186
Thomas Aquinas, 11, 18, 22, 74, 76, 80–81, 84, 88–89, 115, 125, 131–32, 186, 203–4, 209–10, 214–15, 219, 233, 248
throne, 7, 41, 55, 62, 64, 66, 70, 73, 225
Thurian, Max, 11
tinkeritis, 130, 194, 244
tongue, receiving Communion on the, 54, 126, 219–24, 228, 241; baptismal blessing of, 228–30
Tract (Proper), 146, 150, 155, 157, 164
Traditionis Custodes (Francis), 32, 180, 185, 245, 248
transcendence, 15, 20, 22, 24, 65, 74, 77, 83, 168, 172, 175, 178, 191, 219
translation(s), 53, 110, 113, 169, 172–73, 180, 188–89, 198, 204
transparency, 82, 110, 172, 183, 200, 202, 204, 206
transubstantiation, 3, 98, 210; *see also* Real Presence
Trent, Council of, 21, 122–24, 217, 222–23, 244
Trinity, Blessed, 5, 8, 13, 24, 39, 47, 70, 138, 190, 207, 231, 239
triumphalism, 83
Turner, Paul, 99

ugliness, 52, 77, 81, 220
unspontaneity, *see* spontaneity
utilitarianism, 42, 69, 112, 118, 129, 167, 193

Vatican II, 5, 15, 27, 30–34, 36, 42, 49–50, 62–63, 83, 108–9, 114, 119, 133–34, 136–37, 142–43, 156–58, 160, 178, 181–82, 227, 248
veils, 15, 48, 58, 126, 172, 204–5, 208
verbosity, 5, 11, 14–16, 99–100, 113–14, 142–43, 172, 198, 244
Verbum Domini (Benedict XVI), 134
Veritatis Splendor (John Paul II), 180
vernacular, *see* language
versus populum, 1–28, 38, 42, 63, 198
Vespers, 91, 156, 160, 237
vessels, 54, 71, 73–74, 76, 113, 196, 222–23
vestments, 3–6, 28, 30, 41, 52, 54, 58, 64, 71, 76, 90, 105, 108, 113, 121, 130, 169–70, 172, 240
Veterum Sapientia (John XXIII), 179
Vico, Giambattista, 97
Vincent de Paul, 186
Vincent of Lérins, 131
Virgin Mary, Blessed, 5, 39, 41, 43, 45, 52, 59, 62, 87, 99, 102, 114, 123–24, 128, 142, 145, 148, 199, 237
virtue, liturgical formation of, 11, 22, 24, 55, 96, 131, 138, 146, 150, 197–98, 214, 242–43
visibility, 3, 12, 15, 20, 89, 106, 125, 175, 183, 198, 201, 204–5, 207, 210
vocation(s), 25, 35, 50, 61, 235
voluntarism, 87, 100
von Cochem, Martin, 248
Vulgate, 180

Wasserman-Soler, Daniel, 170–71
Wellborn, Amy, 101
west, as symbol of the devil, 9, 16, 26
wonder, 25, 39, 44, 48, 71, 77, 82, 121, 129, 183, 189, 194, 198–204, 209–11
wordiness, *see* verbosity
World War II, 130
Wyoming Catholic College, 185

Zionist movement, 190
Zuhlsdorf, John, 19

About the Author

Peter A. Kwasniewski holds a BA in Liberal Arts from Thomas Aquinas College and an MA and PhD in Philosophy from the Catholic University of America, with a specialization in the thought of St. Thomas Aquinas. After teaching at the International Theological Institute in Austria, he joined the founding team of Wyoming Catholic College, where he taught theology, philosophy, music, and art history and directed the choir and schola until 2018. Today, Kwasniewski is a full-time writer and lecturer known especially for his work in the areas of liturgy and music; his writings have been translated into over twenty languages, and his sacred music compositions have been performed around the world. He regularly posts at his Substack *Tradition & Sanity*, and runs a publishing house, Os Justi Press.

Visit his sites:

www.peterkwasniewski.com
www.CantaboDomino.com
www.osjustipress.com
https://traditionsanity.substack.com/
www.soundcloud.com/drkwasniewski
www.facebook.com/ProfKwasniewski
www.youtube.com/@DrKwasniewski